THE MOTORCYCLE ROAD TESTS 1949-1953

Performance Reports and Technical Data
Reprinted from *The Motor Cycle* magazine

The list of contents is split into 4 sections by vehicle type and each of those sections is arranged alphabetically by manufacturer. However, the pages in the book are in ascending date sequence by year, such that the reader can view the different models that were produced during that year from the various manufacturers. An index sorted by YEAR can be found at the rear of the book.

MOTORCYCLE SECTION

Model	Page
Ariel Four and Sidecar (997 c.c.)	10
Ariel Red Hunter Twin (498 c.c.)	20
Ariel Red Hunter Single (497 c.c.)	50
Ariel Square Four, Mk. II (997 c.c.)	88
Ariel Twin and Sidecar (498 c.c.)	64
Bown Tourist Trophy (122 c.c.)	78
Bown Two-speed (98 c.c.)	54
B.S.A. A7 Twin (495 c.c.)	38
B.S.A. B33 (499 c.c.)	86
B.S.A. Bantam de Luxe (123 c.c.)	18
B.S.A. C10 Side-valve (249 c.c.)	96
B.S.A. C11 (249 c.c.)	52
B.S.A. Golden Flash (646 c.c.)	58
B.S.A. Overhead-valve M33 (499 c.c.)	12
B.S.A. Star Twin (497 c.c.)	68
D.M.W. de Luxe (197 c.c.)	62
D.M.W. Coronation (122 c.c.)	92
Dot Two-stroke (197 c.c.)	2
Excelsior Courier (148 c.c.)	102
Excelsior Talisman (244 c.c.)	42
Excelsior Talisman Sports (244 c.c.)	74
Francis-Barnett Falcon 55 (197 c.c.)	24
Francis-Barnett Falcon 58 (197 c.c.)	70
Greeves de Luxe (197 c.c.)	100
Indian Brave (248 c.c.)	32
James Cadet (122 c.c.)	90
James Captain de Luxe (197 c.c.)	16
James Commodore (98 c.c.)	44
Norman Two-stroke (197 c.c.)	80
Norton Big Four and Sidecar (596 c.c.)	14
Norton Dominator Twin (497 c.c.)	6
Norton Dominator and Sidecar (497 c.c.)	46
Norton Dominator No. 7 (497 c.c.)	94
Norton ES2 (490 c.c.)	82
Royal Enfield Bullet (499 c.c.)	98
Royal Enfield Bullet (346 c.c.)	22
Royal Enfield J2 and Sidecar (499 c.c.)	56
Royal Enfield RE (125 c.c.)	66
Royal Enfield Twin (496 c.c.)	34
Sunbeam S7 with Sidecar (487 c.c.)	72
Sunbeam S8 Twin (487 c.c.)	8
Tandon Supaglid Supreme (197 c.c.)	40
Triumph Speed Twin (498 c.c.)	84
Triumph Thunderbird (649 c.c.)	26
Triumph Tiger 100 (498 c.c.)	76
Velocette LE (192 c.c.)	48
Vincent Comet (449 c.c.)	30
Vincent Rapide and Sidecar (998 c.c.)	36
Vincent Black Shadow (998 c.c.)	4

SCOOTER SECTION

Model	Page
Douglas Vespa Scooter (125 c.c.)	104
Lambretta Scooter (123 c.c.)	106

3 WHEELER SECTION

Model	Page
Bond Minicar, Mk. C (197 c.c.)	108
Reliant Regal Three-wheeler (750 c.c.)	110

CYCLEMOTOR SECTION

Model	Page
Berini Cyclemotor (32 c.c.)	112
Cucciolo Cyclemotor (48 c.c.)	113
Mini-Motor Cyclemotor (49 c.c.)	114
Velo-Solex Motorized Cycle (45 c.c.)	115
Cyclemaster Cyclemotor (32 c.c.)	116
Power Pak Cyclemotor (49 c.c.)	117
B.S.A. Winged Wheel Cyclemotor (35 c.c.)	118

First published 4 August 1949

197 c.c. Dot

A Lightweight

FITTED with the new 197 c.c. two-stroke Villiers engine incorporating the three-speed gear box in unit, the new Dot has a usable cruising speed up to 40–42 m.p.h. The engine of the test machine was quiet mechanically, and the exhaust subdued. With the engine idling, even immediately after a cold start had been made, there was only a slight mechanical whirr and hardly a trace of piston slap. When the machine was ridden at speed on the open road the engine was almost inaudible to the rider, and the exhaust note was low and pleasant to the ear. The engine,

Petrol tank of the test machine was completely chromium-plated; the mudguards are cream

in fact, by virtue of its smoothness and silence, could be said to be completely unobtrusive between speeds of 25 and 40 m.p.h. in top gear. At speeds below 25 m.p.h. in top gear there was a certain transmission roughness. Above 42 m.p.h. there was vibration which was particularly perceptible at the handlebars and saddle.

Apart from the vibration, the engine gave the impression that it was not overstressed when speeds up to 47–48 m.p.h. were held for long periods. It became fussy on one occasion only during the course of the test. That was when an attempt was made to take a petrol consumption reading at a maintained 50 m.p.h. This necessitated driving the machine nearly flat out for some six miles. After four miles the engine showed signs of tightening-up.

Starting, with the engine cold or hot, could generally be accomplished on the second or third dig at the kick-starter assuming the throttle was about two-thirds open. Kick-starting required almost negligible physical effort, but care was required to avoid hitting the footrest with one's instep at the end of the swing of the kick-starter crank.

Slow running on the test model was uncertain. The pick-up on the first quarter of the twistgrip's movement was patchy, whether the engine was running free or under load. Once the engine was pulling on rather more than quarter throttle, it two-stroked regularly and evenly. On level roads two-stroking was regular at speeds of 25 m.p.h. and above.

The relative positions of the saddle and footrests is good, allowing a comfortable leg angle. The handlebar is carried in split clamps, and is adjustable for angle. It is mounted unusually low—for these days. In no position was the angle of the grips such that the rider's wrists were comfortable. The handlebar controls are well placed in relation to the grips. Those for the front brake, clutch and compression-release, are carried on fixed, welded pivot blocks on the handlebar.

The clutch was light and sweet in operation and freed perfectly. Bottom gear could be engaged noiselessly when the machine was stationary with the engine running, and neutral could be positively and effortlessly selected from either bottom or second gears. The gear change was light and smooth. Knife-into-butter gear changes could be made with a slow, leisurely movement of the pedal. So simple were both up and downward gear changes that the gear selector mechanism came in for more use, perhaps, than was strictly necessary.

Both brakes were light in operation and were more powerful by far than those normally associated with the smaller capacity class mount. The braking figure of 28 feet from 30 m.p.h. was achieved on a good surface road just after a heavy shower. Wet though the road surface was, fierce braking gave no cause for concern. Of the handlebar controls, only the

Three light-alloy clamps are used to fix the 197 c.c. Villiers engine in the frame. Simmonds locking nuts are employed

Two-stroke

With a Famous Name

twistgrip was heavy. Also, since it is of the spiral type, there was the almost inevitable trace of backlash.

At speeds below seven or eight m.p.h. the steering was heavy and there was a tendency to rolling. Low-speed negotiation of right-angle corners, when the machine was heeled well over, was not as satisfactory as it might have been. At speeds above 10 m.p.h. the handling gave no grounds for criticism. Corners and bends could be taken effortlessly at speed, and straight-ahead steering was first-class. Road-holding was up to the general standard obtainable with rigid-frame machines.

Throughout the course of the test the engine remained oil-tight. Some oily messiness resulted when the float chamber came loose as a result of vibration during the taking of maximum speed figures. There was also considerable seepage of petrol from the tank filter-cap. There was no oily blowback from the carburettor.

Wet weather encountered in the course of the test provided the opportunity to test the effectiveness of the mudguards. They are wide and of deep section, and afford more protection than the average guard of the present day.

A centre stand with ball-shaped feet is fitted. On one occasion when the machine was parked on a tar-macadam road on a hot day the machine toppled over as a result of the feet of the stand "digging in." The stand was fairly easy to use provided the machine was pulled backwards and upwards by the lifting handle attached to the rear mudguard, and the camber was such that the machine leaned in towards the rider.

Lighting is by Varley "dry" accumulator charged through a Westinghouse rectifier. The illumination provided was good and the horn note loud and clear. Mounted on the handlebar, close to the twistgrip, is a combined horn

The brake pedal is a light-alloy casting. During the course of the test the engine remained oil-tight and the exhaust pipe did not discolour

button and dip switch. The dip switch is conveniently positioned and functioned positively. The horn button, however, required rather too much thumb pressure and is awkwardly placed for delicate operation.

A tool-box of ample proportions is fitted on the side of the rear mudguard and clamped to the lifting handle. A pillion seat was provided on the test model, but there were no pillion footrests and there was no provision for mounting them. The pump is carried out of the way of the elements in a vertical mounting under the saddle. In its position on top of the fork, the lightweight Smith's speedometer is easily read from the saddle. And the head lamp is so mounted that the switch can be easily operated from the saddle without the rider having to fumble below the speedometer. The petrol tank of the test machine was completely chromium plated; the mudguards are cream.

Information Panel

SPECIFICATION

ENGINE: Villiers 197 c.c. (59 x 72 mm) single-cylinder two-stroke with three-speed gear in unit. Roller-bearing big-end: ball bearings supporting mainshafts. Flat-crown, die-cast, aluminium-alloy piston. Detachable light-alloy cylinder head with hemispherical combustion chamber. Petroil lubrication.

CARBURETTOR: Villiers "Middleweight" carburettor, with twistgrip throttle control and separate mixture control operated by handlebar lever. Air-filter standard.

GEAR BOX: Villiers three-speed in unit with engine; positive foot control. Top, 5.87 to 1. Second, 9.98 to 1. Bottom, 19.1 to 1.

TRANSMISSION: Chain, Primary ⅜ x 0.255in.: oil-bath chain case. Secondary, ½ x 0.225in. with guard over top run.

IGNITION: Villiers flywheel magneto.

LIGHTING: By A.C. generator, Varley Dry Accumulator, and Westinghouse Rectifier. Twin-filament 24W main bulb.

PETROIL CAPACITY: 2¾ gallons.

TYRES: Dunlop, 19 x 3.00in front and rear.

BRAKES: 5in dia. internal expanding front, and 6in rear.

SUSPENSION: Webb link-type fork with pressed-steel blades and central compression spring.

WHEELBASE: 52⅜in.

SADDLE: Terry: height, 27in.

WEIGHT: 229 lb fully equipped and with ¼-gallon of fuel.

PRICE: £81. Purchase Tax (in Britain only), £25 17s. 4d. Speedometer, extra £3 3s. 6d. (P.T., 17s. 2d.).

ROAD TAX: £1 17s 6d a year: 10s 4d a quarter.

MAKERS: Dot Cycle and Motor Manufacturing Co., Ltd., Arundel Street, Manchester, 15.

DESCRIPTION: *The Motor Cycle*, 7 April, 1949.

PERFORMANCE DATA

MAXIMUM SPEED: Bottom: 26 m.p.h.
Second: 40 m.p.h.
Top: 54 m.p.h.

ACCELERATION:

	10-20 m.p.h	15-25 m.p.h	20-30 m.p.h
Bottom	2.2 secs	3.4 secs	—
Second	3.2 secs	3 secs	3 secs
Top	—	5.8 secs	6.6 secs

Speed at end of quarter-mile from rest: 52 m.p.h.
Time taken from 0 to 30 m.p.h.: 6.8 secs.

PETROIL CONSUMPTION: At 30 m.p.h., 144 m.p.g. At 40 m.p.h., 120 m.p.g. At 45-50 m.p.h., 104 m.p.g.

BRAKING: From 30 m.p.h. to rest: 28 feet.

MINIMUM NON-SNATCH SPEED: 15 m.p.h.

WEIGHT PER C.C.: 1.11 lb.

> First published 11 August 1949

998 c.c. Vincent-H.R.D.

An Ultra-high Performance Mount for the holding and a Cruising

MERE mention of the name "Black Shadow" is enough to speed the pulse. Since the machine's introduction in 1948 as a super-sports brother to the already famous Rapide, the sombrely finished "Shadow" has achieved wide distinction. It is a connoisseur's machine: one with speed and acceleration far greater than those of any other standard motor cycle; and it is a motor cycle with unique and ingenious features which make it one of the outstanding designs of all time.

So far as the standards of engine performance, handling and braking are concerned—the chief features which can make or mar an otherwise perfect mount—the mighty Black Shadow must

Every line of the 998 c.c. vee-twin Black Shadow is suggestive of powerful urge. Cruising speed is anything up to 100 m.p.h.!

be awarded 99 out of 100 marks; 99 because nothing, it is said, is perfect.

The machine has all the performance at the top end of the scale of a Senior T.T. mount. At the opposite end of the range, notwithstanding the combination of a 3.5 to 1 gear ratio, 7.3 to 1 compression ratio and pool quality fuel, it will "chuff" happily in top at 29-30 m.p.h. Indeed, in top gear, without fuss and with the throttle turned the merest fraction off its closed stop, it will surmount average gradients at 30 m.p.h.

In Britain the machine's cruising speed is not only limited by road conditions, it is severely restricted. It is difficult for the average rider in this country to visualize a route on which the Black Shadow could be driven for any length of time at its limit or near limit. During the test run speeds of 85-90 m.p.h. were commonplace; 100 m.p.h. was held on brief stretches and, occasionally, the needle of the special 150 m.p.h. Smith's speedometer would indicate 110. No airfield or stretch of road could be found which would allow absolute maximum speed to be obtained in two directions, against the watch. Flash readings in two directions of 118 and 114 were obtained, and in neither case had the machine attained its maximum. Acceleration from 100 m.p.h., though not vivid, was markedly good.

The compression ratio of the test model, as has been remarked, was 7.3 to 1. This is the standard ratio, but models for the home market and low-octane fuel are generally fitted with compression plates which reduce the ratio to 6.5 to 1. The greater part of the test was carried out on "pool," though petrol-benzole was used when the attempts were made to obtain the maximum speed figures.

Steering and road-holding were fully in keeping with the exceptionally high engine performance. A soft yet positive movement is provided by the massively proportioned Girdraulic fork. There is a "tautness" and solid feeling about the steering which engenders confidence no matter what the speed and almost irrespective of the condition of the road surface. Corners and bends can be taken stylishly and safely at ultra-high speeds. There was no chopping, no "sawing"; not one of the faults which are sometimes apparent on high-speed machines. Bottoming and consequent clashing of the front fork were, however, experienced once or twice. Low-speed steering was rather heavy.

Any grumble the critics may have had with regard to the Vincent rear suspension has been met by the fitting of the hydraulic damper between the spring plunger units. So efficient is the rear springing now, that never once was the rider bumped off the Dualseat or forced to poise on the rests. Even at speeds around the 100 m.p.h. mark, only the absence of road shocks gave indication that there was any form of rear-springing, such was the smoothness and lateral rigidity.

Straight-ahead steering was in a class by itself. The model could be steered hands off at 15 m.p.h. with engine barely pulling or just as easily at 95 to 100 m.p.h. The steering damper was required only at speeds over 115 m.p.h.

Used in unison, the four brakes (two per wheel) provided immense stopping power. Light pressure of two fingers on the front-brake lever was sufficient to provide all the braking the front wheel would permit. One of the front brakes, incidentally, squealed when in use. The leverage provided at the rear brake is small, and the brake operation was heavy.

The compact engine-gear unit remained exceptionally clean throughout the 700-mile test. Only a faint smear of oil and slight discoloration of the front exhaust pipe close to the port indicated that the model had been ridden at all

Black Shadow

Connoisseur : Magnificent Steering and Road-Speed of Up to 100 m.p.h.

Engine starting from cold was found difficult at first. Cold starting was certain, however, provided that only the front carburettor was flooded and the throttle control was closed. When the engine was hot there was no difficulty.

After a cold or warm start the engine would immediately settle down to a true chuff-chuff tickover. Throughout the course of the test the tickover remained slow, certain and one-hundred per cent reliable. No matter how hard the previous miles had been, the twistgrip could always be rolled back against its closed stop with a positive assurance that a consistent tickover would result.

The engine was only tolerably quiet mechanically. At idling speeds there was a fair amount of clatter, particularly from the valve gear. But so far as the rider was concerned, all mechanical noise disappeared at anything over 40 m.p.h. All that remained audible was the pleasant low-toned burble of the exhaust and the sound of the wind in the rider's ears.

Bottom gear on the Black Shadow is 7.25 to 1. Starting away from rest can seem at first to require a certain amount of skill in handling the throttle and clutch. The servo-assisted clutch had a tendency to bite quickly as it began to engage.

Extreme lateral rigidity is a feature of the massively-proportioned Girdraulic fork. The trail can be altered for sidecar work in a few minutes

The Riding Position

The riding position for the 5ft 7in rider who carried out the greater part of the test proved to be first-class. The saddle height is 31in, which is comfortable for the majority of riders. The footrests are sufficiently high to allow the rider complete peace of mind when the machine is heeled over to the limit, and were sufficiently low to provide a comfortable position for the 5ft 7in rider's legs.

Now famous, the 25½in from tip to tip, almost straight, Vincent-H.R.D. handlebar provides a most comfortable wrist angle and a straight-arm posture. All controls are widely adjustable—the gear pedal and brake pedal for both height and length. Both these controls, incidentally, move with the footrests when the latter are adjusted.

The gear change was instantaneous but slightly heavy in operation. Snap gear changes could be made as rapidly as the controls could be operated. The clutch freed perfectly throughout the test and bottom gear could be noiselessly selected when the machine was at standstill with the engine idling. However, because of the pressure required to raise the pedal it was sometimes necessary to select neutral by means of the hand lever on the side of the gear box, and also to engage bottom gear by hand.

In the 700 miles of the road test the tools were never required. In spite of the high speeds there was no apparent sign of stress. Primary and rear chains remained properly adjusted. There was very slight discolouring of the front exhaust pipe close to the port and a smear of oil from the base of one of the push rod tubes on the rear cylinder. The ammeter showed a charge at 30 m.p.h. in top gear when all the lights were switched on and the road illumination was better than average. An excellent tool-kit is provided and carried in a special tray under the Feridax Dualseat.

There are many ingenious features of the Vincent-H.R.D. which brand it as a luxury mount built by highly skilled engineers who at the same time are knowledgeable motor cycle enthusiasts. The Black Shadow finish is distinctive, obviously durable and very smart; and only a minor reason why the "Shadow" attracts a crowd of interested passers-by wherever it is seen!

Information Panel

SPECIFICATION

ENGINE : 998 c.c. (84 x 90 mm) vee-twin high camshaft o.h.v. with gear box in unit. Fully enclosed valve gear. Dry-sump lubrication : tank capacity, 6 pints. Four main bearings. Roller-bearing big-ends. Specialloid pistons. Cast-iron liners shrunk into aluminium-alloy cylinder barrels. Aluminium-alloy cylinder heads!

CARBURETTORS : Amal : twistgrip throttle control and twin-handlebar-mounted air levers.

TRANSMISSION : Vincent-H.R.D. 4-speed gear box with positive-stop foot control. Gear ratios : Top, 3.5 to 1. Third, 4.2 to 1. Second, 5.5 to 1. Bottom, 7.25 to 1. Servo-assisted clutch. Primary chain, ⅜in pitch triplex, enclosed in aluminium-alloy case. Secondary chain, ⅝ x ⅜in. with guard over top run, R.p.m. at 30 m.p.h. in top gear ; 1,392 approx.

IGNITION AND LIGHTING : Lucas magneto with auto-advance. Miller dynamo : 7in headlamp : stoplight. Dynamo output, 50 watts.

FUEL CAPACITY : 3¾ gallons.

TYRES : Front, 3.00 x 20in Avon ribbed : rear, 3.50 x 19 Avon studded.

BRAKES : Twin on each wheel : drums 7in diameter x ⅞in wide.

SUSPENSION : Girdraulic fork front with twin helical compression springs and hydraulic damping ; link action ; pivot-action rear springing hydraulically damped.

WHEELBASE : 56in. Ground clearance, 5in unladen.

SADDLE : Feridax Dualseat. Unladen height, 31in.

WEIGHT : 476 lb fully equipped and with approximately ¾ gallon of fuel.

PRICE : £315 plus purchase tax (in Britain only) £85 1s. Price includes Smith's speedometer.

ROAD TAX : £3 15s a year (£1 0s 8d a quarter).

DESCRIPTION : *The Motor Cycle* 19 February, 1948.

PERFORMANCE DATA

MEAN MAXIMUM SPEED : Bottom : 68 m.p.h.
Second : 87 m.p.h.
Third : 110 m.p.h.
Top : Not obtained.

ACCELERATION :

	10-30 m.p.h.	20-40 m.p.h.	30-50 m.p.h.
Bottom	2.4 secs	2.8 secs	3 secs
Second	3.6 secs	4.2 secs	3.4 secs
Third	—	5.8 secs	4.8 secs
Top	—	—	7.6 secs

Speed at end of quarter-mile from rest : 96 m.p.h.
Time to cover standing quarter-mile : 14.2 secs.

PETROL CONSUMPTION : At 30 m.p.h., 96 m.p.h. At 40 m.p.h., 91.2 m.p.g. At 50 m.p.h., 86.4 m.p.g. At 60 m.p.h., 70 m.p.g.

BRAKING : From 30 m.p.h. to rest, 26ft 6in (surface, coarse, dry chipping).

TURNING CIRCLE : 14ft.

MINIMUM NON-SNATCH SPEED : 21 m.p.h. in top gear.

WEIGHT PER C.C. : 0.48 lb.

> First published
> 8 December 1949

497 c.c. Dominator

An Attractive Machine With Outstanding All-round Performance

WITH its high standard of mechanical quietness, excellent low-speed torque and smoothness, and rip-snorting top-end performance, the Norton 497 c.c. parallel-twin engine in the Dominator sets a new criterion in its class. When it was started from cold the engine of the test machine was barely audible above the slow, even chuff from the exhausts. Even after it had been driven as hard as possible for four hours, the engine was as quiet as it had been at the beginning, and it would still idle perfectly slowly with complete reliability.

The engine's excellent low-speed torque is one of its most

Zestful performance together with exceptional flexibility are features of the 497 c.c. Norton Dominator

attractive features. It proved so good, in fact, that it gave the impression that the engine was bigger than a 500 c.c. and a "woolly" one at that. It was only necessary to use third gear to accelerate from 20 m.p.h. onward if one was in a real hurry. From idling to full bore the pick-up was clean and rapid. Acceleration right up the range was of the most exhilarating kind. From 60 m.p.h., and even 70 m.p.h., the model would respond instantaneously. There was no marked tendency to pinking.

Acceleration through the gears when the entire engine performance was used was so zestful as to be almost breathtaking and again gave the impression that this was an engine over 500 c.c. The maximum speed available on British roads, when the rider was sitting up and clad in bulky coat and waders, was 80-85 m.p.h., depending on the conditions. Mean maximum speed, with the rider "right down to it," was 92 m.p.h. An enchanting feature, however, was that the machine could be driven for as long as was wanted at 80-85 without giving any hint of stress. No oil leaks were apparent from either engine or gear box. The exhaust pipes did not discolour, even slightly, at the ports. Though at the end of one hard ride, in the course of which 20 miles were covered in 18 minutes, the engine tended to "run on" when the cut-out was operated, other signs of overheating on the road were never evident.

An engine with better balance than that of the Dominator it is difficult to imagine. At low speeds the engine was beautifully and unobtrusively smooth. It remained so throughout its speed range except for a very slight "period" at 60 m.p.h. The transmission smoothness was in keeping with that of the engine. There was also a pleasant "tautness" about the transmission. It was free from snatch at all except inordinately low speeds.

All-round machine performance, however, does not depend on a high b.h.p. engine output alone. The gear ratios must be well suited to engine characteristics. In the case of the Dominator the ratios could not be better chosen. The gear change was light and almost instantaneous, and the pedal movement pleasantly short. Throughout the course of the test the clutch freed perfectly and took up the drive smoothly. Neutral could be simply selected from bottom or second gears (and *vice versa*) when the machine was stationary even if the idling speed of the engine was fairly fast. All the indirect gears were commendably quiet in operation.

Though the engine of the test model had been run-in when the machine was delivered, it was still "tight." It remained so throughout the course of the 600-odd mile test. When cold, it could not be made readily to spin when the kick-starter was operated. Starting from cold was nevertheless generally accomplished without undue physical effort on either the second or third depression of the kick-starter crank. No particularly careful setting of the controls was necessary before making a cold start. When hot the engine was a certain first-kick starter.

On the standard of its exhaust quietness the Norton must again be granted full marks. The machine passed through built-up areas unobtrusively. Only the harshest of harsh driving tactics when the machine was between buildings or walls would make the exhaust noisy; even then the note was low toned and pleasant to the rider.

As would be expected from any Norton, the handling of the Dominator at speed was sheer joy. Fast bends and corners could be

No oil leaks were apparent from either engine or gear box during the course of the test. The sensibly large tool-box will be noted

Norton Twin

Exceptional Standards of Smoothness and Flexibility

A near-side view of the Dominator. The brake lever is long and well positioned

taken cleanly at speed in the classic manner. There was always that "on rails" feeling—even when the model was heeled over at seemingly impossible angles. Straight-ahead steering was of the quality that allowed the machine to be steered hands off at any speed between 20 m.p.h. and 90 m.p.h. Only once was the steering damper used. That was when a long, downhill straight, clear of side-turnings or obstructions, was taken on full throttle, the machine attaining 97 m.p.h. The surface was bumpy, and without the damper there was a tendency to yawing.

Low-speed steering was equally good. In the initial stages of the test a slight roll was apparent at low speeds. It disappeared, however, after the adjustment of the steering-head bearings had been eased. Thereafter, the model could be ridden feet-up at the slowest crawl. Stability on wet and greasy roads was so good as to inspire confidence no matter how bad the surface was. The total weight of 421 lb, plus petrol, was never apparent once the machine was on the move.

The Roadholder telescopic fork and plunger-type rear suspension have rather hard characteristics. Comparatively little comfort is provided at low speeds on poor road surfaces. At speed on the open road, however, the suspension comes into its own and allows pot-holes to be taken hands off or, when the model is heeled over, without allowing the machine to get the slightest bit out of hand.

When used seriously together the brakes provided excellent stopping power. In the early stages of the road test the front brake was poor. It improved as it bedded down, but never quite came up to recognized Norton standard. It was also unduly heavy in operation. Even so, on damp tar macadam a braking figure of 29ft from 30 m.p.h. was the mean of eight attempts. The brakes were both smooth and progressive and they could be confidently used on wet road surfaces. Brake efficiency was unimpaired when the machine was ridden in a rainstorm. There were no signs of fading when the brakes were deliberately abused.

Saddle height is 30½in. This was found to be ideal for riders of average stature. In their delivery position, i.e., with the hangers in the rear-horizontal position, the footrests were well placed in relation to the saddle and handlebars and were high enough to clear the ground when the machine was leant over to the maximum on corners. It was felt that the handlebars could with advantage have been narrower. Tank width across the kneegrips is a mere 9½in and does much to enhance riding comfort on long journeys.

Average protection from road filth was afforded by the mudguards. They were easy to clean and, with their circular stays, provide a smart appearance. Both prop and centre stands could be easily operated. The prop-stand hinges from the nearside front engine plate and is extremely robust. The lifting handles are sensibly placed for centre-stand operation.

Pillion rests and a pillion seat were fitted to the model tested. The position of the rests was too high and too far to the rear for comfort. Both fuel and oil filler caps, incidentally, were liquid tight. The dimensions of the tool-box were ample for the really excellent kit provided, plus a repair outfit and miscellaneous spares such as plugs, chain links, and bulbs.

The head lamp's driving beam was sufficient to allow a cruising speed of up to 60 m.p.h. in the dark. Full battery discharge was balanced at 30 m.p.h. in top gear.

Finish of the machine is black and chromium, and there are silver panels on the tank. The proportion of chrome, silver and black is tasteful and the general appearance very smart.

Information Panel

SPECIFICATION

ENGINE: 497 c.c. (66 x 72.6 mm) o.h.v. vertical twin. Fully enclosed valve gear operated from a single camshaft. Plain bearing big-ends. Roller journal main bearing on driving side; ball journal on timing side. Compression ratio, 6.75 to 1. Dry-sump lubrication; tank capacity, 7 pt.

CARBURETTOR: Amal; twistgrip throttle control; air-slide operated by handlebar control.

IGNITION AND LIGHTING: B.T.-H. or Lucas magneto with auto-advance. Separate 45 W Lucas dynamo. 7in head lamp.

TRANSMISSION: Norton four-speed gear box with positive foot control. Bottom 14.9 to 1. Second, 8.85 to 1. Third, 6.05 to 1. Top, 5.0 to 1. Multi-plate clutch with Ferodo inserts. Primary chain, ⅜in x 0.305in, in pressed-steel oil-bath case. Secondary chain ⅝in x ¼in. R.p.m. at 30 m.p.h. in top gear, 1,940.

FUEL CAPACITY: 3¾ gallons.

TYRES: Dunlop. Front, 21 x 3.00in ribbed. Rear, 19 x 3.50in Universal.

BRAKES: Both 7in diameter x 1¼in wide; hand adjusters.

SUSPENSION: Norton "Roadholder" telescopic fork with hydraulic damping. Plunger-type rear-springing with springs for compression and rebound.

WHEELBASE: 56in. Ground clearance, 5½in unladen.

SADDLE: Lycett. Unladen height, 30½in.

WEIGHT: 421 lb with no fuel and fully equipped.

PRICE: £174, plus Purchase Tax (in Britain only), £46 19s 8d.

ROAD TAX: £3 15s a year; £1 0s 8d a quarter.

MAKERS: Norton Motors, Ltd., Bracebridge Street, Birmingham, 6.

DESCRIPTION: *The Motor Cycle*, 11 November, 1948.

PERFORMANCE DATA

MEAN MAXIMUM SPEED: Bottom : 34 m.p.h.
Second : 61 m.p.h.
Top : 92 m.p.h.

MEAN ACCELERATION:

	10-30 m.p.h.	20-40 m.p.h.	30-50 m.p.h.
Bottom	2.2 secs	—	—
Second	3.8 secs	3 secs	3.2 secs
Third	8.6 secs	6.4 secs	4.8 secs
Top	—	8.8 secs	6.6 secs

Mean speed at end of quarter mile from rest : 79 m.p.h.
Mean time to cover standing quarter mile : 17.4 secs.

PETROL CONSUMPTION: At 30 m.p.h., 79 m.p.g. At 40 m.p.h., 72 m.p.g. At 50 m.p.h., 64 m.p.g. At 60 m.p.h., 52 m.p.g.

BRAKING: From 30 m.p.h. to rest, 29ft (surface, damp tar macadam).

TURNING CIRCLE: 16ft 6in.

MINIMUM NON-SNATCH SPEED: 11-12 m.p.h. in top gear.

WEIGHT PER C.C.: 0.85 lb.

> First published 5 January 1950

487 c.c. Sunbeam

Luxury Tourer with Excellent Steering,

WHEN the first thrilling post-war Sunbeam was announced it was acclaimed as a mount embodying most of the features demanded by the cognoscenti. With its in-line parallel twin-cylinder engine and gear box in unit, shaft drive, coil ignition, unique appearance and many ingenious features it represented a complete breakaway from current motor cycle design.

The Model S8, of course, is the lightened version of the original design. It is a machine which has so many praiseworthy

Numerous detail features of the S8 Sunbeam make it easy to clean and maintain

attributes that it is hardly possible to single out any one of them and say of it that therein lies the model's attraction. But if there is one feature that leaves an outstanding impression after experience with the S8 it is the smoothness of the engine and transmission, especially when the engine is revving in the higher ranges. The end of every run during the test, irrespective of length, and under all but the very worst of weather conditions, was reached with regret.

There was no pace above 30 m.p.h. which could be said with certainty to be the machine's happiest cruising speed. The engine gave the impression that it was working as well within its limits at 75-80 m.p.h. as it was at 45-50 m.p.h. It thrived on hard work and was a glutton for high revs.

A pronounced tendency to pinking on pool fuel was noted when the machine was being accelerated hard in top or in third gears. Therefore, on the occasions when it was wanted to reach B from A just as quickly as the machine could be urged, the engine had to be revved very hard in the indirect ratios. Peak r.p.m. in bottom and second gears, and almost as high r.p.m. as were available in third were frequently used—with the most pleasing results. Steering and road-holding were so good that the rider was encouraged to swing the bends with joie de vivre.

No oil leaks became apparent in the 600-odd miles of the test. The exhaust pipes did not even lightly discolour. Nothing vibrated loose. The toolkit was only removed from its box on one occasion—and that was out of sheer curiosity. Mechanical noise was no more apparent at the end of a hard ride than it was at the beginning. Except on the odd occasions when grit found its way into the jet block, engine idling was slow and certain. When the engine was running at idling speed or only slightly faster it rocked perceptibly on its rubber mounting. This rocking was transmitted to the handlebars in the form of slight vibration and was apparent up to speeds of just over 30 m.p.h. in top gear.

Above, say, 33 m.p.h., there was complete smoothness. Even when the engine was peaking in the indirect ratios the machine was smooth to a degree never hitherto experienced with motor cycles. The harder the engine was revved the smoother and more dynamo-like the machine apparently became. Only the inordinate exhaust noise tended to restrict the use of really high r.p.m.; the exhaust noise, it should perhaps be added, was never obtrusive to the rider.

Starting the engine from cold during a really icy spell, or when it was already hot, was so easy that a child could do it. When the engine was cold it was necessary to close the carburettor air-slide by depressing the easily accessible spring-loaded plunger on top of the carburettor and lightly flood the carburettor; then, with the ignition switched off, to depress the kick-starter twice; switch on the ignition, and the engine would tick-tock quietly into life at the first kick. The air-slide could be opened almost immediately after a cold start.

Because of the combination of well-chosen kick-start gearing and relatively low compression ratio, so little physical effort is required to operate the kick-starter that it can be depressed easily by hand pressure. If there was ever such a thing as tickle-starting, the Sunbeam most certainly has it.

An outstandingly high standard of mechanical quietness was yet another of the Sunbeam's qualities. Only the pistons were audible after a cold start. As near as could be ascertained, the valve-gear was noiseless. Low-speed torque was very good, and the engine would pull away quite happily in top gear from 19-20 m.p.h.

From idling to full throttle the carburation was clean and the pick-up without any trace of hesitation. Acceleration was all that could be expected from a machine which falls into a "luxury fast-touring" rather

Notable features to be seen in this view include the unit-construction, pancake-type dynamo, streamlined air-cleaner, and rear-springing

S8 Twin

Road-holding and Braking

than a "sports" classification. When the mood was there however, and the full engine performance was used in the indirect ratios, acceleration was markedly brisk.

Pressure required to operate the gear change was so light that the pedal could hardly be felt under a bewadered foot. The range of movement of the pedal was delightfully short and allowed upward or downward gear changes to be made merely by pivoting the right foot on the footrest. Clean, delightful gear changing could be effortlessly achieved. Between bottom and second and second and third gears the pedal required a slow, deliberate movement. Between third and top gears the change was all that could be wished for—light and instantaneous. The clutch, too, was light in operation and smooth and positive in its take-up of the drive. It freed perfectly and continued to do so even after six standing-start "quarters." It required no adjustment during the course of the test.

Riding Position

For riders of all but unusually tall or short statures, a better riding position than that provided by the S8 could not be imagined. Saddle height is 30in. The footrests can be ideally situated (they are adjustable through 360 deg.) so that they provide a comfortable knee angle. Even at their lowest position of adjustment they are sufficiently high not to foul the road when the model is banked well over on sharp corners or fast bends, or when it is being turned round in the width of narrow lanes. The wrist angle provided by the handlebars was extremely comfortable.

Handling was at all times beyond criticism. There was no trace of whip from the duplex frame or of lack of lateral rigidity from the plunger-type rear suspension. With plunger-type suspension spring characteristics normally have to be rather "hard." Total movement was approximately 1¼in. The degree of cushioning is therefore not large. The hydraulically damped, telescopic front fork was very light round static load and behaved perfectly under all conditions.

Both brakes provided first-class stopping power. They were light to operate and smooth and progressive in action. They did not fade under conditions of abuse, never required adjustment

During the test, the unit remained free from oil leaks. Exceptional smoothness of running was a feature of the power unit

during the test, and were not adversely affected when the machine was driven hard through heavy rain and snow. The standard of mudguarding was very good. A long, road-width beam was provided by the 8in head lamp. Full lamp load was balanced by the 60-watt pancake generator at 30 m.p.h. in top gear.

Numerous detail features of the machine make it easy to clean and maintain. The ignition coil, voltage control regulator, ammeter and combined ignition and lighting switch are housed in a metal container below the saddle. Opposite to it the battery is housed in a lead-lined box of similar proportions and design. Both front and rear wheels are quickly detachable, the rear especially so. Ignition and oil warning lights are located in the head lamp, one on each side of the speedometer. The speedometer in this position was easily read when the rider was in a normally seated position. The instrument registered approximately seven per cent fast and ceased to function at 589 miles.

Finish of the test machine was black and chromium and the quality fully in keeping with the high engineering standards used on the machine.

Information Panel

SPECIFICATION

ENGINE: 487 c.c. (70 x 63.5 mm) in-line vertical-twin with chain-driven overhead camshaft. Valves set in single row at 22½ deg. to vertical. Squish-type combustion chambers. One-piece aluminium-alloy cylinder head. Crankcase and cylinder block in one-piece aluminium-alloy casting with austenitic cylinder liners. Light-alloy connecting rods with lead-bronze big ends. Wet sump lubrication; sump capacity, 4 pints.

CARBURETTOR: Amal; twistgrip throttle control; air control on carburettor.

TRANSMISSION: Sunbeam four speed gear box in unit with engine: positive-stop foot control. Bottom, 14.5 to 1. Second, 9 to 1. Third, 6.5 to 1. Fourth, 5.3 to 1. Sidecar ratios: Top, 6.13 to 1. Third, 7.4 to 1. Second, 10.3 to 1. Bottom, 16.6 to 1. Single-plate clutch, Final drive by shaft and underslung worm. R.p.m. in top gear at 30 m.p.h. (solo gearing), 2,034.

IGNITION AND LIGHTING: Lucas 60-watt "pancake" dynamo at front end of crankshaft. Coil ignition with auto-advance. 8in diameter head lamp.

FUEL CAPACITY: 3¼ gallons.

TYRES: Dunlop 4.00 x 18in rear; 3.25 x 19in front.

BRAKES: 8in x ⅞in rear. 8in x 1⅛in front.

SUSPENSION: Sunbeam telescopic fork with hydraulic damping Plunger-type rear suspension.

WHEELBASE: 57in. Ground clearance, 5¼in unladen.

SADDLE: Terry, Unladen height 30in.

WEIGHT: 423 lb with empty tanks and fully equipped.

PRICE: £179, plus Purchase Tax (in Britain only) £48 6s 8d. Price includes speedometer.

ROAD TAX: £3 15s a yer; £1 0s 8d a quarter.

MAKERS: Sunbeam Cycles, Ltd., Birmingham, 11.

DESCRIPTION: *The Motor Cycle*, 29 September, 1949

PERFORMANCE DATA

MEAN MAXIMUM SPEEDS: First: *35 m.p.h.
Second: *58 m.p.h
Third: 80 m.p.h.
Top: 83 m.p.h.
*Valve float just beginning.

MEAN ACCELERATION:

	10-30 m.p.h.	20-40 m.p.h.	30-50 m.p.h.
Bottom	3 secs	—	—
Second	5.2 secs	4.2 secs	4 secs
Third	7.6 secs	6.8 secs	5.6 secs
Top	—	9 secs	7.2 secs

Mean speed at end of quarter-mile from rest: 77 m.p.h.
Mean time to cover standing quarter-mile: 18.2 secs.

PETROL CONSUMPTION: At 30 m.p.h., 102 m.p.g. At 40 m.p.h., 92 m.p.g. At 50 m.p.h., 71 m.p.g. At 60 m.p.h., 62 m.p.g.

BRAKING: From 30 m.p.h. to rest, 25ft 6in (surface, coarse-textured tar-macadam).

TURNING CIRCLE: 15ft 9in.

MINIMUM NON-SNATCH SPEED: 12 m.p.h. in top gear.

WEIGHT PER C.C.: 0.9 lb.

> First published 19 January 1950

997 c.c. Ariel Four

A Connoisseur's Outfit With Scintillating

BROADLY speaking, there are two distinct classes of sidecar enthusiast. One is the family man who uses the outfit of his choice as ride-to-work transport during the week and takes his family for an outing on Saturday or Sunday. The other and smaller group comprises the hard-riding enthusiast who delights in having an outfit with something approaching 500 c.c. solo performance—an outfit with which he can cover,

The four-cylinder engine was powerful and flexible

should he so wish, 300–400 miles a day. Though these classes, on the face of it, require machines with vastly different characteristics, the 997 c.c. Ariel Four has traits which make it eminently suitable for both of them. It starts easily, and is quiet, flexible and smooth. On the other hand, it will cruise with such an absence of fuss at 60–65 m.p.h. that as many miles a day can be effortlessly covered as even the most avid enthusiast could desire.

Throughout the course of the test, engine starting was at all times easy. To make a start from cold, it was necessary only to turn the engine over four or five times with the carburettor bi-starter control in the "out" position. Then, with the ignition switched on and the throttle rather less than a quarter open, the engine would respond to the first real dig at the kick-starter. When hot, the engine would start first kick by the rider merely applying his weight on the kick-starter, or, if he were astride the machine, without his having to raise himself from the saddle. There was no need to allow the engine to warm up: as soon as second gear had been engaged the bi-starter control could be moved to its mid-way position and, as soon as top gear was engaged, the control could be pushed right in.

Just after a start from cold the engine was reasonably quiet mechanically. Valve gear and crankshaft gears were audible. The pistons were also audible, but to a lesser degree. When the engine became hot, mechanical noise, from the crankshaft gears especially, increased. The machine had covered some 500 miles in the maker's hands. After a further 600 miles the standard of mechanical quietness had greatly improved. The pleasant drone from the exhausts drowned all traces of mechanical noise so far as the rider was concerned when the machine was at speeds above about 32 m.p.h. Engine idling was satisfactorily reliable, though rather lumpy and irregular.

The clutch took up the drive smoothly and sweetly and was light in operation. The clearance at the cable increased by approximately ⅛in when the standing-start quarter-mile figures were being taken and the clutch, in consequence, was being brutally abused.

Upward gear changes could be executed easily, noiselessly, and lightly. The change from third to top gear could be made just as quickly as the controls could be operated. Downward changes during the first 400 miles of the test were just as sweet and positive. Later, downward gear changes were accompanied by slight clashing unless the speed was allowed to drop right down before the changes were made or the throttle blipped as the clutch was withdrawn.

For two decades the even torque of the Square Four has been something of a byword among enthusiasts. The engine of the test machine was smooth right through the range, except for a slight period at 46–50 m.p.h. From 12–13 m.p.h. in top gear the engine would respond instantaneously to any demands made of it. It appeared to be impossible to make the engine pink, no matter how roughly the throttle was handled and how much the gear box was ignored. If the throttle was snapped open at, say, 13 m.p.h. in top gear, there was faint rumbling from the crankshaft gears and slight transmission flutter until 23 m.p.h. had been reached. At all other times the transmission was beautifully smooth.

At cruising speeds of 60–65 m.p.h., the most often-used speed range on the open road during the test, or when pottering, for example, at 30 m.p.h., the engine produced its power with pleasing smoothness. At speed the exhaust of the test model appeared to be rather noisier than usual with Ariel Square Fours; to the bystander, however, it was an unusually quiet motor cycle.

Acceleration was better than that obtainable from an o.h.v. three-fifty solo and, indeed,

A deeply valanced front mudguard did much to ensure that the machine remained clean. The engine proved oil-tight.

and Sidecar

All-round Performance

almost on a par with that of a good five-hundred solo. It was such that wheelspin could be set up in bottom *and* second gears when the full engine performance was used and the tar-macadam just the slightest shade damp. Harsh tactics were not, however, necessary on the Ariel to obtain high averages. Because of the engine's outstanding flexibility, only medium r.p.m. were called for in the indirect ratios. Acceleration from 30 m.p.h. in top gear was so great that third was seldom necessary for overtaking even on roads where there was heavy traffic and only short straights. Normal main-road hills called for just a shade more throttle to compensate for the gradient. Head winds, or the weight carried in the sidecar, made no appreciable difference to the machine's performance. The indirect ratios, and third gear especially, were audible.

Handling qualities of the outfit were excellent. Corners and bends could be swung with the utmost ease and confidence. On left-hand bends there was at all times power on tap; it was merely a case of twisting the grip farther even if the corner was entered on three-quarters throttle. On left-hand corners at low speeds there was an annoying flat spot.

Outstanding comfort was provided on the Square Four by the combination of the excellent front fork (one of the best of the present day), link-action rear-springing, large saddle, and capital riding position. Steering was hands off when the machine was on the crown of the road at any speed between six and 70 m.p.h. The fork has a long, soft movement and progressive build-up so that it satisfactorily absorbs minor road shocks or potholes. The rear suspension provides a good measure of comfort, though there were occasionally slight traces of pitching between front and rear suspensions on wavy surfaces. Although "solo" fork trail is employed, the steering was not unduly heavy.

Both brakes provided adequate stopping power for the outfit. Hard pressure on the front brake lever was sufficient to squeal the tyre at 50 m.p.h. The rear brake was also light in action and the new pedal position perfect for ease of operation.

A Watsonian Avon sidecar was fitted to the machine tested

What of the sidecar? In most respects the Watsonian Avon fitted for the purpose of the test earned full marks. The body was wide enough to allow the passenger to change his position on long journeys. The windscreen provided sufficient protection in normal weather and, when the hood was raised, the interior was snug, except for slight draughts from between the edges of the screen and hood, where a gap is provided at each side for ventilation purposes. There was no vibration. The suspension on normal main roads was good, but passenger comfort would have been improved on bumpy country lanes if there had been a toe rest in the nose of the body. A roomy glove rack and map pocket are provided inside. The capacious locker and the luggage grid (attached to the locker door) were sufficient to cope with luggage for two or even three people. The hood was quickly and easily erected.

In brief, the Ariel Square Four and Watsonian Avon proved in almost every respect an admirable and most attractive outfit; it is a thrilling mount with a scintillating performance, plus excellent road manners.

Information Panel

SPECIFICATION

ENGINE: 997 c.c. (65 x 75 mm) four-cylinder o.h.v. Aluminium-alloy cylinder cast en bloc in square formation. Detachable light-alloy cylinder head and totally enclosed and positively lubricated valve-gear, with push-rod operation. Twin crankshafts coupled by hardened and ground gears. Light-alloy connecting rods with plain, shell-type big-end bearings. Compression ratio, 6 to 1. Dry-sump lubrication; oil-tank capacity, 6 pints.
CARBURETTOR: Solex, bi-starter type; twistgrip throttle.
GEAR BOX: Burman four-speed with positive-stop foot control. Sidecar ratios: Bottom, 31.2 to 1. Second, 8.4 to 1. Third, 6.2 to 1. Top, 4.9 to 1. Multi-plate clutch. R.p.m. at 30 m.p.h. in top gear, 1,902.
TRANSMISSION: Chain. Primary, $\frac{1}{2}$ x 0.305in in oil-bath chaincase. Secondary chain, $\frac{5}{8}$ x $\frac{3}{8}$in, lubricated by adjustable bleed. Guards over bottom and top runs of secondary chain.
IGNITION: Coil. 70-watt, voltage-controlled Lucas dynamo incorporating distributor with automatic ignition timing: six-bolt coil.
LIGHTING: Lucas 7in head lamp with prefocused light unit; domed glass; 30-watt twin-filament head lamp bulb.
FUEL CAPACITY: $3\frac{3}{4}$ gallons.
TYRES: Dunlop. Front, 3.25 x 19in ribbed. Rear, 4.00 x 18 Universal.
BRAKES: Ariel 7in x 1$\frac{1}{8}$in front and rear. Fulcrum adjusters.
SUSPENSION: Ariel telescopic fork with hydraulic damping. Ariel link-action rear-wheel springing.
WHEELBASE: 56in.
GROUND CLEARANCE: 5in unladen.
SADDLE: Lycett. Height, 29in unladen.
WEIGHT: Complete outfit, 672 lb with $\frac{1}{2}$-gallon of fuel and oil-tank full.
PRICE: Machine, £194, plus Purchase Tax (in Britain only): £52 7s 8d. Spring-frame extra, £15 (Purchase Tax £4 1s).
MAKERS: Ariel Motors, Ltd., Selly Oak, Birmingham.
DESCRIPTION: *The Motor Cycle*, 11 November, 1948.

SIDECAR

MODEL: Watsonian Avon single-seater sports.
CHASSIS: Watsonian VG 21, with quarter elliptic springs at rear, coil springs at front. Silentbloc wheel mounting.
BODY: Overall length, 84in. Width and depth of seat squab, 21$\frac{1}{2}$ x 23in. Cushion measures 20 x 20in. Height inside with hood raised, 33in.

Locker dimensions (approx., since shape is irregular), 26in long x 22in wide x 15in high. Luggage grid on locker door. Black twill hood.
PRICE: Body, £30, plus Purchase Tax, £8. Chassis, £20, plus £5 6s 8d Purchase Tax.

PERFORMANCE DATA

MEAN MAXIMUM SPEED: Bottom* : 44 m.p.h
Second* : 66 m.p.h
Third : 70 m.p.h.
Top : 69 m.p.h.
*Valve float occurring.

MEAN ACCELERATION:

	10-30 m.p.h.	20-40 m.p.h.	30-50 m.p.h
Bottom	3.2 secs	3 secs	—
Second	3.2 secs	4 secs	4.2 secs
Third	6.8 secs	6.4 secs	6 secs
Top	—	8.6 secs	8.4 secs

Mean speed at end of quarter-mile from rest : 67 m.p.h.
Mean time to cover standing quarter-mile : 20.4 secs.
PETROL CONSUMPTION: At 30 m.p.h., 50 m.p.g. At 40 m.p.h., 45 m.p.g. At 50 m.p.h., 40 m.p.g. At 60 m.p.h., 36 m.p.g.
BRAKING: from 30 m.p.h. to rest, 52 feet (surface, wet tar-macadam).
MINIMUM NON-SNATCH SPEED: 12 m.p.h. in top gear.
WEIGHT PER C.C.: 0.68 lb.

| First published 2 February 1950 |

499 c.c. Overhead-valve

A Robust Single-cylinder Mount Tested :

STRAIGHTFORWARD, robust design and construction are, of course, characteristic of all the M group B.S.A.s. The 499 c.c. overhead-valve model M33 is typical and provides the sort of performance which makes it an admirable general-purpose mount for solo or sidecar work. The machine under test was tried in both forms. It was taken over fitted with a B.S.A. sidecar (and sidecar gearing) and run for some 400 miles. Then the sidecar was removed and, without change of engine sprocket,

The M33 B.S.A. was found to handle well in both solo and sidecar forms

a second set of performance figures was taken and a further 300 miles covered. In each case the all-round performance was such that it equalled and, indeed, in solo form, far surpassed the standard which had been anticipated, bearing in mind that the model is an inexpensive-type touring mount.

Cold or hot, the engine started very easily. When the weather was cold, even with temperatures well below freezing point, no especially precise control setting was necessary in order to achieve a cold start. Moreover, with use of the exhaust valve lifter, the muscular effort required to operate the kick-starter was less than that called for to start many a modern multi.

All that was required when making a cold start was to close the handlebar-mounted air lever, retard the ignition about one-fifth, and flood the carburettor. Assuming the throttle were only a fraction open, the engine would fire at the third kick. Immediately after a cold start the air lever could be opened fully and ignored for the remainder of that day. When hot, the engine was a certain "first dab" starter.

The standard of mechanical quietness was moderately good. Piston and valve-gear noises could be identified just after a cold start; they became less audible when the engine was hot. To the rider in a normally seated position on the machine, mechanical noise was not obtrusive and in top gear it was drowned almost completely by the cracking exhaust note at any speed over 40 m.p.h. The exhaust, it should be added, was distinctly "healthy" and may be criticized on the score that it tended to restrict the use of maximum acceleration in built-up areas.

The tickover of the test engine was not 100 per cent reliable unless the carburettor was set to give rather too fast idling on anything except nearly full ignition retard. Throughout the remainder of the throttle range the carburation was entirely clean, and the pick-up, from idling to full throttle, brisk and certain. The gear ratios were well matched to engine performance. In the gears the outfit's acceleration was extremely good. Indeed, as the figures in the panel prove, acceleration was almost on a par with that of a 350 c.c. solo.

The positiveness of the gear change, too, was an aid to acceleration. If desired, snap changes could be made between third and top. The ratios between first and second and second and third were rather wider and a slight pause was necessary when making upward changes.

Downward changes could be quickly and effortlessly accomplished between any pair of gears.

Gear-pedal movement was pleasantly short and "taut," and the lever excellently positioned for ease of operation. During the greater part of the test the clutch freed perfectly and was smooth and sweet in its take-up of the drive. In delivery tune there was hardly sufficient tension on the springs, and there was slip and consequent overheating when the sidecar speed figures were being taken. With the spring pressure increased, however, there was no recurrence of the bother. Lightness of the clutch operation was not noticeably impaired because of the increased spring pressure.

Highest comfortable cruising speed of the outfit was 50-55 m.p.h. with a ten-stone passenger in the sidecar. While, relatively speaking, this may not be excitingly fast, 40 m.p.h. averages were commonplace. Factors largely contributing to good averages were, of course, the machine's good acceleration and excellent handling. Machine and sidecar were perfectly aligned. Normal left- and right-hand turns could be negotiated without appreciable lowering of the speed.

The engine was unusually quick in the

Close-up of the power unit, which has a number of features making for easy maintenance

M33 B.S.A.

Sidecar and Solo Forms

response to the throttle—a feature which made the B.S.A. a very easy machine to drive. A pronounced tendency to pinking on hills, or when the throttle was snapped open quickly, was easily curbed by intelligent use of the ignition control, to which, incidentally, the engine was extremely sensitive.

With the exception of the dip-switch (mounted on the clutch lever clamp block) all controls were well positioned for ease and speed of operation. When the ignition lever was in the full advance position, dip-switch operation was awkward since the two were too close together.

The riding position was felt to be among the best of the present day. Excellent comfort, too, was provided by the B.S.A. telescopic fork, which has just the right spring loading to suit most conditions. Rear-wheel hammer, when the machine was used with the sidecar, was hardly noticeable.

In the early stages of the test, both brakes were rather too spongy. They improved with use, but the rear brake never quite came up to desired efficiency.

Sidecar Commentary

The sidecar earned full marks in all respects, except that the screen offered insufficient protection. In all conditions the suspension was very good and provided excellent comfort over all but the very worst going. The seat and squab are placed at comfortable angles to one another. When the hood was raised the interior was cosy and unusually free from draughts. The hood is of the folding type on a pivoting frame. It can be quickly and easily erected and, when not in use, stows away neatly into a twill "envelope." The lines of the sidecar are such that it looks equally smart with the hood raised or lowered. Finish was all-black.

Removing the sidecar (or refitting it) was the work of a few minutes only. As a solo the M33 was especially impressive. It handled extremely well under all conditions. On greasy cobbles or tramlines and on icy roads it imparted complete confidence. At low speeds the general handling of the model was first-class.

At speed on the open road, straight-ahead steering was beyond criticism. There was, of course, more rear-wheel hop than there had been when the sidecar was fitted, but it was not unduly bad, unless the surface was of the B-class road variety taken at real speed. There appeared to be no obvious limit to the angle to which the model could be heeled over. Only at reckless speeds was there any trace of snaking on corners. The steering-damper was required after the sidecar was removed only when the machine was in the seventies. On bad surfaces the fork occasionally "bottomed" on rebound.

Solo acceleration (with the sidecar gearing) was markedly brisk and made traffic work and hill-climbing sheer joy. Cruising speed could be 70-75 m.p.h. and the maximum speed obtained was 80 m.p.h. Economy was not apparently affected by the low gearing, the fuel consumption working out at 106 m.p.g. at a maintained 40 m.p.h. In fact, except that bottom gear was rather low, there was no impression at all that the gearing was other than standard.

Two oil leaks were apparent at the end of the test. One was at the top push-rod cover tube coupling, and the other was from the oil-tank filler cap. The exhaust pipe discoloured slightly near the port.

The B.S.A. has many features of interest to the enthusiast who carries out his own routine maintenance. Only a lengthy list would encompass them all, but one example is that tappet adjustment is provided at the base of the push-rods and the adjusters are reached merely by removing four screws. The float chamber, and main needle jet, can be easily removed without hindrance to spanner movement. The oil-tank drain plug is accessible and so placed that oil draining out falls clear of the gear box. Cable adjusters on the throttle and air cables are placed near the handlebar levers. A cam-type chain adjuster is fitted to the rear-wheel spindle.

In its position on top of the fork bridge, the speedometer was easily read and did not interfere with the accessibility of the head-lamp switch. The tool-kit provided is excellent—but the tool-box is not large enough to accommodate also a tyre repair outfit, spare plug, bulbs, etc. An excellent driving light was provided by the head lamp. The filaments of two pilot bulbs were fractured, apparently by vibration at peak revs when the performance figures were taken. Protection afforded by the wide-section mudguards was better than average. The standard of the finish is very good.

Information Panel

SPECIFICATION

ENGINE: B.S.A. 499 c.c. (85 mm x 88 mm) single-cylinder o.h.v. with fully enclosed valve-gear. Double journal bearings on mainshaft driving side, single journal bearings on timing side; gear-driven magneto. Dry-sump lubrication with gear pumps; oil-tank capacity, 5 pints.
CARBURETTOR: Amal, with twistgrip throttle. Air-slide operated by handlebar lever.
GEAR BOX: B.S.A. four-speed with positive foot control. Bottom 16.72 to 1. Second, 11.5 to 1. Third, 7.37 to 1. Top, 5.59 to 1. R.p.m. at 30 m.p.h. in top gear, 2,250.
TRANSMISSION: Chain. Primary, ½in x 0.305in in oil-bath chain case. Secondary chain, ⅝in x ¼in, with guards over top and bottom runs.
IGNITION AND LIGHTING: Lucas Magdyno with manual ignition control on handlebar. 7in diameter head lamp with domed glass.
FUEL CAPACITY: 3 gallons.
TYRES: Dunlop Universal—3.25 x 18in front, 3.50 x 19in rear.
BRAKES: 7in diameter front and rear; finger adjusters.
SUSPENSION: B.S.A. telescopic fork front with hydraulic damping.
WHEELBASE: 54in. Ground clearance, 5¼in unladen.
SADDLE: Terry; Unladen height, 30½in.
WEIGHT: 595 lb fully equipped and with 2 gallons of fuel. Machine solo, 387 lb with empty fuel tank.
PRICE: Machine (solo), £218, plus Purchase Tax (in Britain only), £34 11s 4d.
ROAD TAX: £3 15s a year (solo). £1 0s 8d a quarter.
DESCRIPTION: *The Motor Cycle*, 4 November, 1948.
MAKERS: B.S.A. Cycles, Ltd., Small Heath, Birmingham, 11.

SIDECAR

MAKE: B.S.A. Model 22/47.
CHASSIS: Triangular with quarter elliptic springs at rear and twin compression coil springs at front. Four-point attachment.
BODY: Coachbuilt (timber frame with steel panels). Celluloid screen. Folding twill hood. Overall length, 7ft 1in. Cushion, 18in long x 18¼in wide. Squab, width at top, 1ft 10½in; at base, 1ft 5¼in; 1ft 10¼in high. Height inside when hood is raised, 36in. Distance from squab to nose, 34in. Locker dimensions (approximately, since shape is irregular), 17in high x 17in wide x 25in long.
PRICE: Body, £59 5s, plus Purchase Tax (in Britain only), £15 16s. Chassis, £22 10s. Purchase Tax, £6.

PERFORMANCE DATA
Solo figures are quoted in brackets.

MEAN MAXIMUM SPEED: Bottom : *32 (*32) m.p.h.
Second : *45 (*45) m.p.h.
Third : 58 (*66) m.p.h.
Top : 59 (80 m.p.h.)
*Valve float occurring.

MEAN ACCELERATION:

	10-30 m.p.h.	20-50 m.p.h.	30-50 m.p.h.
Bottom	4.6 (3.2) sec		
Second	4.9 (3.2) sec	5.2 (3.4) sec	—
Third	8.6 (4.8) sec	7.0 (4.2) sec	8.0 (4.0) sec
Top	—	11.2 (5.6) sec	11.6 (5.0) sec

Speed at end of quarter-mile from rest: 56 (66) m.p.h.
Time taken to cover standing quarter: 22.4 (18.4 secs).
PETROL CONSUMPTION: At 30 m.p.h., 94 (113) m.p.g. At 40 m.p.h., 68 (106) m.p.g. At 50 m.p.h., 49 (77) m.p.g. At 60 m.p.h., 40 (58) m.p.g.
BRAKING: From 30 m.p.h. to rest, 51 (30) feet.
TURNING CIRCLE: 14ft 3in.
MINIMUM NON-SNATCH SPEED: 14 m.p.h. in top gear with ignition fully retarded.
WEIGHT PER C.C.: 1.2 (0.77) lb.

First published 23 February 1950

596 c.c. Norton Big

A Lusty Side-valve Providing Excellent

FOR day-in, day-out reliability, without the need for constant maintenance, a large section of the sidecar public contends that the side-valve engine provides the perfect answer. Certainly, experience with the 596 c.c. side-valve No. 1 Norton, the famous Big Four, goes a long way towards bearing this out.

The maximum cruising speed of the outfit under test was 50-53 m.p.h. with a 10½-stone passenger in the Swallow all-metal sidecar. Average speeds under fair give-and-take conditions generally worked out at approximately 40 m.p.h. The machine would maintain its 50-53 m.p.h. all day long, apparently without

a sturdy "force" on tap irrespective of the conditions, and irrespective of the number of miles already covered that day. The maximum speed and acceleration figures were taken on a gusty day with a heavily garbed rider and a 10½-stone passenger.

True, as a result of much full-throttle driving, the exhaust pipe discoloured badly below the port and the silencer also discoloured. Nevertheless, signs of overheating were never evident on the road and the engine would idle as reliably at the end of a brutal ride as it would at the beginning. The engine in the test machine was smooth right through the throttle range, though vibration was, of course, apparent when the engine was revved to the point of valve-float.

Low-speed torque developed by the engine was altogether exceptional. The engine would pull slowly and evenly down to speeds of round 15 m.p.h. in top gear, and the outfit would trickle along quietly and effortlessly at 12 m.p.h. in third. On hills, third gear was rarely required. Such was the torque that the outfit would chuff its way up steep gradients in a fussless manner at a steady 30 m.p.h., or accelerate, quite happily, up the speed scale.

The Big Four Norton was found to be almost as lively with a full sidecar load as it was with the sidecar empty

effort. It gobbled up the miles in an easy, effortless fashion, the low-revving characteristics of the engine giving an impression of lusty power.

Acceleration was brisk rather than "sparkling" in the modern sense. But the machine accelerated in a way which again gave that feeling of limitless power. The Norton was almost as lively with a full sidecar load as it was with the sidecar empty. Another feature was that acceleration uphill was not much below that attainable on the level. There was at all times

Starting from Cold

The engine was extremely sensitive to the ignition advance-and-retard control. With the lever in the full-advanced position (forward and with the tension off the cable—a good point), there was a tendency to pinking if the throttle was snapped open or handled hamfistedly on up gradients. With the ignition lever and throttle used in unison, however, pinking could easily be avoided.

Engine starting from cold was easy provided that the air lever was closed and the ignition lever left in the full-advance position. It was unnecessary, and, indeed, undesirable (as with most side-valve engines these days) to flood the carburettor since this could result in wetting the plug. On the side of the carburettor mixing chamber there was a tommy-bar type throttle stop, which, when turned to the right, gave the correct throttle opening for making a cold start. An exhaust valve-lifter lever is fitted on the left handlebar. It was easy to use and, when the valve was raised, the engine could be spun without undue muscular effort or knack. The engine usually fired at the second or third kick when cold and was a certain first-kick starter when warm.

After the engine had been running for a minute or so following a cold start, the air lever could be fully opened and the throttle stop turned to its normal position. With the ignition set at about three-quarters retard, the engine would idle in the best "gas engine" fashion. On full advance the tickover was equally smooth and reliable, though slightly faster, of course.

In delivery tune, the engine was commendably quiet mechanically. When idling, the tappets and piston were barely audible. Later in the test—which embraced over 800 hard miles—the tappets became slightly noisier, but mechanical noise, generally speaking, had not increased. The exhaust noise prohibited the use of maximum acceleration in built-up areas.

The clutch freed perfectly under all conditions and was smooth in its take-up of the drive. Bottom gear could be effortlessly and silently engaged from

The engine was quiet mechanically, and remained oil-tight. Tappets and piston were barely audible when the engine was idling

Four and Sidecar

Engine Characteristics for Sidecar Work

Finish of the Swallow all-metal sidecar was in red and black. The sidecar was roomy and comfortable for a passenger of average build

neutral when the machine was stationary and the engine idling; and neutral was equally easily found from either bottom or second gear. Quiet in operation, the new gear box provided an excellent gear change. Snap changes, if desired, could be noiselessly effected between any pair of gears both upward and downward. Pedal movement was light and short. The pedal could be moved by the rider merely pivoting his right foot easily on the footrest.

A first-class riding position was provided by the relationship between the saddle, handlebars and footrests. All the controls, and especially that for the front brake, were well placed for easy operation. They were light to use, with the exceptions of those for the clutch and front brake, which were rather heavy.

Standard of Comfort

Under dry-weather conditions, the brakes when employed in unison were up to required standard. They were smooth in operation, with just the right degree of "sponginess." When the machine was ridden in the rain, or on roads that were awash, the efficiency of the front brake became seriously impaired.

Steering and road-holding of the test outfit was good, though slightly more sidecar toe-in would have been appreciated. Corners and bends could be swung effortlessly at speed. The standard of comfort provided, too, was high.

Greater than average protection from road water was provided by the deep-section front and rear mudguards. The engine remained oil-tight. Illumination provided by the Lucas head lamp was very good; the dynamo balanced the full lamp load when the machine was being driven at 30 m.p.h. in top gear.

The pilot-bulb filament fractured when the speed figures were being taken. The tool-kit provided is better than average and the tool-box dimensions are really sensible, allowing a repair outfit and other spares to be easily carried.

The sidecar was roomy and comfortable for a passenger of average build. Locker dimensions were adequate for one week-end size suitcase and a travelling valise. It was felt that the entry to the locker could have been wider with advantage. Moderate protection was provided by the celluloid screen. There was considerable draught inside when the hood was raised. The bolts holding the body to the chassis came loose on one occasion. It was not always possible to lock the lid of the locker without a great deal of fumbling because of the tongue of the lock not mating perfectly with its socket. Finish of the sidecar was red and black.

Information Panel

SPECIFICATION

ENGINE: 596 c.c. (82 mm x 113 mm) single-cylinder side-valve. Fully enclosed valve-gear. Detachable aluminium-alloy cylinder head Dry-sump lubrication. Oil capacity, 4 pints.

CARBURETTOR: Amal, with tommy-bar type throttle stops for easy starting. Twistgrip throttle control. Gauze-type flame-trap fitted to air intake.

IGNITION AND LIGHTING: Lucas Magdyno, with manual ignition advance-retard control. 7in diameter Lucas head lamp with pre-focus light unit and domed glass.

TRANSMISSION: Norton four-speed gear box with positive foot control. Top gear 5.47 to 1. Third, 6.61 to 1. Second, 9.67 to 1. Bottom, 16.25 to 1. Multi-plate clutch with Ferodo inserts. Primary chain, ½in x 0.305in in pressed-steel oil-bath. Secondary chain, ⅝in x ¼in; guard over top run. R.p.m. at 30 m.p.h. in top gear, 2,120.

FUEL CAPACITY: 2¾ gallons.

TYRES: 19 x 3.25in Dunlop front and rear.

BRAKES: Both 7in diameter by 1¼in wide; hand adjusters.

SUSPENSION: Norton "Roadholder" telescopic fork with hydraulic damping.

WHEELBASE: 54½in Ground clearance, 5in unladen.

SADDLE: Lycett. Unladen height, 30¼in.

WEIGHT: Complete outfit, 616 lb fully equipped and with full tank.

PRICE: Machine only, £142, plus Purchase Tax (in Britain only), £38 6s 10d.

ROAD TAX: £5 a year; £1 7s 6d a quarter.

MAKERS: Norton Motors, Ltd., Bracebridge Street, Birmingham, 6.

DESCRIPTION: *The Motor Cycle*, 30 October, 1947.

SIDECAR

MODEL: Swallow. Single-seater.

CHASSIS: Norton Model G. Double triangulated steel chassis with cee-springs at rear and laminated leaf springs at front.

BODY: All-welded steel construction. Overall length, 79in. Width, 22in. Squab to toe plate, 40in. Height inside when the hood is raised, 33in. Windscreen measures 21½in x 11in deep. Squab measures

23in x 18½in wide. Seat cushion, 19½in long x 16½in wide. Locker dimensions, 17½in wide x 18in long x 14in high.

PRICE: £57, plus Purchase Tax, £15 4s.

PERFORMANCE DATA

MEAN MAXIMUM SPEED: Bottom : *27 m.p.h.
Second : *41 m.p.h.
Third : 53 m.p.h.
Top : 55 m.p.h.
*Valve float occurring.

MEAN ACCELERATION:

	10-30 m.p.h.	20-40 m.p.h.	30-50 m.p.h.
Bottom	—	—	—
Second	5.8 secs	8.8 secs	—
Third	8.8 secs	8.6 secs	13.4 secs
Top	—	11.4 secs	16.4 secs

Mean speed at end of quarter-mile from rest : 51 m.p.h.
Mean time to cover standing quarter-mile : 24.2 secs.

PETROL CONSUMPTION: At 30 m.p.h., 59 m.p.g. At 40 m.p.h., 48 m.p.g. At 50 m.p.h., 36 m.p.g.

BRAKING: From 30 m.p.h. to rest, 45ft 6in.

TURNING CIRCLE: 16ft 8in.

MINIMUM NON-SNATCH SPEED: 15 m.p.h. in top gear with ignition fully retarded.

WEIGHT PER C.C.: 1.03 lb.

First published 6 April 1950

197 c.c. James Captain

Appealing Two-stroke Fitted with Spring-frame : Lively

A MORE versatile motor cycle than the 197 c.c. rear-sprung Captain de Luxe James is difficult to imagine. With its lightweight and excellent turning lock, the machine can be effortlessly manhandled by almost anyone—be it man or woman, boy or girl. Coupled with the engine's easy starting, economy and cleanliness, these features make the machine an attractive runabout. On the other hand, the model's excellent riding position, plunger-type rear-springing, ruggedness of construction, and 45-48 m.p.h. cruising speed made it suitable for long runs.

Slightly more than an inch of total up-and-down travel is pro-

A de luxe 197 c.c. two-stroke with rear-springing—the James Captain

vided by the rear-springing, which is very light round the static-load position. Since the springing of the front fork is also relatively light round static load, the result is that even the slightest road ripple is satisfactorily dealt with.

Steering and road-holding are at all times very good. Bumpy, twisting country lanes in Worcestershire and Warwickshire could be negotiated confidently and comfortably—probably more quickly and more comfortably than with many larger machines. Had it not been for the fact that the centre stand fouled the road when the model was heeled well over, there seemed to be no limit to the machine's banking angle.

Any selected path on a corner or bend could always be unerringly held. When sunken drain covers and broken road edges near the gutter were ridden over, so well did the suspension do its job that there was never any call for the rider to ease his weight on the rests or take a firmer grip of the bars. In fact, this novel situation was appreciated to such tune that road bumps were deliberately sought out and taken fast.

Outstanding comfort was afforded over cobbles and undulating, rain-swollen wood blocks. On wet surfaces the stability of the "Captain" was good. It was, indeed, very good. The machine was deliberately ridden along wet tramlines set in cobbles. There was only cause for concern on the occasions when the line was sunk to more than average depth. On muddy, three-ply trials going, the machine could not possibly have been more easily controllable.

Another factor which was responsible in large measure for the confidence-engendering character of the James, was the excellence of the riding position. Saddle height is 30⅜in. The position was found to be comfortable, and the rider could effortlessly take his weight on the footrests. Carried in split clamps, the handlebar is adjustable for height, fore-and-aft position, and for angle of the grips.

Apart from a slight oil leak which appeared at the compression-release valve on the final day of the test, the engine remained remarkably clean. There were no other oil leaks or even slight external traces of oil. The standard of mechanical quietness was very good. Slight piston slap was apparent when the engine was started from cold. This disappeared almost completely when the engine's normal working temperature was reached. All that was then audible, apart from the exhaust, was a mechanical whirr. As the revolutions mounted the noise increased, but was never objectionable.

James machines have a reputation for exhaust quietness. The silencer on the test model did not come up to recognized par. However, the exhaust could only be termed obtrusively noisy when the engine was idling and, consequently, firing irregularly.

In delivery tune, the engine was difficult to start, so much so that push-starts were sometimes necessary. Though there appeared to be nothing wrong with the sparking plug fitted, a change of plug proved a remedy. Then, when the engine was hot, it would start at the second depression of the kickstarter provided the throttle was fully one-third open.

Cold starting was equally easy. In this case, of course, it was necessary to move the mixture control lever on the right handlebar forward to its fullest extent and to flood the carburettor. Again the throttle required to be about one-third open. The axes of the kickstarter crank and offside footrest were rather close together. Because of this, care had to be taken to keep one's foot clear of the foot-

Neat legshields-cum-crash-bars fitted to the James were found to give excellent protection in wet weather. Standard of mechanical quietness of the engine was very good

de Luxe

All-round Performance

rest. It was really a question of knack, however, and once the knack of *not* making a "long swinging kick" (which was not, in any case, necessary) was acquired, there was no undue difficulty. The folding kick-starter tucked in nicely out of the way.

On the open road the James would sing along happily at speeds of between 45 and 48 m.p.h.: 45 m.p.h. was comfortably maintained on occasion against strong headwinds.

Power on hills was good, and most main road hills could be breasted at 40 m.p.h. on slightly more than three-quarters throttle. No sign of fatigue or over-driving was ever apparent, though during the test the model was undoubtedly driven harder than it would probably be in the hands of an average, intelligent owner. Vibration was apparent only when the machine was grossly over-revved. The transmission was without any trace of roughness except on those occasions when the engine was running too light to fire regularly or running so slowly as to cause snatch.

Two-stroking was regular at above quarter throttle. Irrespective of the placing of the mixture control, it was not possible to obtain regular firing at smaller throttle openings. Nor was it possible to achieve a pick-up that was entirely clean from idling speeds, even when the engine was under load, and, as might be expected in these circumstances, the tickover was unreliable.

The clutch was light in operation and delightfully smooth in its take-up of the drive. Bottom gear could be easily engaged without noise when the machine was at a standstill with the engine running. Neutral was effortlessly and positively selected from either bottom or second gear. The gear change was light and smooth and the pedal movement short. Clean gear changes were certain provided the gear pedal was moved with a slow, deliberate movement.

Both brakes on the test mount were light in operation and sufficiently in keeping with the performance of the machine. There was a slight tendency to fading when the brakes were used harshly from high speeds. They were progressive in effect and could be used with confidence on wet roads.

All controls were smooth and easy to operate. The throttle twist grip had no tendency to "run back" when released. All hand controls are mounted on split clamps and are adjustable for position on the handlebar as well as for angle. No more than average hand reach was required to operate the clutch and front brake.

Lighting current is supplied by a battery and rectifier set,

Apart from a slight oil leak at the compression-release valve, the engine remained commendably clean. Rear-springing gave outstanding riding comfort

and a 7in Lucas head lamp is employed. The driving light was very good and allowed daylight cruising speeds to be safely maintained after dark. The tool-box fitted on the offside of the machine was large enough to accommodate tools, repair outfit, and so on, without resort to cramming.

A centre stand is the only stand fitted. It is therefore intended for parking purposes as well as for use when puncture repairing. Because of its height and the forward position of its pivot, it is not so easy to operate as might be wished for as a parking stand. A prop-stand would be a welcome additional fitting.

Legshields-cum-crash-bars were fitted to the test model. They were found to give excellent leg protection in bad weather and, in fact, made the wearing of waders unnecessary so far as cleanliness was concerned. A point that was greatly appreciated was that not a seep of petrol appeared outside the tank filler cap, which is scalloped for ease of tightening and slackening. A brake indicator is fitted and operates in conjunction with the rear light. A carrier is part of the standard equipment. There is a lightweight electric horn.

The finish is in maroon with pale-blue panels on the tank, the colours of the famous Airborne regiment. The handlebar, exhaust pipe, and other usually plated parts are chromed.

Information Panel

SPECIFICATION

ENGINE: Villiers 197 c.c. (59 x 77 mm) single-cylinder two-stroke with three-speed gear in unit. Roller-bearing big end; ball bearings supporting mainshafts. Flat-crown, die-cast, aluminium-alloy piston. Detachable, light-alloy cylinder head with hemispherical combustion chamber. Petroil lubrication.
CARBURETTOR: Villiers "Middleweight" with twistgrip throttle control and separate mixture control operated by a handlebar lever. Air-filter standard.
GEAR BOX: Villiers three-speed in unit with engine. Gear ratios: Bottom, 19 to 1. Second, 9.96 to 1. Top, 5.86 to 1
TRANSMISSION: Chain: Primary $\frac{3}{8}$ x 0.225in; oil-bath chain case. Secondary, $\frac{1}{2}$ x 0.225in with guard over top run.
IGNITION AND LIGHTING: Villiers flywheel magneto with lighting coils; Westinghouse rectifier, and Varley or Lucas accumulator. Twin filament 24 W main bulb.
PETROIL CAPACITY: 2½ gallons.
TYRES: Dunlop, 3.00 x 19in front and rear.
BRAKES: 5in x ⅜in internal expanding front and rear. James hubs
SUSPENSION: James-Dunlop rubber telescopic fork. Plunger-type rear suspension.
WHEELBASE: 49in. Ground clearance, 3¾in unladen.
SADDLE: Lycett. Height 30¾in, unladen.
WEIGHT: 215 lb with dry tank and fully equipped with crash-bars leg-shields and carrier.
PRICE: £87 10s, plus Purchase Tax (in Britain only), £23 12s 6d.
ROAD TAX: £1 17s 6d a year; 10s 4d a quarter.
MAKERS: James Cycle Co., Greet, Birmingham.
DESCRIPTION: *The Motor Cycle*, 13 October, 1949.

PERFORMANCE DATA

MEAN MAXIMUM SPEED: Bottom: 21 m.p.h.
Second: 38 m.p.h.
Top: 56 m.p.h.

MEAN ACCELERATION:

	10-20 m.p.h.	15-25 m.p.h.	20-30 m.p.h.
Bottom	2.4 secs	—	—
Second	3.2 secs	3.4 secs	3.4 secs
Top	—	6 secs	6.4 secs

Speed at end of quarter-mile from rest: 51 m.p.h.
Time taken from 0 to 30 m.p.h.: 6.8 secs.
PETROIL CONSUMPTION: At 30 m.p.h., 110 m.p.g. At 40 m.p.h., 102 m.p.g. At 45-50 m.p.h., 92 m.p.g.
BRAKING: From 30 m.p.h. to rest, 30ft 6in (surface, wet tar-macadam).
TURNING CIRCLE: 10ft.
MINIMUM NON-SNATCH SPEED: 16 m.p.h.
WEIGHT PER C.C.: 1.09 lb.

First published 20 April 1950

123 c.c. B.S.A. Bantam

High-performance Two-stroke with Excellent Front and

SINCE the B.S.A. 123 c.c. Bantam was introduced three years ago, it has earned for itself a wide following among two-stroke enthusiasts. Now, with the A.C. generator available and probably more especially the addition of neat, plunger-type rear suspension, the model's appeal has been further enhanced.

The degree of comfort provided by the combination of the telescopic front fork and rear suspension is quite exceptional for a machine in the 125 c.c. class. Badly surfaced, cobbled roads and tram tracks can be traversed at speed without the wheel-

Rear springing gives the 123 c.c. B.S.A. Bantam de Luxe a high degree of comfort

hop sometimes experienced with lightweights. The rear suspension is commendably light round the static load position so that small road shocks—as well as severe ones—are satisfactorily absorbed.

More than this, however; because of the excellent build-up provided, bottoming on full-shock loading was never experienced with a 10½-stone rider in the saddle. Both front and rear suspensions occasionally could be made to bottom on rebound, but never seriously.

Steering and road holding were of the true confidence-instilling variety no matter what the speed and irrespective of the conditions. The angle to which the model could be heeled over was limited only by the height of the footrests, but even that was sufficient not to cause concern except when heeling the model over rather farther than is strictly necessary under normal conditions.

Holding a chosen line on a corner or bend called for no effort and appeared to be all but automatic. On greasy cobbles and wood blocks the handling earned full marks. It was possible to ride the Bantam feet-up at the slowest crawl. Straight-ahead steering was very, very good.

Ignition on the A.C. generator model is, of course, by battery and coil, and the ignition switch is in the head lamp. To make a cold start the drill was to switch on the ignition, flood the carburettor and close the strangler and, with the throttle held rather more than one-third open, operate the kick-starter. Starting from cold generally needed two or perhaps three digs on the pedal. When started from cold the engine required only about a quarter of a mile to warm up. After the first few seconds the strangler could be opened the merest fraction; then, later, it could be fully opened. It was, incidentally, required for each cold start.

When the engine was hot, starting could be accomplished by making only a negligent half- or quarter-swing on the kickstarter. Operating the kickstarter required little muscular effort, but it was necessary to finish the swing early so as not to come up against the footrest with one's foot.

Mechanical quietness of the engine was excellent and at no time at all were traces of two-stroke rattle identified. The standard of exhaust silencing, however, was not all it might have been both for the rider's and pedestrians' comfort.

Best fast cruising speed of the test machine was in the region of 40 m.p.h., though a maximum cruising speed of 45 m.p.h. could be held for hour after hour apparently without detriment to the engine. In fact, the engine just could not be made to tire. It was driven on full throttle, or nearly so, during 300-odd miles of the test and no ill-effects manifested themselves. At the bottom end of the r.p.m. scale the engine pulled very well indeed. It two-stroked smoothly and evenly at speeds down to 23 m.p.h. in top gear on a flat road where there was no appreciable head wind. The engine did not idle reliably at very low tick-over speeds.

Engine balance was very good and unimpaired at all normally used revs. Vibration was only apparent when the engine was screamed mercilessly in bottom and second gears. The transmission, too, was beautifully smooth and "taut," giving the impression, almost, that there was no rear chain there at all.

Acceleration and power on hills were probably rather better than those associated normally with small two-stroke machines. Similar praise might well be used in connection with the brakes. Both were smooth and

Concentric shafts for kick-start and foot gear-change levers are employed. The crankcase has a commendably neat exterior

de Luxe

Rear Suspension

A Lucas A.C. generator, with battery and coil ignition, was fitted to the machine tested

powerful in operation and required only light pressure at the hand, or foot, control, as the case may be. During the course of the test the front brake cable required adjustment on one occasion.

The gear change operates on the up-for-upward changes and down-for-downward changes principle. Except for the fact that it was not possible to position the gear-change lever so that it could be operated without moving the right foot from its footrest, no criticism could be applied to the gear change; even this is a small criticism, since the pedal provides a short, light movement. Noiseless upward changes could be easily effected between any pair of gears, provided that the pedal was moved with a slow, deliberate movement. If desired, upward changes could be made just as quickly as the controls could be operated and, though the gears with this treatment emitted a slight "click" as they engaged, there was no danger of missing a gear, or, apparently, of causing harm.

Downward changes could always be executed quickly, lightly, easily. The clutch freed perfectly; it was smooth in its take-up of the drive and light in operation. Bottom gear could always be selected noiselessly from neutral notwithstanding a rather high idling speed. Neutral was easily located from either first or second gears.

A high standard of comfort was provided by the combination of a good riding position and controls that were smooth and light in operation and well placed. The handlebars are of the rather wide and flat variety and have the grips comfortably positioned in relation to the saddle. Probably an even greater standard of comfort would be provided if the footrests were mounted slightly farther forward.

Apart from the fact that the rear chain appeared to be receiving too much oil and, in delivery tune, the exhaust pipe joints became messy, the only oil which appeared outside the engine-gear unit was that resulting from flooding the carburettor. The petrol filler cap also had a tendency to leak slightly.

A driving beam that allowed full-throttle riding after dark was provided by the 6in head lamp. The dipswitch was conveniently placed on the left handlebar, and the head-lamp switch itself had a sweet, positive action. The ammeter is illuminated when the lights are switched on. The lamp and coil load was balanced at 30 m.p.h. in top gear. An "emergency" position is provided in the combined light and ignition switch. This causes the battery and rectifier to be by-passed, the coil in this case being fed directly from the A.C. generator (so that the machine can be started even if the battery is flat). With the emergency position of the switch in use, sufficient current was available to provide easy starting on the kickstarter.

The tool-box provided is fitted on the seat pillar. It is large enough to accommodate comfortably the tool-kit, but not, in addition, a repair outfit. The colour scheme is green, cream and chromium and the general appearance very smart.

Information Panel

SPECIFICATION

ENGINE: B.S.A. 123 c.c. (52 x 58 mm) single-cylinder two-stroke with three-speed gear in unit. Roller-bearing big-end; ball bearings supporting mainshafts. Domed crown, Lo-Ex, aluminium-alloy piston. Detachable aluminium-alloy cylinder head. Petroil lubrication.

CARBURETTOR: Amal needle-jet type with twistgrip throttle control. Air filter, with external lever for cold-starting strangler.

TRANSMISSION: B.S.A. three-speed gearbox in unit with engine. Positive stop, fully enclosed, foot-change. Top, 7.0 to 1. Second, 11.7 to 1. Bottom, 22.0 to 1. Cork insert clutch running in oil. Primary chain $\frac{3}{8}$ x 0.225in in oil-bath chain case. Secondary chain $\frac{1}{2}$ x 0.305in with guard over top run.

IGNITION and LIGHTING: Coil. Lucas 45-watt A.C. generator, Westinghouse rectifier and Lucas 5 amp. battery. Twin filament, 24 W main bulb.

PETROIL CAPACITY: 1$\frac{5}{8}$ gallons

TYRES: Dunlop, 2.75 x 19in front and rear.

BRAKES: 5in diameter internal expanding front and rear.

SUSPENSION: Telescopic front fork with a single helical spring in each leg. Plunger-type rear-springing.

WHEELBASE: 50$\frac{1}{2}$in. Ground clearance, 5in.

SADDLE: Mansfield. Height, 28in unladen.

WEIGHT: 171lb with dry tank and fully equipped.

PRICE: £74 3s 6d, plus purchase tax (in Britain only), £20 0s 7d.

ROAD TAX: £1 17s 6d a year; 10s 4d a quarter.

MAKERS: B.S.A. Cycles, Ltd., Small Heath, Birmingham, 11.

DESCRIPTION: *The Motor Cycle*, 6 October, 1949.

PERFORMANCE DATA

MEAN MAXIMUM SPEED: Bottom: 22 m.p.h. Second: 40 m.p.h. Top: 46 m.p.h.

MEAN ACCELERATION:

	10-20 m.p.h.	15-25 m.p.h.	20-30 m.p.h.
Bottom	3.2 secs	—	—
Second	4.2 secs	4.4 secs	4.2 secs
Top	—	8.4 secs	8.0 secs

Mean speed at end of quarter-mile from rest: maximum.
Mean time taken from rest to 30 m.p.h.: 7.8 secs.

PETROIL CONSUMPTION: At 20 m.p.h., 160 m.p.g. At 30 m.p.h., 144 m.p.g. At 40 m.p.g., 112 m.p.h.

BRAKING: From 30 m.p.h. to rest, 32 feet. (Surface, dry tar-macadam).

TURNING CIRCLE: 11 feet.

MINIMUM NON-SNATCH SPEED: 13 m.p.h. in top gear.

WEIGHT PER C.C.: 1.4 lb.

First published 11 May 1950

498 c.c. Ariel Red

A Machine With High All-round Performance,

CHIEF among the reasons advanced in favour of the twin over the single are its flexibility, smoothness and quietness. And it is mainly in these respects, as well as, of course, in all-round performance, that one twin is judged against another. The 498 c.c. Ariel Red Hunter Twin, therefore, because of its excellence in all these regards, must be considered as one of the outstanding mounts in the modern 500 c.c. class.

Mechanical silence of a high order was a feature of the Ariel Twin tested

Probably the machine's most noteworthy feature is its very high standard of mechanical quietness. Hot or cold, the engine on being started would settle down immediately to a beautifully slow, regular tick-over. The valve-gear was all but inaudible, and the only noises that could be identified with certainty were from the pistons. Such was the exhaust quietness that the machine's full acceleration could be used at all times. Indeed, it was possible to take the machine right up to 30 m.p.h. in bottom or second gear without the machine's passage being at all ostentatious.

There was no unduly marked tendency for the engine to pink.

Throughout the period of the test, the air slide was never required for cold-starting, which called for merely two easy depressions of the kick-starter pedal. When warm, the engine started with a light, easy half-swing on the pedal.

From idling speed, right through the throttle range, the carburation was clean and the pick-up brisk. The acceleration through the gears, when the engine performance was used to the full, was sparkling. There was at all times an impression of excellent smoothness of the transmission — a characteristic maintained throughout the 500 miles of the test. Neither chain required any adjustment. Low-speed torque was exceptional for a 500 c.c. twin.

Engine balance was wellnigh perfect. It was one hundred per cent throughout the speed range except that, between 60 and 65 m.p.h., slight vibration could be felt at the handlebars, saddle and footrests— so slight, however, as to be hardly worthy of note.

Where rapid acceleration is wanted, necessary attributes are a quick, upward gear change and ratios that are well suited to the engine characteristics. In these respects the Ariel again earned full marks. Upward gear changes could be made cleanly and in what might almost be described as racing fashion. The clutch was light in operation and delightfully smooth in its take-up of the drive. It freed perfectly at all times and withstood all but the most callous abuse. It required adjustment once: when the standing-start acceleration figures were being taken. Bottom gear could be selected from neutral with the ease of a warm wire slicing into a slab of butter. When the machine was stationary and the engine idling, neutral could be equally easily selected from bottom or second gear.

The upward change, it has been stated, was extremely quick. Care was required if "scrunchless" downward changes were to be obtained. Engine speed had to be carefully matched to the road speed and a pause made at mid-travel of the pedal movement. The indirect ratios were commendably quiet.

Average speeds in the region of 50 m.p.h. proved possible even on journeys of no more than, say, 70 miles which were not without their quota of built-up area. Factors contributing to this were the model's brisk acceleration, the available 70-75 m.p.h. cruising speed, the excellent handling, and powerful braking.

Not a trace of oil appeared at any of the engine joints during the course of the test. Finish of the machine was: red and chromium tank, with black frame and mudguards

Hunter Twin

Excellent Steering and Road-holding

In the early stages of the test, the engine tended to tire if full throttle was used indiscriminately. After 1,000 miles, when the engine was completely run-in, speeds of 70-75 m.p.h. could be held for mile after mile. Not a trace of oil appeared at any of the engine joints. One exhaust pipe became straw-coloured, but not blue, in the neighbourhood of the port. The handling of the machine at speed was sheer joy. There was never any pitching or wavering, nor chopping or snaking. Straight-ahead steering at high speed was perfect. The steering damper was never required. At very low speeds the steering was rather heavy and there was a slight tendency for the machine to roll. This disappeared at speeds over 30 m.p.h. and was never so pronounced as to cause concern on greasy surfaces. Indeed, the handling on grease was first class.

Riding Position

The relationship between saddle, footrests and handlebars is such that the riding position is excellent. It was a position which proved to be equally suitable for fast main-road work or about-town pottering. A taper fit on their hangers, the footrests are adjustable for height and also, of course, move fore and aft. The saddle height was dead right for riders of average stature. The handlebars are clipped to the head lug, forward of the steering axis, and provide a straight-arm posture and a good angle for the wrists. The handlebar controls are of the clip-on type. Though they may be positioned to suit individual riders, the hand-reach necessary for operating the brake and clutch levers was felt to be too great. The gear pedal is adjustable for height, but could have been two inches shorter with advantage. The brake pedal fell immediately beneath the left foot.

The brakes were powerful, smooth, and progressive in action, with just the right amount of sponginess. They

Nearside close-up of the power unit, which was found to be both flexible and smooth

required fairly frequent adjustment if used to the point of abuse. Fulcrum adjusters for the shoes and finger adjusters for the cable or rod (front and rear respectively) are provided, and adjustment is very simply carried out.

In its position on top of the fork legs, the speedometer was easily read by a normally seated rider. Incidentally, it was 5 m.p.h. fast at 50 m.p.h. The position of the headlamp switch in the tank-top instrument panel was appreciated, since the switch is so easily operated.

Better than average protection is provided by the rather wide-section Ariel mudguards. Two separate petrol taps are fitted and each has a reserve position. Full lamp load was balanced by the dynamo at a speed of 30 m.p.h. in top gear. The driving beam was long and flat, but rather too narrow to allow speeds of more than 60 m.p.h. after dark. A pillion seat and pillion footrests were fitted to the test model, and the relationship between the seat and footrests was such as to provide a comfortable riding position. The machine has pleasing lines, and the red and chromium tank and black frame and guards provide a distinctive appearance.

Ariel Red Hunter Twin

Information Panel

SPECIFICATION

ENGINE: Ariel 498 c.c. (63 x 80 mm) twin-cylinder o.h.v. Cylinder heads and rocker boxes in one casting. Forged, one-piece crankshaft; roller bearing on drive side, and plain, white-metal bearing on timing side. Light-alloy connecting rods, with shell, white-metal, big-end bearings. Compression ratio, 6.8 to 1. Dry-sump lubrication; oil-tank capacity, 5 pints.
CARBURETTOR: Amal; twistgrip throttle; air valve operated plunger on top of mixing chamber.
TRANSMISSION: Burman four-speed gear box, with positive-stop foot control. Gear ratios: Bottom, 13.3 to 1. Second, 8.8 to 1. Third 6.4 to 1. Top, 5 to 1. Multi-plate clutch. Primary chain, $\frac{1}{2}$ x 0.305in in oil-bath case. Secondary chain, $\frac{5}{8}$ x $\frac{3}{8}$in lubricated by bleed from primary case and crankcase breather. R.p.m. at 30 m.p.h. in top gear, 1,934.
IGNITION AND LIGHTING: Lucas or B.T.-H. magneto with auto-advance. Separate Lucas dynamo. 7in diameter head lamp.
FUEL CAPACITY: 3¾ gallons. Reserve taps.
TYRES: Dunlop. Front, 3.25 x 20in ribbed. Rear, 3.50 x 19in.
BRAKES: Ariel, 7 x 1⅛, front and rear. Fulcrum adjusters.
SUSPENSION: Ariel telescopic front fork with hydraulic damping. Ariel link-type rear-wheel springing.
WHEELBASE: 56in. Ground clearance, 5in unladen.
SADDLE: Terry. Unladen height, 28in.
WEIGHT: 402lb with dry tank and fully equipped.
TURNING CIRCLE: 14ft.
PRICE: £159, plus Purchase Tax (in Great Britain only), £42 18s 8d.
ROAD TAX: £3 15s a year; £1 0s 8d a quarter.
MAKERS: Ariel Motors, Ltd., Selly Oak, Birmingham, 29.
DESCRIPTION: *The Motor Cycle*, 27 November, 1947.

PERFORMANCE DATA

MEAN MAXIMUM SPEED: Bottom : 40 m.p.h.*
Second : 60 m.p.h.*
Third : 74 m.p.h.
Top : 84 m.p.h.
*Valve float occurring.

MEAN ACCELERATION:

	10-30 m.p.h.	20-40 m.p.h.	30-50 m.p.h.
Bottom	2.8 secs	—	—
Second	4.4 secs	4.0 secs	4.4 secs
Third	7.4 secs	5.2 secs	5.2 secs
Top	—	9.2 secs	7.8 secs

Mean speed at end of quarter-mile from rest : 72 m.p.h.
Mean time to cover standing quarter mile : 17.2 secs.
PETROL CONSUMPTION: At 30 m.p.h., 93 m.p.g. At 40 m.p.h., 82 m.p.g. At 50 m.p.h., 70 m.p.g. At 60 m.p.h., 58 m.p.g.
BRAKING: From 30 m.p.h. to rest, 29ft 3in.
MINIMUM NON-SNATCH SPEED: 11-12 m.p.h. in top gear.
WEIGHT PER C.C.: 0.81 lb.

First published 25 May 1950

346 c.c. Royal Enfield

Overhead-valve Three-fifty With Sporting Performance and

BEFORE the war there were several sports three-fifties on the market. Their engines thrived on revs and could withstand full-throttle driving all day long; they had manual ignition control, full-blooded exhausts, and slick gear changes. The performance approached that available from a 500 c.c. machine. In short, they were "enthusiasts' mounts," which paid dividends when handled by an expert rider.

The Royal Enfield 346 c.c. Bullet revives the spirit of the type and has the advantage over its predecessors of ten years' research. With its excellent telescopic front fork and pivot-action rear suspension, the machine is endowed with handling qualities that are second to none. At the bottom end of the scale, the engine will pull uncommonly well, with a degree of smoothness surpassing that of many a modern parallel twin.

Minimum non-snatch speed of the Royal Enfield was a genuine 15-16 m.p.h. in top gear. From this speed the machine would accelerate quite happily, assuming intelligent, co-ordinated handling of ignition lever and throttle. Above 20 m.p.h. in top gear, the ignition lever was required only if very hard acceleration was wanted. Above 25 m.p.h. in top, the ignition control was not called for at all. It was next to impossible to make the engine pink.

In restricted areas, on gradients that are sufficient of a drag to demand third gear from several five-hundred twins, the Bullet would climb effortlessly and smoothly in top gear, and it was even possible to shut off and open up again without the need to change down. Outstandingly good flexibility was one of the machine's most endearing characteristics. At the opposite end of the range, there was no limit that need be imposed to save the engine from being overdriven. Fifty m.p.h. averages were obtained without fuss or bother. If desired, the model would cruise in the upper sixties, and it was apparently as happy and effortless at that gait as it was at 45 m.p.h.

Engine characteristics were of the most pleasing kind. Use of small throttle openings and changing up at comparatively low revs gave a performance of the most gentlemanly character; the machine was then as docile as the most genteel tourer. In traffic, top gear was generally engaged at between 22 and 25 m.p.h. Out of restricted areas, with the machine given its head, the engine came into its own. Affection for the machine built up into high admiration.

The power comes in with a surge when the engine is revving in the higher ranges. Full performance in the gears results in remarkably good acceleration. During fast road work on the test machine, upward gear changes were best made at about 48 m.p.h. and 65 m.p.h. The exhaust was loud with this type of riding and, though having a note that was stirring to the enthusiast, was probably objectionable to non-motor cyclists.

An aid to brisk acceleration was the excellent gear change. Upward or downward changes could be achieved by making an easy, short, light movement of the right foot. The change was entirely positive and it appeared to be impossible to "scrunch" a change or to miss a gear.

Starting from cold was generally accomplished at the third or fourth dig on the kick-starter, assuming a fairly accurate control setting and no flooding. It was necessary to close the air lever, set the ignition at three-quarters advance, and open the throttle fractionally. The correct throttle setting was very important

Front and rear suspension systems of the Bullet provided a high standard of riding comfort

A neutral selector operated by a separate pedal on the end of the gear box is a feature of the machine

Bullet

Excellent Suspension

if an easy start was to be achieved with certainty. The Bullet is fitted with a special compression-release valve in place of the more usual exhaust-valve lifter. The valve has the same effect as an exhaust-lifter; the control was well placed for ease of operation.

The same cannot be said of the front brake and clutch controls, which required considerably too great a hand reach. The clutch was rather heavy in operation. It freed perfectly at all times and did not appear to be adversely affected by abuse. It was sweet and smooth in its take-up of the drive. Bottom gear could be effortlessly selected from neutral when the engine was running and the machine stationary. The Royal Enfield is, of course, fitted with a neutral selector. This is operated by a separate pedal on the end of the gear box. To select neutral from any gear except bottom it is only necessary to lift the clutch and depress the pedal to the limit of its travel.

The engine was moderately quiet mechanically. There was a fair amount of noise from the valve gear. The piston was audible just after a cold start. Towards the end of the 600-mile test, a slight oil-leak appeared at the cylinder-head joint and there was oil seepage, too, from the oil-filler cap. Apart from this, the engine—and, indeed, the whole machine—remained remarkably clean.

No praise is too high for the steering and road-holding. The telescopic fork has a long, easy movement that suits the characteristics of the pivot-action rear-springing—which itself provides a higher standard of comfort than the majority of spring-frames available today. Whether the machine was being ridden slowly or at high speeds, the suspension absorbed road shocks most satisfactorily.

This excellent suspension has great advantages during bend-swinging or cornering at speed. Wavy- or bumpy-surfaced bends could be taken fast with the knowledge

A sturdy centre stand as well as a prop stand is fitted. The tool-box is of ample size

that the rear wheel would follow the front one with unerring accuracy. Excellent comfort was provided over cobbled city streets. Low-speed steering was first-class, allowing the rider to raise his feet to the rests the instant the clutch began to bite and to keep them there at the slowest crawl without resort to body lean or other balancing tricks.

Fitted as standard is a neat air cleaner. There are sturdy centre and prop stands, both of which are easy to use and both of which, when in use, ensure that the machine is absolutely safe from falling. The tool-box is of sensible proportions. The speedometer in its light-alloy forged housing is neatly mounted and easily read. Pillion footrests are fitted as standard.

Probably most outstanding of all is the machine's smart appearance coupled with its complete "functionality." Finish of the frame and mudguards is battleship grey; the tank is chrome and silver, and the usual parts are chromium-plated.

346 c.c. Royal Enfield Bullet

Information Panel

SPECIFICATION

ENGINE: 346 c.c. (70 x 90 mm) single-cylinder o.h.v. Fully enclosed valve-gear operated by push-rods. Plain big-ends bearing. Double-ball bearing on drive-side of mainshaft. Large-diameter plain bearing on timing side. Compression ratio, 6.5 to 1. Dry-sump lubrication. Oil-tank cast integral with crankcase; capacity, 4 pints.

CARBURETTOR: Amal; twistgrip throttle control; air slide operated by handlebar control.

IGNITION AND LIGHTING: Lucas Magdyno with manual ignition control head lamp with pre-focus light unit.

TRANSMISSION: Royal Enfield four-speed gear box with positive-stop foot-change incorporating patented neutral finder. Bottom, 15.8 to 1. Second, 10.2 to 1. Third, 7.37 to 1. Top, 5.67 to 1. Multi-plate clutch with bonded and cork inserts. Primary chain, ⅜in duplex, with hard-chromed slipper-type adjuster. Secondary chain, ⅝ x ⅜in, with guard over top run. R.p.m. at 30 m.p.h. in top gear, 2,250.

FUEL CAPACITY: 3½ gallons.

TYRES: Dunlop, 3.25 x 19in. Ribbed front, Universal rear.

BRAKES: 6in diameter front and rear.

SUSPENSION: Royal Enfield hydraulically damped front fork. Swinging-fork rear suspension with hydraulic damping.

WHEELBASE: 54in. Ground clearance, 6¼in unladen.

SADDLE: Terry. Unladen height, 29½in.

WEIGHT: 351 lb with empty fuel tank (oil-tank full) and fully equipped.

PRICE: £140, plus Purchase Tax (in Britain only), £37 16s 0d

ROAD TAX: £3 15s a year. £1 0s 8d a quarter.

MAKERS: Enfield Cycle Co., Ltd., Redditch, Worcs.

DESCRIPTION: *The Motor Cycle*, 11 March, 1943.

PERFORMANCE DATA

MEAN MAXIMUM SPEED: Bottom: 34 m.p.h.*
Second: 54 m.p.h.*
Third: 68 m.p.h.
Top: 73 m.p.h.
*Valve float starting.

MEAN ACCELERATION:

	10-30 m.p.h.	20-40 m.p.h.	30-50 m.p.h.
Bottom	4.0 secs	—	—
Second	5.0 secs	5.2 secs	5.8 secs
Third	8.2 secs	6.4 secs	6.6 secs
Top	—	8.8 secs	8.2 secs

Mean speed at end of quarter-mile from rest: 68 m.p.h.
Mean time to cover standing quarter mile: 20.4 secs

PETROL CONSUMPTION: At 30 m.p.h., 102.4 m.p.g. At 40 m.p.h., 96 m.p.g. At 50 m.p.h., 80 m.p.g. At 60 m.p.h., 64 m.p.g.

BRAKING: From 30 m.p.h. to rest, 32ft 6in (surface, dry tar macadam).

TURNING CIRCLE: 12ft 9in.

MINIMUM NON-SNATCH SPEED: 15-16 m.p.h. in top gear with ignition fully retarded.

WEIGHT PER C.C.: 1.01 lb.

197 c.c. Francis-Barnett

First published 6 July 1950

A Robust, Well-finished Lightweight With

FOR many years the name Francis-Barnett has held an illustrious place in the lightweight sphere. The reputation is based on such features as robustness of construction and a high standard of finish, and it is predominantly in these respects that the 197 c.c. Francis-Barnett Falcon 55 merits praise.

In addition, the all-round performance provided by the 197 c.c. Villiers Mark 6E engine, with three-speed gear in unit, is exceptionally good. Irrespective of night temperature during the course of the test, starting from cold in the morning was simplicity itself. The pre-starting drill consisted merely of flooding the carburettor, moving the separate, handlebar-mounted mixture control forward to the "rich" position and then, with a throttle opening of slightly less than one-third, prodding the kick-starter. The engine would usually fire at the second kick.

Immediately the engine had started, the mixture control could be moved back to about one-eighth from the "full-weak" position and then forgotten, for there was no need to alter its position at all while the machine was under way.

Saddle of the Falcon can be easily adjusted between heights of 27¾ in and 29 in

Starting from hot was even more simple and accomplished with an easy swing on the kick-starter, again with the throttle about one-third open.

The standard of mechanical quietness of the engine was exceptionally high. After a cold start, the piston was just audible. Apart from that there was only a pleasantly subdued whirr, characteristic of a two-stroke unit. In its exhaust quietness the Francis-Barnett also scored heavily. The exhaust could only be said to be noisy when the engine was firing irregularly as, for example, when the machine was running downhill on a light throttle opening.

Maximum cruising speed of the model ranged from 45 to 50 m.p.h., depending on the conditions. At these speeds the engine gave no signs of being driven "on the limit" and there was no indication of fussiness. In the course of a 400-mile test, the exhaust pipe did not discolour even slightly near the port, but the silencer became stained with burnt oil. There was a marked absence of leaks from the upper part of the engine, but oil appeared on the exhaust pipe and silencer, the oil coming from the underside of the engine; oil was also thrown from the rear chain and silencer mouth on to the rear tyre and rim.

At speeds above about 28 m.p.h. in top gear, under light load, the engine would two-stroke quite happily. Acceleration from this speed was sufficient for normal road work. Power on hills was markedly good and average main-road gradients were generally breasted without the speed dropping much below 40 m.p.h. In the early days of the test, slight transmission roughness was apparent throughout the speed scale. Later this disappeared almost completely. Engine balance was good, and only slight vibration was felt at speeds over 50 m.p.h.

It was not possible to obtain a tickover that was slow and, at the same time, perfectly reliable. The pick-up from idling to full-bore, however, was brisk and clean without, as has been mentioned, the need to use the separate mixture control.

The clutch freed perfectly. It was beautifully light in operation and silky smooth in its take-up of the drive. It required no adjustment during the test, although when the speed-test figures were taken it was subjected to a degree of abuse unlikely to be encountered normally.

Bottom gear could be faultlessly selected from neutral when the machine was stationary and the engine running. Neutral was easily located from bottom or second gears under similar conditions. The gear pedal was extremely well posi-

Front fork has three-rate coil springs. Lighting equipment includes a rectifier and battery

Falcon 55

Lively Performance

tioned in relation to the right footrest. Light, leisurely pressure of the foot was all that was necessary to make clean, noiseless, upward gear changes. Clean downward changes could be made as quickly as the clutch and gear controls could be operated.

A noteworthy feature of the Falcon is that the saddle can be quickly and easily adjusted between heights of 27¾in and 29in. At its lowest setting, the riding position provided was as near perfect as might be for a rider of average stature. Distances of over 100 miles could be covered without the need for a leg-stretching stop. It was also a riding position which caused the rider to sit "over" rather than "in" the machine, thus giving absolute control at all speeds regardless of all but trials-type conditions (for which the footrests were rather too far forward).

Wide Steering Fork

Wood blocks, tramlines and cobbles in their trickiest of moods could be negotiated with entire confidence. On the open road, corners and bends could be entered with the certain knowledge that any chosen line could be unerringly held. Straight-ahead steering was equally good at 1 m.p.h and 50 m.p.h. The steering lock was worthy of a trials machine and very useful when turning the machine in confined spaces or when manhandling it.

All controls were light and quite well placed for ease of operation. Slightly less reach of the front brake and clutch levers, however, would have been appreciated. Used together, the brakes provided adequate stopping power, but the front brake was not so effective as could be desired.

A rear stand is fitted for parking purposes. The lifting handles on the sides of the standard rear carrier made parking of the machine easy. Fitted between the seat and chain stays on the nearside of the machine is a 3-pint

The rear-brake pedal has an adjustable stop. Note the 3-pint capacity oil-tank, which allows a separate supply of oil to be carried

capacity oil-tank to allow a separate supply of oil to be carried. The tool-box is mounted on the opposite side of the machine. A two-compartment container, it is rather too small to accommodate both the excellent tool-kit provided and a repair outfit.

Lighting is by Lucas battery and A.C. rectifier. The driving beam was good and allowed the use of daylight speeds after dark. The full lamp-load was never balanced by the output from the flywheel lighting coils no matter how high the engine speed. Both front and rear mudguards are of wide section and provided more than average protection in wet weather. The tank filler cap was petroil tight. Mounted on top of the front fork, the speedometer was easily read and the instrument, for all practical purposes, accurate. The finish is black with chromium plating, and the tank is gold-lined. The effect is quite distinctive and the proportion of black to chrome, tasteful.

Information Panel

SPECIFICATION

ENGINE: Villiers 197 c.c. (59 x 72 mm) single-cylinder two-stroke with three-speed gear in unit. Roller bearing big-end ; ball bearings supporting mainshafts. Flat-crown, die-cast aluminium-alloy piston. Detachable, light-alloy cylinder head with hemispherical combustion chamber. Petroil lubrication.

CARBURETTOR: Villiers "Middleweight" with twistgrip throttle control and separate mixture control operated by a handlebar lever. Air-filter fitted as standard.

TRANSMISSION: Villiers three-speed gear in unit with engine. Gear ratios : Bottom, 15.6 to 1. Second, 8.2 to 1. Top, 5.87 to 1. Primary drive by ⅜ x 0.225in chain ; oil-bath chain case. Secondary, ½ x 0.225in chain with guard over top run.

IGNITION AND LIGHTING: Villiers flywheel magneto. Lighting by flywheel generator, battery and Westinghouse rectifier. Twin filament 24 W. main bulb.

PETROIL CAPACITY: 2¼ gallons.

TYRES: Dunlop 3.00 x 19in front and rear (ribbed front tyre).

BRAKES: 5in diameter front and rear. Finger adjusters.

SUSPENSION: Francis-Barnett telescopic, three-rate-spring fork.

WHEELBASE: 49in. Ground clearance, 5in, unladen.

SADDLE: Lycett. Height, 27¾-29in, unladen.

WEIGHT: 203lb fully equipped and with dry tanks.

PRICE: £81 plus Purchase Tax (in Britain only), £21 17s 5d.

ROAD TAX: £1 17s 6d a year ; 10s 4d a quarter.

MAKERS: Francis and Barnett, Ltd., Lower Ford Street, Coventry.

DESCRIPTION: *The Motor Cycle*, 22 September, 1949.

197 c.c. Francis-Barnett Falcon

PERFORMANCE DATA

MEAN MAXIMUM SPEED: Bottom : 26 m.p.h. Second : 48 m.p.h. Top : 58 m.p.h.

MEAN ACCELERATION:

	10-20 m.p.h.	15-25 m.p.h.	20-30 m.p.h.
Bottom	2.6 secs	3.0 secs	—
Second	4.2 secs	4.2 secs	4.2 secs
Top	—	6.4 secs	6.4 secs

Mean speed at end of quarter-mile from rest : 51 m.p.h.
Mean time taken from 0-30 m.p.h. : 7 secs.

PETROIL CONSUMPTION: At 30 m.p.h., 128 m.p.g. At 40 m.p.h., 101 m.p.g. At 45-50 m.p.h., 88 m.p.g.

BRAKING: From 30 m.p.h. to rest : 36ft 6in (surface, dry tar macadam).

TURNING CIRCLE: 12ft.

MINIMUM NON-SNATCH SPEED: 15-16 m.p.h. in top gear.

WEIGHT PER C.C.: 1.03lb.

First published 19 October 1950

649 c.c. Triumph

Enthralling Vertical Twin Tested in

OVER many years, Triumph machines have earned a reputation without parallel in the motor cycle world. It is a reputation based, probably above all, on such features as zestful performance and first-class standard of quality, though it goes deeper than that. For instance, in sum total, the modern Triumph has a greater number of "desirable features" than most. The youngest member of the breed, the 650 c.c. Thunderbird, has all

The Thunderbird tested was fitted with the spring hub and tandem seat

these in good measure; and, in addition, the obvious advantages accruing from increased engine capacity.

In general dimension and feel, when one straddles the machine, the Thunderbird is to all intents and purposes a 500 c.c. This is partly due to the compactness of the riding position (which proved equally comfortable for riders of tall or short stature).

Height from the ground of the new twinseat is 31½in, and the width across the knee-grips, in spite of the fuel tank having a capacity of rather more than four gallons, is no more than 11in. The handlebar sweeps back from the steering head rather more than is usual on British machines, and brings the grips to within comfortable reach of the very comfortable seat. On first acquaintance, the impression is that the angle of the grips, in relation to the machine's transverse axis, is too great, but later, when the strangeness that accompanies any marked change in riding position has been overcome, an angle that is more comfortable or gives a greater degree of control at high or low speeds is difficult to imagine.

Controllability of the first order is, of course, one of the primary essentials of a machine capable of cruising at speeds in the region of 90 m.p.h. So fast is the Thunderbird that during the test the maximum speed at which the machine could be cruised, without engine fatigue becoming apparent, was never determined. When road conditions permitted, speeds of 80, 85, 90 m.p.h. were often held for as long as the rider could withstand the buffeting force of wind pressure. It is perfectly true to say that the cruising speed of the model was limited only by the physical strength of the rider.

However, at normal cruising speeds the Thunderbird rustles along in the most effortless manner imaginable. At 50 m.p.h. in top gear the engine is turning over at little more than a fast tickover. At 60 m.p.h. or at 70, the machine will cruise with a degree of quietness and smoothness that is quite exceptional. Above 70 m.p.h. there was vibration; high-frequency vibration which became less and less noticeable as the test progressed. Towards the end it was so slight that it was all but imperceptible if waders and gloves were worn. Severe vibration was only evident when the engine was revved to the point of valve float in the indirect gears.

Considerable difficulty was experienced in finding a section of road providing a straight of sufficient length to allow the solo maximum-speed figures to be taken. On the road ultimately selected, the maximum timed speeds recorded gave a mean of 97 m.p.h. So far as could be ascertained by careful checking at speeds varying between 30 m.p.h. and 60 m.p.h., the speedometer was spot-on accurate, and on several occasions with three different riders, it registered speeds of 105 m.p.h. in one direction and 100 m.p.h.

Throughout the test the power unit remained free from oil leaks. The gear box was exceptionally quiet in operation

Thunderbird

Both Solo and Sidecar Forms

in the other which, of course, gives a mean speed of 102.5 m.p.h. However, these speeds were not recorded over the timed quarter-mile, and it is the timed figure which is quoted in the information panel. In any case, closely calculated maximum-speed figures of over, say, of 90 to 95 m.p.h. are purely academical and have little practical value; the general trend today is to aim rather more at achieving a high, tireless cruising speed.

During the days when attempts were made to obtain the maximum-speed figures, the engine took such a flogging as is unlikely ever to come the way of a machine in the hands of even the hardest of everyday riders. Because different sections of road were tried and because, also, on one occasion, trouble was experienced with a magneto, the engine was on full-bore almost continuously for three or four hours at a stretch on four consecutive days. It gave no signs of abuse and, indeed, caused despair among hard-riding members of the Staff because of the difficulty experienced in even slightly discolouring the exhaust pipes! Not the faintest trace of oil appeared outside the engine or gear box.

Starting the 650 c.c. engine from cold was positive and generally accomplished on the second or third kick, assuming that the throttle was opened the merest fraction, and the carburettor flooded copiously. Throughout the test, the air lever was never used. Starting required rather more muscular effort than was desirable, and it was felt that the fitting of an exhaust-valve lifter or some other form of compression-release would be an advantage.

A high-output dynamo is fitted. The lever under the seat operates the carburettor air valve

Immediately it had fired, the engine could be driven off without warming up. It would idle as perfectly after a cold start as it would after reaching its working temperature. Once the engine had warmed up, it could generally be started with an easy half-swing on the kick-starter.

The carburettor air-intake is normally fitted to a Vokes air-filter, which completely eliminates suction hiss. Maximum speed with the filter in position and a 130 jet fitted was found to be only three or four miles per hour down on that obtained when the filter was removed and a 190 jet employed. The filter was removed when the maximum-speed figures were taken.

Engine idling was satisfactory, though the pick-up from pilot to needle jet not as clean as might be desired. There

Information Panel

649 c.c. Triumph Thunderbird

SPECIFICATION

ENGINE: 649 c.c. (71 x 82 mm) o.h.v. vertical twin. Fully enclosed valve-gear operated by push-rods and twin camshafts. Plain big-ends (steel white-metal caps and light-alloy connecting rods) running directly on crankpins. Roller and ball-bearings supporting main-shafts. Dry-sump lubrication; tank capacity, 5 pints.
CARBURETTOR: Amal; Triumph twistgrip throttle control; air-slide operated by lever under seat.
IGNITION AND LIGHTING: B.T.-H. or Lucas magneto with auto-advance. Separate 60 W Lucas dynamo. 6in head lamp.
TRANSMISSION: Triumph four-speed gear box with positive foot control. Gear ratios: Bottom, 11.2 to 1. Second, 7.75 to 1. Third, 5.45 to 1. Top, 4.57 to 1. Sidecar: Bottom, 12.8 to 1. Second, 8.85 to 1. Third, 6.24 to 1. Top, 5.24 to 1. Five-plate clutch with cork inserts running in oil. Primary chain ½ x 0.305in in cast aluminium oil-bath case. Secondary chain, ⅝ x ⅜in, with guard over top and bottom runs. R.p.m. at 30 m.p.h. in top gear—Solo, 1,742; sidecar, 2,046.
FUEL CAPACITY: 4 gallons.
TYRES: Dunlop. Front, 3.25 x 19in ribbed. Rear, 3.50 x 19in studded.
BRAKES: 7in front x 1⅛in wide. Rear (with spring hub), 8in diameter x 1⅜in wide.
SUSPENSION: Triumph telescopic fork front with hydraulic damping; and Triumph Spring Wheel with helical springs for compression and rebound. (Duplex springs for compression and single for rebound).
WHEELBASE: 55in. Ground clearance, 6in unladen.
SEAT: Triumph Twinseat. Unladen height, 31½in.
WEIGHT: 397 lb, fully equipped and with no fuel.
PRICE: £153; plus Purchase Tax (in Britain only), £41 6s 3d. Spring Hub extra £16; plus P.T., £4 6s 5d. Twinseat, £1 15s; plus P.T., 9s 6d.
ROAD TAX: £5 a year; £1 7s 6d a quarter.
MAKERS: Triumph Engineering Co., Ltd., Meriden Works, Allesley, Coventry.
DESCRIPTION: *The Motor Cycle*, 29 September, 1949.

SIDECAR

MODEL: Watsonian Avon, single-seater sports.
CHASSIS: Watsonian VG 21, with quarter elliptic springs at rear, coil springs at front; Silentbloc wheel mounting.
BODY: Overall length, 84in width and depth of seat squab 21½ x 23in. Cushion measures 20 x 20in. Height inside with hood raised, 33in. Locker dimensions (approx., since shape is irregular), 26in long x 22in wide x 15in high. Luggage grid on locker door. Black twill hood.

PRICE: Body, £30; plus Purchase Tax, £8. Chassis, £20; plus £5 6s 8d Purchase Tax.
WEIGHT: 210 lb complete with chassis and wheel.

PERFORMANCE DATA
(Sidecar figures in brackets)

MEAN MAXIMUM SPEED: Bottom: *45 (36) m.p.h.
Second: *61 (51) m.p.h.
Third: *90 (71) m.p.h.
Top: 97 (73) m.p.h.
*Valve float occurring.

MEAN ACCELERATION:

	10-30 m.p.h. secs	20-40 m.p.h. secs	30-50 m.p.h. secs
Bottom	2.4 (3.4)	3.0 (—)	—
Second	4.2 (5.5)	3.2 (4.9)	3.4 (5.2)
Third	6.8 (9.7)	5.4 (7.4)	4.8 (7.5)
Top	—	— (10.8)	6.4 (12.5)

Mean speed at end of quarter-mile from rest: 85 (66) m.p.h.
Mean time to cover standing quarter-mile: 15.4 (20.7) secs.
PETROL CONSUMPTION: At 30 m.p.h., 88 (65) m.p.g. At 40 m.p.h. 72 (57) m.p.g. At 50 m.p.h., 64 (50) m.p.g. At 60 m.p.h., 57 (40) m.p.g.
BRAKING: From 30 m.p.h. to rest, 29ft (52ft). (Surface, solo, dry tarmacadam; sidecar, wet tarmacadam).
TURNING CIRCLE: 14ft 6in (14ft 6in).
MINIMUM NON-SNATCH SPEED: 22 m.p.h. (19 m.p.h.).
WEIGHT PER C.C.: 0.61 lb (0.94 lb).

649 c.c. TRIUMPH THUNDERBIRD

was always the chance that the engine would stall unless the throttle were opened gently through its initial phase. As mentioned previously, the Triumph is happy at any speed above 50 m.p.h. Below, say, 40 m.p.h. there was roughness in power delivery which was more pronounced at lower speeds. It was thought that the fitting of a manual ignition control would be an advantage.

With the engine idling and the machine stationary, bottom gear could be engaged easily and noiselessly. Clutch operation was so light that it permitted two-finger control, and the take-up of the drive was smooth and sweet. Clean, entirely positive upward gear changes could be accomplished by moving the pedal with the merest trace of "leisureliness." Downward changes could be made as quickly as the controls could be operated. Very rapid upward changes could also be made, but they were accompanied by a suggestion of clashing of the pinions.

Exceptional quietness of running in the indirect gears was a feature of the Triumph gear box. Mechanical noise from the engine was not excessive and not apparent to the rider at speeds of above 35 m.p.h.

Acceleration of the Thunderbird is in a class by itself; because of the effectiveness of the exhaust silencing, full-bore acceleration could be used almost with impunity. The mean figure of 85 m.p.h. over a quarter-mile from a standing start speaks for itself.

Very Efficient Brakes

Front and rear brakes were outstanding in efficiency and proved entirely adequate for the machine's ultra-high performance. The rear brake was excellently positioned for operation with the minimum of movement of the left foot. Though the front-brake lever required rather more than an easy span of the fingers, it was not unduly heavy in operation. Fading was never experienced no matter how hard and how often the brakes were used.

Handling on average-good road surfaces was exemplary at all speeds. The Triumph could be heeled over round turns at 100 m.p.h. with the utmost facility; the machine clung accurately to the selected line in a most satisfactory manner. Straight-ahead steering and cornering at speeds of over 70 m.p.h. on irregular road surfaces was good without being exceptional, and a touch of friction on the steering damper was found to be desirable.

At speeds of around 30 m.p.h. the standard of comfort provided over the worst of city surfaces by the Triumph telescopic fork and spring wheel was well up to the desired standard. Handling at low speeds was excellent, and the machine could be ridden easily feet-up at the slowest, clutch-slipping and brake-biting crawl.

After the machine had been tested in solo form, it was returned to the works, where it was fitted with sidecar fork springs, the standard 24-tooth engine sprocket was replaced by a 21-tooth sprocket, and a Watsonian Avon sidecar fitted.

The result was a sidecar outfit with few equals in all-round performance. A 10½-stone passenger was carried when the speed and petrol consumption figures were taken. Acceleration was such that wheelspin could readily be set up if the road surface was the merest shade damp. Head winds or gradients, or the weight carried in the sidecar, made little difference to the way in which the outfit gobbled up the miles. With the sidecar fitted, there was no critical vibration at any speed and, with the lower gearing, low-speed pulling was sweet in the extreme. Neither was the tendency to pinking so marked as to cause annoyance unless, of course, the throttle was brutally used at low speeds.

Best maximum cruising speed appeared to be in the region of 65 to 70 m.p.h., though the outfit could be driven flat-out for mile after mile without the engine's giving the slightest hint that it was being overworked. The riding position for sidecar work could not be better; the relationship between the seat and the footrests provided a comfortable knee angle, and the handlebars furnished just the desired leverage.

Sidecar Features

Adequate stopping power for the outfit was provided by the brakes; fierce pressure on the front brake at 55 m.p.h. was sufficient to cause the tyre to scream a protest. Lining-up of the outfit was such that there was a tendency for it to steer to the left. The tendency was slight, however, and in no way impaired zestful swinging on curves.

The sidecar itself was praiseworthy in nearly every respect. Seat and squab cushions are wider than average and provide a high standard of comfort. The windscreen fitted was wider than that employed on the previous road test Avon and afforded good protection for the passenger.

When the hood was raised, the interior was markedly free from draughts. The suspension was sufficiently good on all normally encountered road surfaces, though a toe-rest inside the body would have enhanced passenger comfort. A map-pocket is provided in the right-hand side of the body, and in the dash there is a roomy glove and small parcels rack. The locker and the luggage grid are sufficient to cope with reasonable luggage for two people for a fortnight's tour. A tonneau cover is provided. When lowered, the hood and its frame stow neatly out of sight behind the seat squab. The hood could be raised without hurry in 60 to 90 seconds.

The Thunderbird, then, is a high-speed touring solo-cum-sidecar machine *par excellence*, with all the outstanding quality of production and finish which have made Triumphs famous over the years. It is a worthy addition to such a famous range, and one which must inevitably establish a reputation as high as that of its smaller-capacity sisters.

A Watsonian Avon, single-seater body on the VG21 chassis was fitted for tests with a sidecar

TRIUMPH
The Best Motorcycle in the World

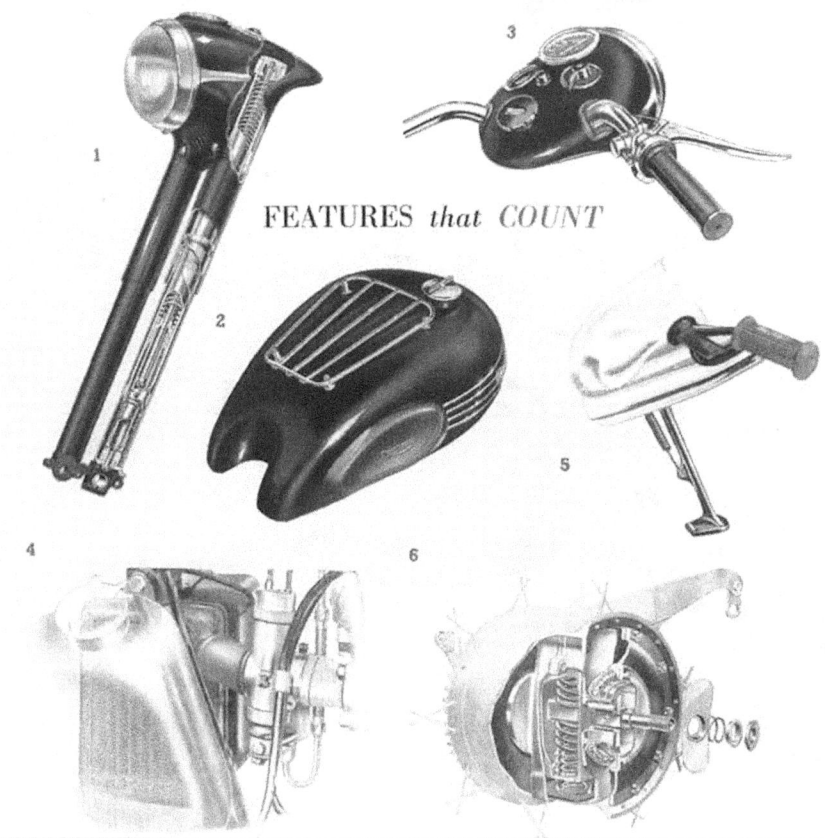

FEATURES that COUNT

1. THE TRIUMPH TELESCOPIC FORK: With six inches of hydraulically damped movement these forks set a high standard of controllability and comfort. The sectioned drawing shows how long supple fork springs are enclosed inside the stanchions which enables these vital components to be of maximum diameter and strength. No adjustments of any kind have to be made by the rider.

2. PARCEL GRID: A useful chromium-plated tank-top fitting standard on all models. Particularly valuable to the long distance solo rider.

3. THE TRIUMPH INSTRUMENT "NACELLE": Groups all instruments and switchgear where they can most easily be seen and used. Integral with the top of the forks and therefore fully sprung the nacelle incorporates the headlamp (rim adjustable), speedometer, ammeter, lighting switch, cut-out button and horn. All instruments rubber mounted, internally illuminated and readily accessible.

4. AIR CLEANER: Triumph design patented Vokes air cleaner. A "transparent" oil tank shows how neatly this piece of equipment fits between the oil tank and battery. Very efficient oil-wetted muslin filament readily detachable for cleaning.

EXTRAS :

5. PROP STAND: Extra on all models. A spring retains the stand out as a prop or in folded back position. Can be fitted to all Triumph models from 1937. State whether over or under 350 c.c. when ordering.

6. THE FAMOUS TRIUMPH SPRING WHEEL (Patent No. 824885). Available as an extra on all models. This remarkable springing system has achieved great popularity in all parts of the world. The massive aluminium alloy hub shell totally encloses all moving parts and has a powerful eight-inch brake attached. Mounted in the frame exactly like a normal wheel.

HOW IT OPERATES: The spindle remains stationary, bolted into the frame as usual, while the wheel and hub move on a curved path taken from the centre of the gearbox sprocket. Chain tension remains constant. Movement controlled by springs, two below the spindle and one above.

> First published
> 16 November 1950

449 c.c. Vincent

High-performance Single With Magnificent Roadholding,

ABOUT two years ago Vincents added single-cylinder models to their range of famous vee-twins. This fact in itself called for no special comment since there were Vincent singles and twins in pre-war years, but there was an unusual aspect in the policy announced at the end of 1948. The new singles comprise a very high proportion of the components employed for the twins; indeed, it might almost be said that the singles are twins modified as necessary.

It is to be expected, therefore, that many of the outstanding characteristics of the larger machines are retained with the

Most of the distinctive features of the Vincent twins are retained with the Comet

singles. Frame and Girdraulic fork of the Series C Comet are, as near as can be, identical with those of the Series C twins, the handling of which is of that high order which has earned praise from experienced riders throughout the world.

At very low speeds there is a slight heaviness in the steering—a steering-head roll that might be thought to be caused by damper friction—but this sensation is lost as soon as the speed is above 10 m.p.h. and, in any event, is unnoticed when the rider has had a few hours' experience with the machine. Apart from this minor fault, the steering is superbly precise and light.

The link-type fork gives about five inches of movement at the wheel spindle and its action is soft yet entirely free from flutter. At the one extreme, small surface ripples are efficiently absorbed and, at the other extreme, even the worst of shocks, such as sunken roadside drains purposely taken at speed, are minimized to only a minor movement felt at the handlebar.

A feeling of tautness and rigidity is provided by the frame of the Comet. The rear wheel, controlled by the twin spring cylinders and the separate hydraulic unit, maintains contact with the road in a leech-like fashion, but so effective is the hydraulic damper that, as with the front fork, there is never any suggestion of excessive reaction or patter. Front and rear suspension characteristics harmonize in an exemplary manner and result in steering and roadholding which is not only a sheer delight, especially at high speeds, but which also makes the maximum mechanical contribution to safety.

At all times there is a pleasing rigidity about the handling which gives a precision that means so much when the machine is cornering.

As with all Vincent models, the rider sits high on the comfortable, Dunlopillo-filled, Feridax Dualseat with the layout of the footrests and the narrow, almost straight handlebar such that he is over the machine in a slightly crouching position. This riding position plays an important part in inspiring confident, fast travel for which Vincents are renowned. The model under test was particularly stable and handled as well as the best on slippery surfaces.

The Comet is an uncompromising, high-speed, sporting single with the disadvantages and advantages of that type of machine. Standard compression ratio of 6.8 to 1 means that on pool petrol the rider has to be gentle-handed with the twistgrip if pinking is to be avoided, and the top gear ratio of 4.64 to 1 is too high for the utmost in maximum speed to be achieved except in very favourable circumstances. Under average driving conditions the engine repays for skilled handling of the throttle and frequent gear changing.

For the purposes of experiment, 50/50 petrol/benzole fuel was tried. The change in the behaviour of the engine was marked, with pinking eliminated, acceleration slightly improved, and power delivery made smoother. The major part of the road mileage and the performance figures were, however, completed on straight pool fuel.

High gearing gives a soothing, easy sensation to high-speed riding. At 60 m.p.h. in top gear, for example, engine revolutions are only about 3,600 a minute; the machine is free from vibration, the engine has the feeling of running at no more than a fast tickover, and the throttle twistgrip is only about a quarter open. The engine is, in fact, a lusty slogger with a remarkably powerful punch that means tireless travel—high performance at relatively low revs. It seemed impossible to over-drive the engine, which

Light-alloys are extensively employed. The gear box is a four-speed Burman

Comet

Steering and Brakes

Enclosed by the light-alloy cover in front of the crankcase is the magneto with auto-advance. The separate Miller dynamo has a rated output of 50 watts

under all conditions of usage during the test remained noticeably cool. As a corollary, the engine maintains its tune for very long periods and, it might confidently be supposed, would give long service before replacements would be necessary.

As mentioned earlier, the machine is singularly free from engine vibration; there is a remote feel about the power unit, which seems to be working lazily and easily. Power delivery through the transmission is slightly harsh unless engine r.p.m. is higher than about 2,000, and it was thought that a manual ignition control, knowledgeably used, would provide smoother low-speed pulling. A certain amount of valve clatter can be heard, although other common sources of noise such as the piston, the primary drive, and the indirect gear ratios were commendably quiet. The exhaust note was dull-toned, but staccato, and considered to be too raucous for town use, especially if hard acceleration was used.

Starting required a fairly lusty swing on the pedal and then a first-time response was usual if the engine was hot. Under cold-starting conditions, a flooded carburettor and a closed air slide, together with a fractionally open throttle (as for a hot engine) gave the same quick start. The engine attained a working temperature quickly and would then idle slowly and reliably, as it would also on being throttled-down after long-distance, hard riding.

Unlike the twin-cylinder models, the single-cylinder Comet has a Burman gear box and clutch. Average handlebar lever pressure was required to disengage the clutch, which freed cleanly and quickly so that bottom-gear engagement with the machine stationary and the engine ticking over could be made noiselessly. Take-up of the drive by the clutch was sweet and progressive, with just the right amount of lever movement for easy control.

The positive-stop gear-change mechanism was decisive in movement and pleasurable to use; neutral could be selected from either bottom or second gears very readily. Upward gear changes were accomplished neatly and quietly provided there was just a suggestion of pause in pedal movement before engagement of the higher ratio; clean downward changes could be made as smartly as the controls could be operated.

The Vincent has two inter-connected brakes for each wheel. On the machine tested, the front wheel brakes were strikingly efficient—light to operate and powerful, and progressive in action. Rear-wheel brakes were most effective, but required slightly heavy pedal pressure—this heavy pressure is the result of the small leverage provided intentionally in the design as a precaution against inadvertent locking of the rear wheel. As the figures show, the Comet can be stopped from 30 m.p.h. in the unusually short distance of 26ft; more than this, the pleasure of using the silky deceleration of the front brakes is enhanced by a fork which does not deflect markedly under braking.

Driving light provided by the Miller equipment with a rated 50-watt output dynamo was very good and the deflection of beam of the off-focus filament sufficient to prevent dazzle of oncoming motorists. During the test, the bulb-holder in the tail light fractured and a battery lead short-circuited. The speedometer registered approximately six per cent fast throughout the range. Two prop-stands are fitted, one on each side; they are sturdy and hold the machine safely, provided the front wheel is turned in the direction of lean.

Finish of the Comet is stoved black enamel for tank, frame, fork blades and chain guard, with light-alloy mudguards and chromium plate for handlebar, controls, wheelrims and exhaust system.

Information Panel

Vincent 499 c.c. Comet

SPECIFICATION

ENGINE: 499 c.c. (84 x 90 mm) single-cylinder high camshaft, overhead valves. Light-alloy cylinder head with integral rocker housings; light-alloy cylinder barrel with shrunk-in cast-iron liner. Dry-sump lubrication; 6 pt. oil-tank. Four main bearings. Compression ratio, 6.8 to 1.
CARBURETTOR: Amal, two-lever, 1⅛in choke; twistgrip throttle control.
TRANSMISSION: Burman four-speed gear box with positive-stop foot control. Gear ratios: Bottom, 12.4 to 1. Second, 8.17 to 1. Third, 5.94 to 1. Top, 4.64 to 1. Multi-plate clutch. Primary chain ½ x 7⁄16in, in oil-bath case. Secondary chain ⅝ x ⅜in, with guard over top run. R.p.m. at 30 m.p.h. in top gear, approximately 1,800.
IGNITION AND LIGHTING: Lucas magneto with automatic advance. Miller dynamo; 7in head lamp; stop-light.
FUEL CAPACITY: 3½ gallons.
TYRES: Avon. 3.00 x 20in ribbed, front; 3.50 x 19in studded, rear.
SUSPENSION: Girdraulic front fork with twin helical compression springs and hydraulic damping; link action. Pivot-action rear-springing hydraulically damped.
BRAKES: Twin on each wheel; 7 x ⅞in front and rear.
WHEELBASE: 56in. Ground clearance 6in, unladen.
SADDLE: Feridax Dualseat. Unladen height, 31in.
WEIGHT: 413 lb, with approximately one gallon of fuel.
TURNING CIRCLE: 15ft.
PRICE: £190, plus Purchase Tax, £51 6s.
ROAD TAX: £3 15s a year; £1 0s 8d a quarter.
MAKERS: Vincent H.R.D. Co., Ltd., Stevenage, Herts.

PERFORMANCE DATA

MEAN MAXIMUM SPEED: Bottom: 38 m.p.h. Second: 63 m.p.h. Third: 78 m.p.h. Top: 84 m.p.h.

MEAN ACCELERATION:

	10-30 m.p.h.	20-40 m.p.h.	30-50 m.p.h.
Bottom	3.0 secs	—	—
Second	—	3.8 secs	4.2 secs
Third	—	7.2 secs	6.0 secs
Top	—	—	8.4 secs

Mean speed at end of quarter mile from rest: 71 m.p.h.
Mean time to cover standing quarter mile: 18.2 secs.
PETROL CONSUMPTION: At 30 m.p.h., 122 m.p.g. At 40 m.p.h., 104 m.p.g. At 50 m.p.h. 79 m.p.g. At 60 m.p.h., 55 m.p.g.
BRAKING: From 30 m.p.h. to rest, 26ft (surface, dry tar macadam).
MINIMUM NON-SNATCH SPEED: 22 m.p.h. in top gear.
WEIGHT PER C.C.: 0.83 lb.

> First published
> 23 November 1950

248 c.c. Side-valve

A New Machine Produced in Great Britain for the

A FAVOURABLE impression is conveyed by the Indian Brave immediately it is seen. The dimensions of the machine as a whole belie its capacity of only 248 c.c.; the power unit is of exceptionally clean external design; the finish has a quality appearance about it and, though attractive, is not garish.

The machine is unusual in many respects, not the least is the fact that it is of absolutely new design and is produced by a very large engineering organization whose activities have not previously been associated with motor cycles of this type. Essentially the Brave was conceived and designed, and is now in production, for the American market and carries the name Indian which, for decades, has been the proud hall-mark of a line of famous U.S. machines.

This does not mean that the characteristics of heaviness and adornment associated with American big-twins are embodied in the Indian Brave. The reverse is the case and the new model is on British lines with only a few uncommon features such as the gear change and kick-starter on the left and the rear brake pedal on the right, coil ignition, a compression ratio suitable for American fuel, and a high top-gear ratio.

The 6.3 to 1 compression was too high for normal British pool petrol and although most of the mileage of the test and the performance figures were obtained on this fuel, a mixture of 60/40, petrol/benzole, was tried to get some idea of what the performance would be like on a fuel akin to the approximately 80-octane available in U.S.

The mixed fuel resulted in sweeter running, but it was in the higher speed range that the benefit was most marked. On pool, at speeds above 40 m.p.h. in top gear, the throttle had to be opened slowly if pinking was to be avoided. With the slower-burning, benzole-laced pool, pinking was eliminated and the pick-up from the forties to the fifties noticeably smart for a 250 c.c. side-valve power unit—this despite a top-gear ratio of 5.73 to 1 which, for British usage, would be considered about right for a three-fifty. There is no doubt that had the performance figures been attempted with the petrol/benzole fuel, better results would have been obtained.

It is perhaps inevitable that the first comments regarding the Brave should be devoted to top-end performance. These arise because, as intimated earlier, the machine gives the impression of being bigger and of larger capacity than it is in fact. On the open road the tendency to ride consistently at speeds near the maximum was inescapable because, aside from the pinking when running on straight-pool fuel, the high top gear meant that the engine was turning over comparatively slowly, there was no palpable vibration, and the engine remained remarkably cool.

Two of these characteristics might well be enlarged upon. It is rare to encounter a motor cycle free from at least a short vibration period somewhere in the speed range. The Brave is one of the exceptions, although this attractive feature was to some extent nullified by a hardness in the transmission at lowish speeds. The engine has a lusty punch in power delivery that can be felt under load until crankshaft revolutions are approaching 2,500.

Carburettor settings were such as to give a mixture considered to be slightly weak, yet so cool did the engine remain at all times that at the end of the test, extending to 750 miles, cylinder, cylinder head and exhaust pipe were not only free from any appearance of having been hot but retained the "bloom" of newness.

At all speeds and under all road conditions the steering was impeccable—light, positive and entirely free from any suggestion of waver. The front fork has a long, progressive travel which is satisfactory except that the springing is slightly hard at static loading and does not absorb minor road irregularities traversed at very low

The Indian Brave is a full-size machine with a lusty performance for a two-fifty

Unit-construction of engine and gear box is a feature. Foot-change and kick-starter controls are on the left

Indian Brave

United States and Other Dollar Markets

speeds; occasionally during the test the rubber limit stops were reached on both shock and rebound. Road-holding was about average for a solid frame, with the machine perhaps less prone to rear-wheel hop than most and notably free from chopping out on fast, bumpy curves.

Starting was uncommonly easy. The crank on the left side of the machine has a long travel but is geared low so that the crankshaft is turned rather than spun. Nevertheless, one gentle, unhurried depression on the crank was always sufficient to bring the engine to life, assuming that the throttle grip was only fractionally open and that, when the engine was cold, the carburettor had been flooded. It was never found necessary to employ the spring-loaded air-slide plunger. No coil ignition warning lamp is fitted and on two occasions the rider forgot to switch on the ignition before attempting to start.

It would be difficult to suggest any motor cycle engine in production to-day that idles slower and more reliably than the Indian Brave. The consistent regularity of the tickover called to mind stationary engines rather than lively power units designed for operating over a wide range of speeds. At idling speeds timing-gear clatter obtruded, but became almost unnoticeable when the machine was under way.

Standard unladen height of the saddle is 28in, but adjustments may be made by means of the bottom spring bolts and a set of alternative pivoting holes in the saddle frame at the nose. Footrests are readily adjustable and the handlebar may be swivelled in its clamps.

Handlebar levers are clamped to the bar and fully adjustable, and no more than an average hand-span is required to operate them; the rear-brake pedal, on the right side of the machine, and the gear-change pedal on the left are both well positioned for operation without removing the foot from its footrest.

The clutch freed satisfactorily and took up the drive smoothly though rather rapidly; in other words, the clutch was disengaged or engaged by a comparatively short movement of the handlebar lever, which was slightly heavy in operation.

With the machine stationary and the engine idling, bottom gear could be engaged noiselessly. Pedal travel for selecting all gears—downward for lower gears and upward for higher—was short. Pedal movement was stiff; this was probably due to newness, although the mechanism showed no signs of freeing-off during the test. This stiffness sometimes made it difficult

Handlebar measures 28 inches from tip to tip. The machine has first-class steering properties and the absence of a damper was never detrimental

to select neutral. Indirect gears were audible at very low speeds on both drive and overrun.

Both brakes required only light pressure on the controls and were remarkably powerful in operation. Both were a delight to use and were in a class usually associated with only the most expensive, powerful machines.

The driving light provided by the Lucas sealed-beam unit was first-rate and the stop-light, when operated by the rear brake, was of such brilliance that it could hardly be unnoticed even in sunny weather. Maximum output of the alternator was insufficient by one ampère to balance the main, tail and speedometer lights and coil ignition—the normal, night-lighting load.

Until the last few miles of the test, when the tappet cover washer split, the power unit remained absolutely oil-free. Mudguarding gave reasonably adequate protection and was perhaps better than average. The lower run of final-drive chain was rather too close to the valance of the rear mudguard and though adjusted correctly, the chain occasionally scraped the guard. The prop stand is sturdy, effective and easily operated; there is no rear stand and no means of lifting either wheel clear of the ground.

Finish of the machine tested was black enamel with polychromatic pale blue wheel rims and chromium-plated handlebar controls, exhaust system and head lamp rim.

Information Panel

248 c.c. Indian Brave

SPECIFICATION

ENGINE Brockhouse 248 c.c. (64.5 x 76 mm) single-cylinder, side-by-side valves. Detachable light-alloy cylinder head with cast-iron barrel. Flat-crown light-alloy piston. Roller bearing big-end; three bearings supporting crankshaft. Oil reservoir, 1½ pt. in crankcase. Force-feed lubrication through gear type pump. Compression ratio, 6.3 to 1.

CARBURETTOR Amal, with twist grip throttle control and air-slide control on carburettor. Air filter is standard.

TRANSMISSION Albion three-speed gear box in unit with engine. Positive-stop foot control. Gear ratios: Bottom, 16.2 to 1. Second, 9 to 1. Top, 5.73 to 1. Three-plate cork-insert clutch incorporating rubber block shock absorber. Primary drive by ⅜ x 0.25in chain enclosed in crankcase-gear box casting. Secondary, ½ x 0.335in, with guard over top run. R.p.m. at 30 m.o.h. in top gear, 2,450.

IGNITION AND LIGHTING: Lucas 6-volt coil. Automatic advance. Lucas 45w alternator mounted on nearside crankshaft, charging battery through Westinghouse rectifier. Lucas 30.24w sealed-beam headlamp with separate parking light. Combined stop and tail lights.

FUEL CAPACITY: 2¼ gallons.
TYRES: Dunlop, 3.25 x 18in studded front and rear.
BRAKES: 5 x 1in front and rear.
SUSPENSION: Telescopic front fork, with coil springs and rubber limit stops.
WHEELBASE: 52in. Ground clearance, 5⅜in unladen.
SADDLE: Lycett. Height, 28in unladen.
WEIGHT: 241 lb, with 1 gallon fuel.
PRICE: Not yet available in this country.
ROAD TAX: £1 17s 6d a year; 10s 4d a quarter.
MAKERS: Brockhouse Engineering (Southport) Ltd., Crossens, Southport, Lancs.
DESCRIPTION: *The Motor Cycle*, September 28, 1950.

PERFORMANCE DATA

MEAN MAXIMUM SPEED: Bottom: 21
Second: 47.
Top: 56.

MEAN ACCELERATION: 10-30 m.p.h. 20-40 m.p.h. 30-50 m.p.h.
Bottom ... ... — — —
Second ... ... 5.2 secs 5.8 secs —
Top ... ... — 13.8 secs 14 secs
Mean speed at end of quarter mile from rest: 53 m.p.h.
Mean time to cover standing quarter mile: 22.2 sec.

PETROL CONSUMPTION: At 30 m.p.h., 145 m.p.g. At 40 m.p.h., 119 m.p.g.
BRAKING: From 30 m.p.h. to rest, 26ft (surface, dry tar macadam).
TURNING CIRCLE: 15ft.
MINIMUM NON-SNATCH SPEED: 20 mph in top gear.
WEIGHT PER C.C.: 0.96 lb.

First published 7 December 1950

496 c.c. Royal

High Performance Allied to Excellent Handling

WHEN deciding as to whether this machine or that meets one's requirements it is usual to assess good and bad features and make comparisons. In the main—where five-hundreds are considered—the features mostly concerned in the check-up are: handling, braking, gear change, highest comfortable cruising speed, acceleration and smoothness. In all of these, with possibly one exception, the 496 c.c. Royal Enfield Twin gains full marks; which makes it all the more disappointing that, because of problems of supply and export demands, delivery to the home market is still severely restricted.

The Royal Enfield Twin is a good-looker. Finish is in light grey

So good are the majority of the Royal Enfield's features that it is difficult to select one and say of it that herein lies the model's most magnetic attribute. The engine started easily from hot or cold, requiring no particularly meticulous setting of the controls. To start from cold it was merely necessary to flood lightly, close the air lever, switch on the ignition and give a gentle prod on the kickstarter. The air lever could be opened almost immediately the engine had started. The engine would idle as slowly and reliably after a cold start as it would after its normal working temperature had been reached. Mechanical noises were not marked and were inaudible to the rider when he was astride the machine.

From idling right up the throttle scale the pick-up was clean-cut and lively. Bottom gear could be selected effortlessly and noiselessly when the machine was stationary with the engine idling. At all times the clutch freed perfectly and it was silky smooth throughout the engagement period. The gear change proved to be perfect. No delay in pedal-movement was necessary when making upward or downward changes between any pair of gears. All that was required was a quick, light flick of the right toe. Neutral could be selected easily from bottom or second gears by means of the gear lever. The neutral selector could not be readily operated by a bewadered foot, because of its height and proximity to the kickstarter

At traffic speeds the Royal Enfield proved to be tractable to an extent not hitherto experienced with a modern parallel twin. It would trickle happily at 15 m.p.h. in top gear—and indeed at an even lower speed if care was used in the manipulation of the twistgrip. From 20 m.p.h. in top gear, acceleration was all that was required under normal driving conditions. At such low speeds the combination of the engine's smooth power delivery and the famous Enfield cush-hub in the rear wheel eliminated any suggestion of roughness. Vibration was negligible throughout the speed range.

Acceleration through the gears was such as to give a favourable impression of the engine's capabilities. Cruising speeds of 60, 70 and 75 m.p.h. were commonplace throughout the test. There was at no time the slightest indication of excessive heat. The engine remained free from oil leaks until the performance data were being obtained; then cylinder-head seepage occurred. When the maximum-speed figures were being recorded there was a hindering diagonal wind.

Another factor contributing to the high average speeds obtainable was the good standard of the exhaust silencing. Only when the engine was revving at high r.p.m., such as when the road speed was in the region of 55-60 m.p.h. in third gear, was it felt that the exhaust noise might prove objectionable to pedestrians. Be-

Power unit is up-to-the-minute in design. Cylinder heads and cylinders are separate castings

Enfield Twin

A Machine With Numerous Attractive Features

Coil ignition is employed. The high-output dynamo is chain-driven

cause of the engine's excellent low-speed torque, acceleration in the higher gears is particularly good.

It is widely held in these days that the best rear suspension is achieved with the oil-damped, pivot-fork design. The excellence of the Royal Enfield suspension bears this out in every respect; a high standard of comfort is provided and high speeds are possible on the worst of surfaces. The test machine was driven over the time-section used in the British Experts' Trial and the time taken was within minutes only of that of the faster five-hundreds competing in the event. Corners and bends could be taken stylishly at speed, the wheels hugging the chosen line in the highest, confidence-instilling manner. The machine cornered with the effortless ease of a lightweight. Low-speed steering was equally good; the model could be ridden feet-up, slowly, and to a standstill. Handling on greasy surfaces was markedly good. The worst of road shocks were well cushioned from the rider—to such an extent, indeed, that there was a deliberate tendency between to ride over broken road edges, and seek out sunken man-hole covers.

Both brakes proved to be rather spongy. The front brake lacked real power, no matter how hard it was applied.

A comfortable riding position, as well as one which provided excellent control of the machine at high or low speeds, was furnished by the relationship between saddle, footrests and handlebar. The handlebar is mounted to the rear of the facia and has an orthodox bend, providing a sensible wrist angle. The reach was such that the rider naturally adopted a straight-arm posture. Relationship between the saddle and footrest was such that an angle of more than 90 deg was formed at the knee; but a disadvantage was that, in their optimum position, the footrests were not sufficiently high from the road and were often grounded during fast cornering or when the machine was being turned in narrow lanes. Riding comfort, it was felt, would have been enhanced had the tank width been less across the kneegrips.

The controls were reasonably well positioned for ease of operation. More hand reach than is desirable for easy and rapid manipulation was required to operate the clutch and front-brake controls. Throttle, rear-brake and gear controls were all light in operation; both rear-brake and gear pedals are readily adjustable relative to the footrests.

Two stands are fitted, a prop and a centre stand. The propstand leg was too long for easy manipulation and general machine safety. Moreover, it was weak at the hinge, the welding fracturing during the test. Operation of the centre stand required knack plus considerable effort.

Finish of the machine is a smart battleship grey and chromium. The combination of an attractive colour scheme and trim lines make the machine æsthetically right. More important, however, is that with its good all-round performance and excellent handling the Royal Enfield Twin takes its place proudly among the foremost machines in its capacity class.

Information Panel

496 c.c. Royal Enfield Twin

SPECIFICATION

ENGINE: 496 c.c. (64 x 76 mm) parallel twin o.h.v. with separate cylinders and heads. Fully enclosed valve-gear Ball and roller bearings supporting one-piece alloy-iron cast crankshaft. Plain, split big-end bearings. Light-alloy connecting rods. Slightly-domed aluminium-alloy pistons. Standard compression ratio, 6.5 to 1. Dry-sump lubrication with the oil compartment cast integral with, and at rear of crankcase: capacity, 4 pints.
CARBURETTOR: Amal, twistgrip throttle control and handlebar-mounted air lever.
IGNITION AND LIGHTING: Coil through vertical distributor incorporating auto-advance and retard. Lucas 3¼in dia. dynamo. Switch ammeter, voltage control and ignition warning light carried in box alongside seat tube. Lucas 7in headlamp.
TRANSMISSION: Royal Enfield four-speed gear box with positive-stop foot-change incorporating neutral-finder. Bottom, 13.9 to 1 Second 9.0 to 1. Third, 6.5 to 1. Top, 5.0 to 1 Multi-plate clutch with bonded and cork inserts. Primary chain, ⅜in duplex with hard-chromed, slipper-type adjuster Secondary chain, ⅝ x ⅜in with guard over top run. R.p.m. at 30 m.p.h. in top gear, 1,950.
FUEL CAPACITY: 3¼ gallons.
TYRES: Both Dunlop. Front, 3.25 x 19in ribbed. Rear, 3.50 x 19in Universal.
BRAKES: 6in diameter front and rear.
SUSPENSION: Royal Enfield hydraulically damped front fork. Swinging-arm rear suspension with hydraulic damping.
WHEELBASE: 54in.
SADDLE: Terry. Unladen height, 29½in.
WEIGHT: 410lb fully equipped and with full fuel and oil tanks.
PRICE: £167 10s plus Purchase Tax (in Great Britain only), £45 4s 6d.
ROAD TAX: £3 15s a year; £1 0s 8d a quarter.
MAKERS: Enfield Cycle Company Ltd., Redditch, Worcs.
DESCRIPTION: *The Motor Cycle*, 4 November, 1948.

PERFORMANCE DATA

MEAN MAXIMUM SPEED: Bottom : *35 m.p.h.
Second : *56 m.p.h
Third : *75 m.p.h.
Top : *85 m.p.h
*Valve float starting.

MEAN ACCELERATION:

	10-30 m.p.h.	20-40 m.p.h.	30-50 m.p.h.
Bottom	2.4 secs	—	—
Second	4 secs	3.2 secs	3.8 secs
Third	6.2 secs	5 secs	4.8 secs
Top	—	6.8 secs	6.4 secs

Mean speed at end of quarter-mile from rest : 75 m.p.h.
Mean time to cover standing quarter-mile : 16.2 secs.
PETROL CONSUMPTION: At 30 m.p.h., 81 m.p.g. At 40 m.p.h. 74 m.p.g. At 50 m.p.h. 65 m.p.g. At 60 m.p.h., 57 m.p.g.
BRAKING · From 30 m.p.h. to rest, 38ft (surface, damp tar macadam).
TURNING CIRCLE · 13ft.
MINIMUM NON-SNATCH SPEED: 12 m.p.h. in top gear
WEIGHT PER C.C.: 0.83 lb.

> First published 4 January 1951

998 c.c. Vincent Rapide

An Enthralling, High-performance Big-twin With

SPEEDS in excess of 80 m.p.h. are apt to be talked of glibly. Yet if the truth be admitted, the number of riders who have, in fact, bettered 80 m.p.h. are without doubt in the minority—and for many of those who have, it has been a once- or twice-only experience. So far as the vast majority of sidecar men are concerned, 80 m.p.h. is probably at least 10 m.p.h. faster than anything within their ken. The exceptions, racing men and freak conditions aside, are only those who have sampled the o.h.v big-twin type outfit exemplified by the modern Vincent, the Rapide edition of which, wedded to a sidecar, will

Hydraulically damped rear-springing is fitted to the Vincent Rapide

cruise effortlessly and without fuss at "eighty" and indeed exceed that gait in third gear.

High, tireless cruising speed was certainly not the sole attribute, or even the most likeable one, of the outfit under test. It was described by Vincents as a "semi-sporting outfit"—a standard Series C Rapide with a Swallow Jet 80 sidecar. On first acquaintance it appeared to be just that: semi-sporting—with a lusty, smooth and vibrationless performance at low speeds, and starting as effortless as that of the most docile tourer.

From idling speeds right up the engine speed scale, the pick-up was clean-cut and brisk, and acceleration such that, in this respect, the outfit had few equals on the road—whether they were two-wheelers or four. The big-twin's power meant that wheel-spin was easily set up in first or second gears. It was such, too, that it sent the blood coursing quickly through the arteries and engendered an enthusiastic feeling of thrilled anticipation.

In view of the inordinately high gearing of the outfit—bottom gear was 10.66 to 1 and second as high as 6.35 to 1—the darting acceleration comes rather as a surprise. But the fact is that the mighty Vincent engine has characteristics which make it ideally suited for pulling high gear ratios. Though it is true that the road speed had to be as high as 6 or 7 m.p.h. before the clutch could be fully engaged, unless transmission snatch was to be experienced, there was no lack of power at engine speeds so low that the firing strokes could almost be counted. The combination of high gearing and a large-capacity engine spells effortlessness at high speeds and the avoidance of rapid wear and tear on engine and transmission. At 60 m.p.h. the engine is turning over at only 3,240 r.p.m.

During the normal course of the test, on which over 1,000 miles were covered, the tools were never once required. Later, when the performance figures were being taken and the engine grossly over-revved, the valve collars moved up on the valve stems. This trouble was rectified at the Works and gave no sign of recurring when the figures were obtained finally.

Speeds in the 80 m.p.h. region were used with the outfit whenever practicable—the engine turning over with no more fuss than at 50 m.p.h. Indeed, when the mood was one of seeking real sport, the engine was quite often driven as near flat-out as maybe. It was commonplace, for instance, to run the outfit up to 75 m.p.h. before engaging top gear. Yet, the rear chain was only once adjusted—no tools are necessary to do this—and no other form of adjustment whatever was necessary. No oil leaks manifested themselves. The slow and reliable tickover persisted no matter how severe the treatment of the engine had been.

Naturally, an imperative requirement of a sidecar outfit in this class is that the fork possesses a high degree of lateral rigidity. In this respect the massive Girdraulic fork earned full marks. Corners and bends could be entered with a zest approaching abandon, the driver at all times confident that any chosen line could be effortlessly held. The handling was such that only the slightest trace of damper was required at speeds over 35 m.p.h. Below that speed, considerably more damping was necessary to curb the tendency of the front wheel to wobble. The Girdraulic fork has numerous novel features, one of them being the ease with which it may be altered to provide solo or sidecar trial. For sidecar work, steering was delightfully light at high speeds. At low speeds it was naturally heavier, but never unduly so.

Contributing to the excellent handling of the outfit, the Vincent riding position is one that causes the driver to sit well over the machine, in a straight-arm posture, body leaning slightly forward and with the feet well back. It is a

The Vincent power unit is of most advanced design. Light-alloy components are extensively employed

and Sidecar

Connoisseur's Features

position which afforded excellent control at high or low speeds. Both the standard Vincent handlebar—the famous short, almost straight bar—and the touring one which has a rather more orthodox bend were tried. In each case there was ample leverage, though it was felt that, for sidecar work, slightly greater angle of the grips in relation to the machine's lateral axis would have been preferred.

All controls are fully adjustable and may be perfectly positioned for ease of operation. The Servo-assisted clutch was remarkably light to use—so light, indeed, that the pressure of one finger was sufficient—and it required very little travel. The front brakes, too, were light in operation. In contrast, the twistgrip proved "heavy," and inordinately heavy pressure was required at the rear brake pedal in order to obtain maximum braking efficiency. Once the four brakes—there are two per wheel—had bedded down, they came well up to the recognized Vincent standard—which means, of course, that they were in keeping with the outfit's colossal performance.

Gear Changing

Even in these enlightened times, many an otherwise excellent machine is condemned because of its having a poor gear change. With the Vincent there was no question of this. A slight pause was necessary—because of the rather wide jump in ratios—when changing between first and second gears, but all other changes could be made quite effortlessly, and just as rapidly as the controls could be moved. The gear pedal is pleasantly short, well positioned and it has a brief travel. The only criticism that could be levelled at the gear box was that the change was

The Swallow Jet 80 sidecar has elegant, sporting lines Suspension is by means of rubber bushes

rather heavy. None of the indirect ratios was more than just audible.

The driving beam from the 7in Miller head lamp was adequate for speeds up to 50 m.p.h. under average night conditions. Surprisingly good protection from water and road filth was provided by the polished light-alloy mudguards. In its position under the Feridax Dualseat, the tool tray was easily accessible, but rather too small to accommodate a full list of tools, with spare plugs, bulbs, and a puncture repair outfit.

What of the Swallow Jet 80 sidecar? There is probably no sports sidecar with cleaner lines in production in the world today. The chassis was fitted with an excellent four-point attachment and proved completely rigid. Average comfort was provided by the rubber suspension. For Britain's capricious climate the windscreen was rather too small; the height inside when the hood was raised was, for all but passengers of smaller than average stature, rather inadequate. Finish of the outfit was black, chromium and silver.

Information Panel

998 c.c. Vincent with Swallow sidecar

SPECIFICATION

ENGINE: 998 c.c. (84 x 90 mm) vee-twin high-camshaft o.h.v., with gear box in unit. Fully enclosed valve-gear. Dry-sump lubrication: tank capacity 6 pints. Four main bearings. Roller-bearing big-ends. Specialloid pistons. Cast-iron liners shrunk into aluminium-alloy cylinder barrels. Aluminium-alloy cylinder heads.
CARBURETTORS: Amal: Twistgrip throttle control and twin handle-bar-mounted air levers.
IGNITION AND LIGHTING: Lucas magneto with auto-advance. Miller dynamo: 7in head lamp: stoplight. Dynamo output, 50 watts.
TRANSMISSION: Vincent four-speed gear box with positive-stop foot control. Gear ratios: Top, 4.1 to 1. Third, 4.88 to 1. Second, 6.35 to 1. Bottom, 10.66. Alternative ratios (available by reversing rear wheel): Top, 3.96 to 1. Third, 4.71 to 1. Second, 6.14 to 1. Bottom, 10.30 to 1. Servo-assisted clutch. Primary chain, in triplex, enclosed in aluminium-alloy oil-bath case. Secondary chain, ⅝ x ⅜in with guard over top run. R.p.m. at 30 m.p.h. in top gear (with higher ratios), 1,620.
FUEL CAPACITY: 3¾ gallons.
TYRES: Front, 3.00 x 20in. Avon ribbed, rear 3.50 x 19in Avon studded.
BRAKES: Twin on each wheel; drums 7in diameter x ⅞in wide.
SUSPENSION: Girdraulic link-action front fork with twin helical compression springs and hydraulic damping; pivot-action rear-springing hydraulically damped.
WHEELBASE: 56in. Ground clearance, 5in unladen.
SEAT: Feridax Dualseat. Unladen height, 31in.
WEIGHT: 728lb, fully equipped and with one gallon of fuel and oil-tank full.
PRICE: Machine only, £255, plus (in Great Britain only), £69 17s. P.T.
ROAD TAX: £5 a year; £1 7s 6d a quarter.
DESCRIPTION: *The Motor Cycle*, 31 August, 1950.
MAKERS: The Vincent H.R.D. Co., Ltd., Stevenage, Herts.

SIDECAR

MODEL: Swallow Jet 80.
CHASSIS: Swallow "Silk" tubular chassis with forward pivot mounting for body at front and torsion arms on bonded rubber bushes at rear. Wheel is also carried on rubber-bushed mounting.
BODY: All-steel welded construction with no doors. Length is 82in; width, 25½in; distance from squab to nose, 42½in; height inside with hood raised, 30in. Locker dimensions are 24in long x 19½in wide x 15in deep. Black twill hood.
PRICE: £70 13s 2d (complete) plus (in Great Britain only), £13 16s 10d P.T. **MAKERS:** Swallow Coachbuilding Co. (1935), Ltd., The Airport, Walsall, Staffs.

PERFORMANCE DATA

MEAN MAXIMUM SPEED: Bottom: 45 m.p.h.
Second: 72 m.p.h.
Third: 81 m.p.h.
Top: 88 m.p.h.

ACCELERATION:

	10-30 m.p.h.	20-40 m.p.h.	30-50 m.p.h.
Bottom	2.8 secs	3 secs	—
Second	—	4 secs	4 secs
Third	—	6.2 secs	5.6 secs
Top	—	10 secs	7.6 secs

Speed at end of quarter mile from rest: 77 m.p.h.
Time to cover standing quarter-mile: 16.8 secs.
PETROL CONSUMPTION: At 30 m.p.h., 75 m.p.g. At 40 m.p.h. 64 m.p.g. At 50 m.p.h., 54 m.p.g. At 60 m.p.h., 46 m.p.g.
BRAKING: From 30 m.p.h. to rest, 36ft 6in (surface, wet tar-macadam).
TURNING CIRCLE: 16ft.
MINIMUM NON-SNATCH SPEED: 20 m.p.h. in top gear.
WEIGHT PER C.C.: 0.73lb.

> First published 8 February 1951

495 c.c. B.S.A. Model

Latest Edition of an Established High-performance Five-hundred:

THE original 495 c.c. A7 B.S.A. was introduced to an eager, war-weary market in 1946 and retained its basic and detail design features almost without change until the end of last year. Though even to an experienced eye the 1951 engine and gear box exteriors are largely unchanged, both units are, in fact, new and almost identical in internal detail design with those of the already illustrious Golden Flash model. The result of the change-

The 1951 A7 is a cobby, neat, businesslike mount

over is such that many will immediately class the new A7 as being the best 500 c.c. B.S.A. yet; in terms of all-round engine performance, handling, braking and gear change—particularly the last—the new A7 is without doubt one of the best of two, or perhaps three, machines in its particular capacity class.

During the course of the Road Test, the B.S.A. was generally driven in a manner calculated to bring to light—and quickly—any indication that the engine might "fuss" or tire. In other words, the engine was revved very hard in the indirect ratios, and speeds wherever possible were just as high as road conditions permitted. On one particular occasion a run of 150 miles in Warwickshire and Shropshire was completed in a few minutes over three hours.

Speeds on the main roads were regularly in the 70-75 m.p.h. region, and 80 m.p.h. was maintained and held effortlessly on several occasions—this by a heavily garbed rider sitting in an orthodox position. When the machine was stopped after several miles on full bore, a hand could be placed on the cylinder finning. The exhaust pipes had not even discoloured near the ports; they later became slightly straw coloured, but never blue. Throughout the entire test the engine and gear box remained absolutely oil-tight. Transmission smoothness was of a high order. The rear chain, however, tended to run dry.

When motor cycling, there are naturally occasions when one begins a run with some fixed idea, such as: "I am going to potter," or, "I am out for a whang." Such were the A7's characteristics that, irrespective of the state of one's mind at the beginning of a run, speeds generally rose and rose throughout the run's duration. Reasons for this are not hard to seek; for instance, at 70 m.p.h. there is as complete lack of fuss as there is at 50-55 m.p.h. From 50 m.p.h. onwards, high-frequency vibration could be felt at the handlebar, but it was slight and would not worry even fastidious riders. Vibration was marked only when the engine was revved to the point of valve float.

A slow, reliable tick-over was one of the A7's most attractive features. At idling speeds, the engine was beautifully quiet mechanically, the only certainly identified noises being piston slap and slight "rustling" from the valve-gear. The built-in air cleaner completely eliminates induction hiss. Performance figures, incidentally, were taken with the filter in use. Pick-up throughout the entire throttle range was clean and brisk, and there was no undue tendency to pinking.

Slightly heavy in operation, the clutch freed perfectly at all times, required no adjustment even after the high stresses imposed when performance figures were being taken, and was delightfully smooth in its take-up. Bottom gear could be engaged noiselessly and certainly when the machine was stationary with the engine idling. Clean and entirely positive upward gear changes were accomplished by moving

New twin-cylinder power unit follows closely the design of the 650 c.c. A10

A7 Twin

An Enthralling Machine

the pedal without due attention to making a deliberate lag in pedal movement. Snap racing-type changes could be made with certainty and with or without freeing the clutch. When snap changes were made, the pinions engaged with the merest suggestion of a "clonk." In the indirect ratios, notably in third gear, there was considerable gear whine. Clean, sweet, downward changes could be accomplished just as quickly as the controls could be operated. Pedal movement was short and light, and the pedal could be moved up or down by lightly pivoting the right foot on the footrest. The combination of positive gear change, clean pick-up and reliable idling made the B.S.A. particularly useful for safe, effortless traffic threading.

The front fork has a long, soft movement, allowing the front wheel to follow the road surface accurately, be it bumpy or smooth, be the speed high or low. Greasy cobbles and wet tramlines could be traversed with complete confidence. The rear suspension (which on the A7 is an extra) provided reasonable comfort, though slightly more travel, it was felt, would have been appreciated.

Light Brake Operation

Both brakes were smooth and progressive in operation, and provided adequate stopping power. Fade was never experienced under hard-driving conditions on the road, but it did occur when the braking figures were being taken —a quick succession of crash stops in this instance being made from 30 m.p.h. Both brakes were light in operation.

The only point of criticism applying to the riding position was that the top corners of the knee pads were slightly sharp and caused discomfort towards the end of a day in the saddle. Relationship between saddle, footrests and handlebar provided a comfortable knee angle and arm reach, and the angle of the grips allowed a natural position for the wrists. Both footrests and handlebar are, of course, adjustable. All controls were delightfully sweet in operation.

Primary drive is by a duplex chain with a slipper for adjustment. Gear box is bolted to the rear of the crankcase

An intense and commendably wide driving beam was furnished by the 7in Lucas head lamp. In its position on the fork bridge, the speedometer was easily read by a normally seated rider. The instrument read approximately seven per cent fast. Mudguarding provided above-average protection for rider and machine. The centre stand could be operated without undue muscular effort, but required knack. The prop stand (which is an extra) was easily operated and held the machine safely.

Engine starting from cold (during some of the coldest weather experienced this winter) was certain at the third or fourth dig on the kick-starter. Kick-starting required commendably little physical effort or knack, and engendered the thought: "A child could do it." Finish of the A7 is black and chromium, with the tank finished in red and chromium.

B.S.A. 495 c.c. Model A7 twin

Information Panel

SPECIFICATION

ENGINE: 495 c.c. (66 x 72.6 mm) o.h.v. vertical twin. Fully enclosed valve gear operated by push rods from a single camshaft. Plain-bearing big-ends. Mainshaft supported by roller and plain bearings. Compression ratio, 6.7 to 1. Dry-sump lubrication; tank capacity, 4 pints.
CARBURETTOR: Amal; twistgrip throttle control; air-slide operated by handlebar lever. Built-in air cleaner.
IGNITION AND LIGHTING: Lucas magneto with auto-advance. Separate 45w Lucas dynamo. 7in. head lamp. 30/24w head lamp bulb.
TRANSMISSION: B.S.A. four-speed gear box with positive-stop foot control. Bottom, 13.2 to 1. Second, 9.0 to 1. Third, 6.2 to 1. Top, 5.1 to 1. Multi-plate clutch with fabric inserts. Primary chain, ⅜in duplex in cast-aluminium, light-alloy case. Secondary chain, ⅝ x ⅜in. R.p.m at 30 m.p.h. in top gear, 1,990 approx.
FUEL CAPACITY: 3½ gallons.
TYRES: Dunlop, Front 3.25 x 19in. Rear 3.50 x 19in. Both studded tread
BRAKES: 7 x 1⅛in front and rear.
SUSPENSION: B.S.A. telescopic front fork with hydraulic damping. Plunger-type rear springing.
WHEELBASE: 54½in. Ground clearance, 4⅛in unladen.
SADDLE: Lycett. Unladen height, 30in
WEIGHT: 436lb with fuel and oil tanks full and machine fully equipped.
PRICE: £144 plus Purchase Tax (in Britain only), £38 17s 8d. Spring frame extra, £10, plus P.T £2 14s.
ROAD TAX: £3 15s a year; £1 0s 8d a quarter.
MAKERS: B.S.A. Cycles, Ltd., Small Heath, Birmingham, 11.
DESCRIPTION: The Motor Cycle, 19 October, 1950.

PERFORMANCE DATA

MEAN MAXIMUM SPEED: Bottom : 36 m.p.h.*
  Second : 54 m.p.h.*
  Third : 78 m.p.h.
  Top : 88 m.p.h.
  *Valve floating starting

MEAN ACCELERATION:

	10-30 m.p.h.	20-40 m.p.h.	30-50 m.p.h.
Bottom	2.4 secs	—	—
Second	4 secs	3 secs	3.2 secs.
Third	—	5.4 secs	5 secs
Top	—	8.2 secs	7.4 secs

Mean speed at end of quarter mile from rest : 76 m.p.h.
Mean time to cover standing quarter mile : 17.6 secs.
PETROL CONSUMPTION: At 30 m.p.h., 92 m.p.g. At 40 m.p.h. 81 m.p.g. At 50 m.p.h., 72 m.p.g. At 60 m.p.h., 64 m.p.g.
BRAKING: From 30 m.p.h. to rest, 29ft 6in (surface, wet tar macadam)
TURNING CIRCLE: 13ft 6in.
MINIMUM NON-SNATCH SPEED: 18-19 m.p.h. in top gear.
WEIGHT PER C.C.: 0.88lb.

First published 22 February 1951

197 c.c. Tandon Supaglid

A Powerful Lightweight with Outstandingly Good Suspension and

THE Tandon Supaglid Supreme is almost identical with the already proved 122 c.c. Supaglid model except that the Supreme is fitted with the 197 c.c. Villiers engine-gear unit. The result is a machine which retains the outstanding road-holding and steering qualities and the attractive appearance of the smaller model, but which has what to some riders will be the added advantage of a higher performance.

This higher performance is pleasing, especially in the way it endows the new Tandon with the capacity for sustained hard work. For its size, the engine has lusty power—one might almost use the word "punch"—and it is never happier than when being driven hard.

Under average, open-road conditions, a pleasant, effortless gait was around 45 m.p.h. Adverse conditions such as strong head-winds and hills would have an effect, of course, but to a less marked extent than might be anticipated. Top gear at 5.32 to 1 is on the high side, and at 45 m.p.h. the engine speed is well below 4,000 r.p.m. The engine pulls this gear admirably, and this feature makes its contribution to the effortlessness of cruising in the middle forties. On no occasion did the engine get "fussy" or give any other indication of over-driving.

Front suspension of the Tandon is by means of a straight-forward telescopic fork with coil springs, and the pivoting-fork rear suspension is controlled by a rubber cartridge situated under the rear of the engine-gear unit. The suspensions mate in well together and give what must be as good a standard of road-holding and comfort as do the suspensions on any other light-weight machine available. An unusually deep pot-hole or corrugation had to be traversed before the rider felt the impact, and over all other surfaces the rider was fully insulated from irregularities. The only criticism that could be applied in the context of suspension was that on full fork depression the front number plate fouled the lamp rim. The result on the model under test was a shattered lamp glass. This fault could easily be remedied by repositioning the plate about ½in nearer the nose of the mudguard.

Tandon Supaglid Supreme—a robust lightweight of balanced proportions

Steering was light, positive, and precise at all speeds. The machine handled particularly well when cornering and was noticeably free from the sensation of skittishness sometimes experienced with light-weights. In adverse conditions—and there was a good deal of riding on wet, greasy roads during the test—the machine showed itself to have excellent stability; no suggestion of skidding was ever experienced.

The engine started readily in hot or cold conditions and no special setting of the controls or knack in operating the kick-starter was necessary. As often experienced with the close-coupled Villiers engine-gear unit, the kick-starter pedal at the bottom of its arc was slightly too close to the footrest, but if the ball of the bewadered foot was applied to the pedal there was sufficient clearance. The engine warmed up quickly; then the mixture control on the handlebar, in the "rich" position for starting, could be moved towards the "weak" setting. The correct setting of this control was inclined to be critical, and under all hot-engine conditions the best results were obtained with the lever about three-quarters of its travel towards "weak."

Four-stroking was less noticeable than with many engines of this type and, furthermore, there was only a minor degree of intermittent firing when the engine was on the overrun with the throttle closed. Carburation was clean and the pick-up as the throttle was opened crisp and lively. Low-speed pulling power, and acceleration from low speeds in relation to the gear engaged, was lusty and positive, though inclined to cause a slight transmission harshness.

Very light in operation, the clutch freed cleanly and was progressive in its take-up of the drive—in fact, it was an excellent example of the high standard achieved by Villiers clutches. The gear change was light to operate and the pedal movement short. Clean and positive selection of the ratios, higher or lower, was certain, even if the pedal was moved rather

The 197 c.c. Villiers engine has extremely good pulling powers and cruises happily at 45 m.p.h.

Supreme

Attractive Appearance

Fully adjustable footrests are fitted. The pivoting rear fork is controlled by a rubber cartridge

more smartly than is the practice of the average rider. Only if racing-type changes were made was there any suggestion of a "scrunch" as the gears were engaged. A clearly felt pedal movement from bottom or second gear selected neutral.

Exhaust silencing was pleasingly subdued at speeds up to about 45 m.p.h. and provided full-throttle acceleration was not used. At higher top-gear speeds and when the engine was being given its head in the indirect gear ratios, the exhaust became slightly on the noisy side, but probably not objectionably so. The orifice of the silencer tail pipe is blanked off; the gas outlet is provided by a longitudinal slit in the underside of the tail pipe. This arrangement has the merit of preventing an oily deposit on the rim and tyre.

Both brakes were disappointing. They lacked power and there was a disconcerting sponginess in operation; to some extent this sponginess derived from the inefficiency of the brakes in the sense that there was the irresistible tendency to employ excessively high application pressures. When an endeavour was made to obtain the best stopping performance figure, the front-brake cable nipple pulled off. The figure given relates to the mean of only two runs, whereas with the majority of machines tested the figure will be the mean of eight to a dozen runs.

Inherent Balance

Disposition of the handlebar, saddle and footrests provides a satisfactory position for riders of a wide variety of stature, and contributes to the "man-size" feel of the machine. In point of fact, with the Tandon there is never any sensation of smallness or "flimsiness." The handlebar can be swivelled in its clamps and the footrests have a 360deg range of adjustment.

Inherent balance of the machine is good, and when it is being manoeuvred manually or being ridden at minimum speed, it feels even lighter than it is and is most handleable. The central stand is reasonably easy to operate and raises the front wheel. Weight on the steering head—such as a couple of riding coats—brings the front wheel down and the rear wheel well clear of the ground.

A good, white driving light adequate for cruising up to the limits of the machine was provided by the Lucas head lamp.

Standard equipment includes the Westinghouse rectifier and a battery, and although the output registered by the ammeter never appeared to be more than about three amps., and seemed a fraction below balancing the full lighting load, the battery remained well charged throughout the test, which included a considerable amount of night riding. The battery is neatly mounted between the frame tubes and below the saddle, where it is readily accessible and can be removed without the use of tools.

Ample accommodation for tools, the tyre pump, and incidental equipment is provided by the container in the tank, which has a large chromium-plated cover detachable after one knurled nut is unscrewed. As becomes a machine of such pleasing lines as the Tandon, the colour finish—a polychromatic light blue—is distinctive. Exhaust system, handlebar, controls, wheel rims, head-lamp rim, saddle springs and other detail components are chromium-plated.

This new, more powerful Tandon in no way supersedes its excellent smaller-capacity brother; it broadens the range and thereby enhances the appeal of the marque.

Information Panel

197 c.c. Tandon Supaglid Supreme

SPECIFICATION

ENGINE: Villiers 197 c.c. (59 x 72 mm.) single-cylinder two-stroke with three-speed gear in unit; flat crown, die-cast aluminium-alloy piston; roller-bearing big-end; ball bearings supporting mainshafts. Detachable, light-alloy cylinder head with hemispherical combustion chamber. Petroil lubrication.

CARBURETTOR: Villiers "Middleweight" double lever, with twist-grip throttle control. Air filter standard.

TRANSMISSION: Villiers, three-speed, foot-operated gear box in unit with engine. Overall gear ratios: Bottom, 14.15 to 1. Second, 7.45 to 1. Top, 5.32 to 1. Primary chain, ½ x 0.335in in oil-bath; secondary chain, ½ x 0.335in, with guard over top run. R.p.m. at 30 m.p.h. in top gear, 2,580.

IGNITION AND LIGHTING: Villiers flywheel magneto, with lighting coils. Lucas accumulator and Westinghouse rectifier. Lucas 6in head lamp; twin-filament, 18-watt main bulb.

PETROIL CAPACITY: 2¼ gallons.

TYRES: 3.00 x 19in Dunlop ribbed front, and 3.00 x 19in Speed Universal rear.

BRAKES: 5 x ⅞in front and rear.

SUSPENSION: Tandon telescopic front fork. Pivoting fork rear suspension, with rubber as the resilient medium.

WHEELBASE: 49in. Ground clearance, 7in unladen.

SADDLE: Wrights. Height, 27in, unladen.

WEIGHT: 184lb with one gallon of fuel and full equipment.

PRICE: £98 10s (in Great Britain, with £26 11s 11d P.T., £125 1s 11d).

ROAD TAX: £1 17s 6d a year; 10s 4d a quarter.

MAKERS: Tandon Motors, Ltd., Colne Way, By-Pass Road, Watford (Works); and 29, Ludgate Hill, London, E.C.4 (Offices).

DESCRIPTION: *The Motor Cycle*, 14 December, 1950.

PERFORMANCE DATA

MEAN MAXIMUM SPEED: Bottom: 25 m.p.h. Second: 49 m.p.h. Top: 55 m.p.h.

MEAN ACCELERATION:

	10-20 m.p.h	15-25 m.p.h.	20-30 m.p.h.
Bottom	2.2 secs	2.4 secs	
Second	4.8 secs	4.2 secs	4.4 secs
Top	—	8.6 secs	8.0 secs

Speed at end of quarter-mile from rest: 52 m.p.h.
Time taken from 0 to 30 m.p.h.: 6.4 secs.

PETROIL CONSUMPTION: At 30 m.p.h., 98 m.p.g.; at 40 m.p.h., 80 m.p.g. (Figures obtained under adverse weather conditions.)

BRAKING: From 30 m.p.h. to rest, 39ft (surface, dry tar macadam).

TURNING CIRCLE: Left, 14ft; right, 12ft 6in.

MINIMUM NON-SNATCH SPEED: 17 m.p.h. in top gear.

WEIGHT PER C.C.: 0.94lb.

First published 1 March 1951

244 c.c. Excelsior

Lively Performance Allied to Smooth Torque :

"FOUR-CYLINDER torque" with its consequent "top-gear performance" has for many years been an eagerly sought characteristic in motor cycles. Hitherto, however, almost without exception it has been available only in expensive, luxury mounts. Today the 244 c.c. Excelsior two-stroke twin, the Talisman, introduced at the 1949 Earls Court Show, offers four-cylinder torque at a price within the range of many. Exceptional smoothness of engine and transmission is one of the Talisman's most impressive features. True, like all

A neat telescopic fork and plunger-type rear suspension give good riding comfort

normal three-port two-strokes, the Excelsior engine suffers from erratic firing when it is running on light load. But the low-speed torque is so good that, with intelligent handling of the throttle, the occasions during which uneven firing need occur are so few as to render the criticism nebulous.

The two-cylinder two-stroke, of course, pays dividends in other directions as well as in terms of smoothness. It also provides excellent flexibility and surging power during acceleration. The Talisman has these attributes in full measure. Such was the engine's flexibility that it was not practicable to determine a true minimum non-snatch figure. Provided the engine was under load it would pull sweetly down to speeds as low as, and even below, 10 m.p.h. in top gear. Speeds of this order in top gear were frequently used in city traffic; and the subsequent acceleration was all that was required.

Irrespective of how abruptly the throttle was opened when the engine was pulling hard on a high gear, there was at no time any indication of engine knock or hesitation during pick-up.

The response, indeed, was in the form of a surge of smooth, effortless power of a character that is unique to this type of engine. The degree of flexibility was such as to make the provision of a four-speed gearbox seem superfluous.

Power on hills was very good indeed. One particular hill in the city of Birmingham, the well-known Bull Ring, which has a gradient of 1 in 11, was frequently climbed in third gear; from a walking pace at the bottom the machine would accelerate briskly and cleanly in third, and, if desired, top could be engaged about half-way up. An over-500 c.c. machine used by a member of the staff requires bottom and second gears at these speeds in similar circumstances.

At a maintained 30 m.p.h. on a level road, the engine was under only light load, of course, and there was a tendency to four-stroking. Minimum comfortable cruising speed, therefore, was, say, 32-33 m.p.h., at which gait the engine hummed with dynamo-like smoothness. There was no trace of vibration or engine roughness at any cruising speed. At 40 m.p.h. on top gear the acceleration was well in keeping with that expected from a 250 c.c. Even from 50 m.p.h. the machine would perceptibly accelerate if the throttle was snapped open. Highest comfortable cruising speed was 50 m.p.h.

For some of the test mileage the cruising speed was higher than that, say, 55-60 m.p.h., but at these speeds slight two-stroke rattle was apparent. At no time did the engine become unduly hot and, indeed, it was felt that for maximum efficiency it ran too cool. After one 30-mile journey, when the engine was on full-bore whenever possible, a hand could be placed lightly on the cylinder heads and held there. No oil leaks became apparent and the exhaust pipes did not discolour in the slightest degree. The exhaust note, even at the highest speeds possible, was a pleasant, subdued, quite unexceptionable hum.

A factor contributing to the Talisman's zooming acceleration was the instantaneous gear change. No lag in pedal movement was necessary when making upward changes. Pedal movement was inordinately brief—so brief, in fact, that one was not always certain that a change had been effected. The gear change was slightly heavy, and this fault coupled with the short movement made the selection of neutral from bottom or second gears not always positive. The clutch required "unsticking" by means of the kick-starter

Cylinder heads and barrels are separate castings. The generator rotor is mounted on the mainshaft

Talisman

Good Handling and Braking

before the first engine start of the day was made, but thereafter it freed perfectly at all times.

Engine starting from cold with the test machine was not so effortless as might be desired. The drill which gave best results called for copious flooding, air lever closed, and a throttle opening of between one-third and a half. One snag contributing to the starting difficulty was that with the footrests in the farthest forward position commensurate with ease of operation of the rear brake, the kick-starter and footrest axis were too close, so that only an ineffectual dab at the kick-starter was possible with a bewadered foot. Starting the engine once it was warm required only an easy dab, provided the throttle was about one-third open.

Three-and-a-half inches total movement was provided by the front fork and 1½in by the plunger-type rear-springing. The action of the front fork was rather too stiff around the static load position to provide maximum comfort on cobbled surfaces at low speeds. At high speeds on the open road the standard of comfort provided by the fork was all that was desired. In delivery tune the rear-springing was unusually stiff owing to binding on the centre post by the rubber seals. This was remedied by slackening the end-caps by approximately half a turn each. This done, the rear-springing was found to be most effective, cushioning road shocks in the most satisfactory manner.

Steering and road-holding were of a high order, allowing any selected line on corners and bends to be held effortlessly, at high or low speeds. Straight-ahead steering was first class and the machine could be steered hands-off at full speed, or at 15 m.p.h. with the engine barely pulling.

The only criticism applying to the riding position was that the top corners of the tank pads were too sharp, causing discomfort on quite brief journeys. Most of the test riding was carried out with them removed. Relationship between saddle, footrests and handlebar was sensible, and provided a riding position that was comfortable while at the same time permitting the straight-arm posture which contributes so much to absolute control. The saddle is intelligently provided with adjustment for height, the alteration being effected in such a way that as the

A three-position range of adjustment is provided for the saddle

saddle is raised so it moves farther back. There are three positions.

Used in unison, both brakes provided adequate stopping power. Both were equally powerful, with just the desired degree of sponginess, and neither faded under conditions of hard usage.

The driving beam provided by the 7in headlamp with prefocus light unit was adequate for road speeds of up to 50 m.p.h. At no speed did the ammeter indicate that the lamp load was balanced while the on-focus filament was in use. On the dip filament, the discharge was balanced at 30 m.p.h. in top gear. In its position on top of the fork bridge the speedometer was easily read from a normally seated position; the instrument registered approximately 10 per cent fast. A spring-up type centre stand is provided for parking purposes. It was very difficult to operate from either side of the machine. Ample room for a comprehensive tool-kit, with repair outfit, spare plugs and bulbs, is furnished by the provision of a tool-box on each side of the machine. The finish is red and chromium plate, and there is a cream panel on each side of the tank.

Information Panel

244 c.c. Excelsior Talisman Twin

SPECIFICATION

ENGINE: 244 c.c. (50 x 62 mm) two-stroke parallel twin. Separate cylinder barrels and heads; crank throws at 180 deg; crankshaft supported on five ball bearings; roller-bearing big-ends; aluminium-alloy, flat-top pistons. Petroil lubrication.

CARBURETTOR: Amal; twistgrip throttle control; air-slide operated by handlebar lever; air-cleaner standard.

IGNITION AND LIGHTING: Wico-Pacy Mag-generator driven direct from crankshaft. 7in headlamp with pre-focus light unit. 30/24w headlamp bulb.

TRANSMISSION: Four-speed gear box with positive-stop foot control. Bottom, 16 to 1. Second, 9.9 to 1. Third, 7.42 to 1. Top, 5.5 to 1. Two-plate cork-insert clutch running in oil. Primary chain, ¼ x 3/16in. in cast-aluminium case. Rear chain, ½ x ⅛in with guard over top run. R.p.m. at 30 m.p.h. in top gear, 2,145 approx.

FUEL CAPACITY: 2¾ gallons.

TYRES: Dunlops, 3.00 x 19in front and rear.

BRAKES: 5in diameter front and 6in rear.

SUSPENSION: Excelsior undamped telescopic front fork. Plunger-type rear-springing.

WHEELBASE: 49in. Ground clearance, 5in unladen.

SADDLE: Terry. Unladen height, 29in approx.

WEIGHT: 263lb with full tank and fully equipped.

PRICE: £113 3s 6d plus Purchase Tax (in Britain only), £30 11s 2d.

ROAD TAX: £1 17s 6d a year; 10s 4d a quarter.

MAKERS: Excelsior Motor Co., Ltd., King's Road, Tyseley, Birmingham, 11.

DESCRIPTION: *The Motor Cycle*, 13 October, 1949.

PERFORMANCE DATA

MEAN MAXIMUM SPEED: Bottom: 37 m.p.h.
Second: 48 m.p.h.
Third: 56 m.p.h.
Top: 61 m.p.h.

MEAN ACCELERATION:

	10-30 m.p.h	20-40 m.p.h	30-50 m.p.h
Bottom	4.2 secs.	—	—
Second	4.4 secs.	5.6 secs.	—
Third	5.4 secs.	6.4 secs.	9 secs.
Top	8 secs.	7 secs.	10.4 secs.

Mean speed at end of quarter mile from rest: 57 m.p.h
Mean time to cover standing quarter-mile: 23 secs.

PETROIL CONSUMPTION: At 30 m.p.h., 119 m.p.g. At 40 m.p.h., 110 m.p.g. At 50 m.p.h., 92 m.p.g. At 55-60 m.p.h., 80 m.p.g.

BRAKING: From 30 m.p.h. to rest, 29ft 6in (surface, wet tar-macadam).

TURNING CIRCLE: 13 feet.

WEIGHT PER C.C.: 1.08 lb.

First published 10 May 1951

98 c.c. James

Villiers-engine Lightweight with

WHERE economy and cleanliness from the riding aspect are among the chief requirements, thoughts inevitably turn to the 98 c.c. James Commodore, which costs £60, plus Purchase Tax, is taxed at 17s 6d a year, will cover at a speed of 30 m.p.h. over 140 miles per gallon of petroil and which, with its shielded engine and large-area legshields, requires the use of no special motor cycle clothing. The 98 c.c. Villiers engine is inherently clean and, in the case of the Commodore, it is enclosed.

Throughout the test the tools were never required; and, because of the robust and simple character of the engine and cycle parts, there was every indication that trouble-free running over long periods could be confidently expected. All-round performance had not reached its peak at the end of the test and undoubtedly the fuel consumption and speed figures would have been improved had an additional 1,000 miles been possible. Starting from cold was at all times easily accomplished at the third or fourth kick-starter depression—with a warm engine starting was certain at the first kick.

A shielded engine is the distinctive feature of the Commodore. The machine weighs little over 150 lb

The cold-starting procedure was quite simple, involving merely flooding the carburettor, closing the strangler by lowering the lever on the side of the air filter and, with the throttle approximately one-half open, depressing the kick-starter. "Depressing" is the operative term, since starting proved so effortless that "spinning" the engine was quite unnecessary.

After a cold start the strangler required to be opened partially and left thus for roughly a quarter of a mile. Then it could be opened fully and forgotten about till the next cold start was required. As soon as it had reached its normal working temperature the engine would idle slowly and reliably with the twistgrip turned the merest fraction off its closed stop.

The two-speed gear is operated by means of a lever on the right handlebar connected to the gear box through a Bowden cable. Moving the lever forward to the limit of its travel engages bottom gear, and top gear is selected by drawing the lever backwards with a leisurely movement of the right forefinger.

Only light pressure and no special skill was required to make clean, sweet, upward or downward gear changes. Because of slight clutch drag bottom gear generally engaged with an audible "clonk" when the machine was stationary with the engine idling.

Clutch drag, it was felt, was due to inadequate movement at the handlebar lever—movement which was such that the cable had to be adjusted without free play if excessive drag was to be avoided. No trouble from clutch slip was, however, experienced during the test. Light enough in operation to be easily disengaged by an eight-year-old boy, the clutch was silky-sweet in its take-up of the drive.

All controls were light and smooth and well placed for ease of employment. The clutch and front-brake levers required unusually little hand reach. In its position close to the twistgrip, the gear control could be operated by the forefinger and thumb of the right hand—there was no need to take a hand off the bar. Neutral, though not "positive," was easily selected from bottom or top gear. The brake pedal could be depressed by pivoting the left foot on the footrest—there was no need to lift the foot in order to apply it.

James machines are, of course, noted for their comfortable riding position. The Commodore is no exception, the test mount proving outstandingly comfortable for a machine in this particular capacity class. The saddle height is 28½in and the relationship between the saddle and footrests was such as to permit a satisfactory knee angle for riders of average stature. Footrests on the Commodore are non-adjustable. The handlebars are carried in split clamps which provide adjustment for height, fore and aft position (or "reach"), and angle of the grips.

Scaling little over 150lb, the Commodore is the type of machine which instils confidence in the veriest novice. All manner of vile road surfaces were encountered during the test. Stability on greasy surfaces was exceptionally good. Wood blocks and slippery tramlines

Protection from road dirt in wet weather proved to be entirely adequate

Commodore

First-class Weather Protection

could be traversed with complete confidence. Traffic threading on wet roads could be indulged in almost with impunity just as it could when it was dry. The Commodore is easily manœuvred in traffic and, with its low weight and excellent turning lock, it can be pushed in and out of awkward garages or passages with ease.

In the wet, the measure of protection from water and road dirt proved entirely adequate. Waders or any other form of waterproof leggings were never required. Goggles and gauntlet gloves were the only items of out-of-the-ordinary wear that were indulged in when the machine was used as a ride-to-work "hack."

Front suspension is by means of a link-type fork with a single compression spring. The degree of comfort provided was adequate on roads of average poor surface; on very bad city cobbles, severe jolting was experienced unless the speed was kept down to, say, 15 m.p.h. At this speed in top gear, the engine is entirely happy, whether it is pulling hard or running under only light load.

Hill-climbing Capabilities

The engine's flexibility, indeed, was such that bottom gear was seldom required except for starting away from rest or when the speed had to be dropped very low (because of traffic conditions) on severe gradients. All main-road hills encountered during the test, irrespective of head winds, were surmounted (given a no-baulk run) on top gear. The average up-grade would be topped at 28-30 m.p.h., and the more severe gradients at seldom below 20-25 m.p.h. Restarts were made on an estimated 1 in 10 gradient without difficulty.

Throughout the test circumstances generally demanded that the model had to be driven flat-out or all but flat-out. It gave no indication of being unduly stressed even with this treatment and, indeed, the engine never became really hot. Maximum comfortable cruising speed was in the region of 35 m.p.h., at which gait the engine was buzzing quickly, but not to an extent which suggested unduly high revs or fuss. Minimum practicable cruising speed in top gear was about 14-15 m.p.h.

At the beginning of the test both brakes proved to be spongy in operation and lacking in real power. They improved steadily

An appreciated rider's feature of the James—the wide legshields

with use, however, and at the conclusion of the test they were satisfactorily in keeping with the machine's performance.

A particularly pleasing feature of the James is the fact that the exhaust is subdued to a degree in excess of average standards. At speed on the open road it was no more than a pleasant purr. Even when the machine was running downhill on a small throttle opening (and there was firing in the silencer), the exhaust noise was not at all objectionable.

For parking purposes—or for use when removing either wheel—a centre stand is provided. It was extremely easy to operate, but unless the joint at the detachable part of the silencer was kept clean, a spot of oil was liable to find its way on to one's shoe each time the stand was used. The petroil filler cap was liquid-tight even when the tank was filled almost brimful, which is, of course, as it should be on a machine of this type. So that the oily exhaust gases are not ejected on to the rear tyre and rim, the silencer outlet is turned outward; a measure which proved most effective.

Tools are carried in a neat, easily-accessible, cylindrical container under the rear of the tank, and the pump is carried on clips on the top of the safety bars. The finish is in James maroon and chromium (though the wheel rims are argenized silver), and the tank panel is blue with gold lining.

The 98 c.c. James Commodore

Information Panel

SPECIFICATION

ENGINE: Villiers 98 c.c. (47 × 57 mm) single-cylinder two-stroke, with two-speed gear in unit. Roller-bearing big-end; ball-bearings supporting mainshafts. Flat-crown die-cast, aluminium-alloy piston. Detachable light-alloy cylinder head. Petroil lubrication.

CARBURETTOR: Villiers "Junior" single-lever type with air-filter and strangler. Twistgrip throttle control.

TRANSMISSION: Villiers two-speed gear in unit with the engine; gear change operated by handlebar lever through Bowden control cable. Top, 8.47 to 1; bottom, 13.04 to 1. Cork-insert clutch running in oil. Primary chain, ⅜ × 0.225in; oil-bath chain case. Secondary, ½ × 0.305in, with guard over top run.

IGNITION: Villiers flywheel-magneto.

LIGHTING: Villiers direct. Twin-filament 18w main bulb. Dry battery in headlamp for parking.

PETROIL CAPACITY: 1¾ gallons.

TYRES: Dunlop studded, 19 × 2.50in front and rear.

BRAKES: 4in internal expanding front and rear.

SUSPENSION: James link-type fork with single compression spring.

WHEELBASE: 46½in. Ground clearance, 5in.

SADDLE: James. Height, 28½in.

WEIGHT: 161lb, with full tank and fully equipped.

PRICE: £60, plus Purchase Tax (in Britain only), £16 4s.

ROAD TAX: 17s 6d a year, 4s 10d a quarter.

MAKERS: The James Cycle Co., Ltd., Greet, Birmingham.

DESCRIPTION: *The Motor Cycle*, 16 November, 1950.

PERFORMANCE DATA

MAXIMUM SPEED: Bottom: 30 m.p.h. Top: 39 m.p.h.

ACCELERATION:

	10-20 m.p.h.	15-25 m.p.h.	20-30 m.p.h.
Bottom	4 secs	5.6 secs	9.6 secs
Top	4.6 secs	4.4 secs	6.2 secs

Speed at end of quarter-mile from rest: 37 m.p.h.
Time taken from rest to 30 m.p.h.: 11.6 secs.

PETROIL CONSUMPTION: At 20 m.p.h., 172 m.p.g. At 30 m.p.h., 144 m.p.g. At 35 m.p.h. (full throttle running), 104 m.p.g.

BRAKING: From 30 m.p.h. to rest, 35 feet

TURNING CIRCLE: 11ft 6in.

MINIMUM NON-SNATCH SPEED: 12 m.p.h.

WEIGHT PER C.C.: 1.6lb.

> First published
> 31 May 1951

Norton Dominator

Famous Twin and Garrard S90 Occasional Two-seater

Handling of the outfit proved first-class

ROAD-TESTED in solo form in December, 1949, the 497 c.c. Norton Dominator proved to be among the best of high-quality, high-performance machines. Further, members of the Staff who from time to time have sampled the machine in sidecar form have commented upon their experiences with keen appreciation. The outfit submitted for test, a Dominator coupled to an S90 Garrard sidecar, amply justified all previous enthusiasm. Indeed, it indicated that as well as being right in the front rank as a solo, the Dominator is an excellent machine for sidecar work.

The chief reason for the Norton's success as a sidecar machine lay undoubtedly in the fact that there was excellent torque at low and medium r.p.m. At 18-20 m.p.h. on its 5.9 to 1 top gear the engine ran smoothly and sweetly, without any indication of transmission harshness, and acceleration in top gear from that speed, though by no means brisk, was good enough for town-driving requirements.

At 30 m.p.h. the outfit was well into its stride, the engine turning over with silky smoothness and developing so much power that average gradients could be climbed at that speed. Between 40 and 50 m.p.h. the engine felt to be at its best, revving quietly and even more smoothly than at lower speeds.

The outfit's highest practicable cruising speed was really its maximum speed. Certainly, for much of the test mileage, 60-65 m.p.h. was held under average conditions. Full throttle was frequently used without indication of over-driving. On one particular occasion, along a by-pass with a long, downhill straight, 80 m.p.h. was held for approximately a mile, and the throttle kept against the stop on the following mile-long rise. The engine gave indications by severe pinking, of being abused.

This episode came towards the end of the day on which the performance figures were taken; a day on which brutally hard driving had been the rule rather than the exception. Yet at the end of it the engine was as clean as it had been in the morning; indeed, it was as clean as it had been at the start of the test. Only a faint blemish marred the exhaust pipes' pristine brilliance. Not the faintest oily trace appeared externally. In the early stages oil from the oil-tank breather tended to make the base of the crankcase and gear box messy, but this was because the oil-tank had been overfilled. Draining off approximately one pint of oil eliminated the bother.

Total mileage recorded on the speedometer at the conclusion of the test was 734, and even then the engine felt to be "tight" when it was started from cold. This tightness, allied to the engine compression, would hold a 10-stone rider on the kick-starter for half a minute. Consequently, especially in the early stages of the test, starting from cold involved considerable muscular effort as well as knack. Starting was at all times positive, however, the engine generally firing on the second or third swing of the kick-starter. The effort required to spin the engine decreased as the miles totted up.

Starting from Cold

No particularly careful control setting was necessary in order to make a cold start. The carburettor required flooding and the air lever had to be closed, but the engine was not too critical as regards the throttle opening. The air lever could be opened almost directly after a cold start and was thereafter not required for the remainder of that day. The test, incidentally, was carried out in average May temperatures with no extremes of cold—and certainly none of heat.

Almost immediately after a cold start the engine would idle in a manner that was quite exceptional for a 500 c.c. parallel twin. It is no exaggeration to say that it "chuffed"—almost in a manner reminiscent of the famous Norton side-valves. Mechanical noises when the engine was idling were not marked. Piston slap and valve-gear noises were just audible.

From tickover engine speeds the pick-up in delivery tune was unusually brisk, though not quite clean, since there was an annoying flat-spot just off the pilot jet. This was cured by enriching the pilot mixture setting and raising the throttle stop slightly, but idling thereafter was not quite so slow—though perfectly even and reliable. When the engine was under heavy load, the throttle had to be handled discriminately if pinking was to be avoided.

The riding position proved nearly 100 per cent comfortable. The only points of criticism were that the right heel of a bewadered foot came up against the kick-starter and the left foot had to be kept clear of the inside of the rest (or held at an angle) because of the brake pedal. It was considered that the pedal could be more

An exceptionally slow and even tickover was a feature of the power unit

and Sidecar

Combine to Provide a Thrilling Outfit

A view showing the S90 Garrard sidecar

"tucked in" with advantage. A comfortable knee angle is provided by the relative positions of saddle and footrests. Carried in the excellent Norton split clamps, the handlebar is widely adjustable for fore and aft position, height and angle of the grips.

All the controls are excellently positioned for ease of operation. No great hand reach is necessary in using the clutch or front brake. Levers are of the solid type, which can be adjusted to operate smoothly and without "flap." Clutch withdrawal required rather less than average pressure on the lever; but the front brake, potent enough in itself, needed considerable pressure for maximum effect.

The twistgrip was beautifully light and smooth in operation; light enough to be manipulated by the palm of the hand while the fingers were grasping the brake lever—an excellent feature. Both the brake and gear pedals could be used without raising the operating foot from its footrest. Clean, sweet upward or downward gear changes could be made as quickly or as leisurely as desired. Pedal movement was pleasantly light.

Assuming the full travel permitted by the handlebar lever was used, the clutch just freed on withdrawal. Bottom gear could be engaged quietly when the engine was idling and the machine stationary, but engagement was slightly heavy and the gear generally had to be "fed in." Similarly, some knack was necessary in selecting neutral.

Both brakes provided smooth, progressive braking and came well up to the recognized standard. Illumination from the headlamp was sufficient to allow cruising speeds of 50-55 m.p.h. after dark. The tool-box is sufficiently capacious for a complete and comprehensive tool-kit, together with a repair outfit, spare plugs and bulbs.

The sidecar was fitted by the Garrard people in London. Delivery alignment was poor, the machine "leaning-in" perceptibly. Under these conditions the handling was unsatisfactory, but re-aligning the outfit transformed it into one "which could be made do anything but talk." No flexing took place between the machine and sidecar and, since it sits on a pivot mounting at the front, neither was there any sideways sway of the body.

Standard of comfort provided by the sidecar was very high. The tension coil springs at the rear effectively absorb road shocks and the generous windscreen and side-screens provide nearly 100 per cent protection from the elements. There was, too, all but complete freedom from draughts.

With the additional weight of a sidecar the Norton suspension appeared to work even better than it does when the machine is in solo form. Road shocks were effectively damped from the rider. The handling at high speeds or low, on bumpy or smooth surface, was absolutely first class. A quarter to one-half of a turn was all that was required on the steering damper.

Finish of the machine and sidecar was black, silver and chromium plate, and a better-looking outfit would be difficult to imagine. One that would give greater all-round satisfaction to the discriminating enthusiast would be very difficult indeed to find.

Information Panel

SPECIFICATION

ENGINE: 497 c.c. (66 x 72.6 mm) o.h.v. parallel twin. Fully enclosed valve-gear operated by a single camshaft. Plain bearing big-ends. Roller journal main bearing on drive side ; ball journal bearing on timing side. Compression ratio, 6.75 to 1. Dry-sump lubrication ; tank capacity, 7pt.
CARBURETTOR: Amal ; twistgrip throttle control ; air-slide operated by handlebar control.
IGNITION AND LIGHTING: B.T.-H. or Lucas magneto with auto-advance. Separate 45-watt Lucas dynamo. 7in headlamp.
TRANSMISSION: Norton four-speed gear box with positive-stop foot control. Bottom, 17.75 to 1. Second, 10.43 to 1. Third, 7.14 to 1. Top, 5.9 to 1. Multi-plate clutch with Ferodo inserts. Primary chain, $\frac{3}{8}$in x 0.305in in pressed-steel oil-bath case. Secondary chain, $\frac{5}{8}$in x $\frac{1}{4}$in. R.p.m. at 30 m.p.h. in top gear, 2,300 approx.
FUEL CAPACITY: $3\frac{3}{4}$ gallons.
TYRES: Avon. Front, 21 x 3.00in ribbed. Rear, 19 x 3.50in studded.
BRAKES: Both 7in diameter x 1$\frac{1}{8}$in wide ; hand adjusters.
SUSPENSION: Norton Roadholder telescopic fork with hydraulic damping. Plunger-type rear-suspension with springs for shock and reaction.
WHEELBASE: 56in. Ground clearance, 5$\frac{1}{4}$in unladen.
SADDLE: Lycett. Unladen height, 30$\frac{1}{2}$in.
WEIGHT: Complete outfit, 616lb (machine only, 421lb).
PRICE: £183, plus Purchase Tax (in Britain only), £49 8s 2d.
ROAD TAX: £5 a year. £1 7s 6d a quarter.
MAKERS: Norton Motors, Ltd., Bracebridge Street, Birmingham, 6.
DESCRIPTION: *The Motor Cycle*, 11 November, 1948.

SIDECAR

MODEL: Garrard S90 Occasional Two-seater.
CHASSIS: Tubular section with wheel spindle supported at both ends. Body carried on pivot mounting at front and coil springs in tension at rear. Pre-loading of springs adjustable. Wheel has W.M.3-19 rim with 3.50 x 19in tyre.
BODY: Ash framework with sheet aluminium panelling. Safety glass windscreen ; large-area celluloid side screens and black twill hood. Overall length, 7ft 9in ; front squab to nose, 5ft 6in ; squab measures 20 x 20in ; height inside when hood is raised, 31in. Rear seat accommodation suitable for child up to 12-13 years.

Norton Dominator and sidecar

PRICE: Body, £51, plus Purchase Tax (in Great Britain only), £13 12s. Chassis, £35, plus Purchase Tax, £9 6s 8d.
DESCRIPTION: *The Motor Cycle*, 14 October, 1948.

PERFORMANCE DATA

MEAN MAXIMUM SPEED: Bottom* : 27 m.p.h.
Second* : 46 m.p.h.
Third : 66 m.p.h.
Top : 68 m.p.h.
* Valve float just starting.

MEAN ACCELERATION :

	10-30 m.p.h.	20-40 m.p.h.	30-50 m.p.h.
Second	4.2 secs	4 secs	—
Third	7.4 secs	5.6 secs	6.2 secs
Top	—	8.4 secs	8.2 secs

Mean speed at end of quarter-mile from rest : 62 m.p.h.
Mean time to cover standing quarter-mile : 19.4 secs.
PETROL CONSUMPTION : At 30 m.p.h., 62 m.p.g. At 40 m.p.h., 53 m.p.g. At 50 m.p.h., 44 m.p.g. At 60 m.p.h., 37 m.p.g.
BRAKING : From 30 m.p.h. to rest, 51 feet (surface: dry, smooth tar macadam).
TURNING CIRCLE : 19 feet 5 inches.
MINIMUM NON-SNATCH SPEED : 14 m.p.h. in top gear.
WEIGHT PER C.C. : 1.24lb.

> First published 12 July 1951

192 c.c. LE

Much Enhanced Performance : Latest Model Sets a New

THE motor cycle world was fascinated when, in 1948, Velocettes introduced the 149 c.c. model LE. Its specification embodied nearly every luxury feature desired by the discriminating rider. The LE, however, was designed for use by the layman, as distinct from the motor cyclist, and it was criticized by the latter, and to some extent by the former, because, it was said, the engine was lacking in power. Velocettes paid heed to the call for enhanced performance and, towards the end of 1950, increased the capacity by approximately one-third—

Increased engine capacity has not altered the appearance of the LE

to 192 c.c. Further increase was decreed undesirable and, in any case, would have involved extensive redesigning.

A result of the modification has been to transform the LE—to increase the machine's speed and climb to a degree that is entirely unsuspected by the majority of informed motor cyclists as well as by the not-so-knowledgeable general public. But, equally important, the LE has not lost in the change-over a single one of its endearing characteristics, such as smoothness, silence, freedom from pinking and low fuel consumption.

Motor cyclists are notorious for their conservatism. The test of the LE was approached in the light that the machine was one in the small-power, low-capacity class and "100 miles would be adequate for both machine and rider in an afternoon.' Yet on one occasion early in the test, when the machine was taken out after lunch without prior thought or preparation, 254 miles were covered before 9.30 p.m. Every mile was sheer delight Cruising speed at the beginning of this particular trip was 40-45 m.p.h. As the miles totted up this was increased to 50 m.p.h. and on the following day, when a further 150 miles were added, numerous road stretches were effortlessly covered at 55 m.p.h.

Fifty miles per hour on top gear represents approximately 5,000 r.p.m., which is described by Velocettes as being the maximum desirable engine speed commensurate with long engine life. Certainly, at 50 m.p.h., the engine felt to be working well within its limits. The machine hummed along without the slightest vibration or fuss, easily tucking 40 miles inside the hour, the engine turning over all the while with a degree of smoothness that has surely never been equalled in motor cycle history. Main-road hills were generally topped at 40-45 m.p.h., depending on their gradient. Second gear was rarely required on main roads in the southern half of England and, when it was needed, 36-38 m.p.h. could generally be maintained if desired.

At the lower end of the scale the LE again excelled. It would trickle through traffic in a manner that attracted attention from pedestrians because it was so quiet, and so obviously smooth and comfortable to ride.

At no time is the exhaust apparent to the rider, and the engine, with its water-jacketed cylinders, is audible only by reason of a faint, pleasant hum, which is superseded by the sound of the wind at speeds in excess of, say, 30 m.p.h. None of the indirect gear ratios is audible. With shaft drive there is, of course, no chain swish, and the large-area carburettor air intake effectively silences the ingoing charge. It is no exaggeration to say that the LE is quieter than all but the more expensive type of car; and it is quieter probably than even that, because tyre swish and wind roar are noticeable where cars are concerned, and they are negligible factors to one aboard the Velocette.

The riding position is of the sit-up-and-beg type, that is to say, the saddle is relatively low (its height from the ground is 28in) and the handlebar is swept back so that the grips come within comfortable reach. The footooards are long and, with the stepped-up position provided for the pillion rider, furnish a variety of positions for the feet. Using the slopes towards the rear provides the rider with a leg position that would be difficult to improve upon. For general town-work or for long journeys the riding position proved as near perfect as might be.

All manner of road surfaces were encountered during the test. Rough city cobbles and broken asphalt could be traversed with equanimity, the front and rear suspension systems doing their jobs so well as to cause the word " glide " to suggest itself. Straight-ahead steering proved faultless, irrespective of how bad the road surface was and whether the speed was in the fifties

Hand-starter and hand-operated gear lever; note the stepped-up footboard

Velocette

and Most Enviable Standard in Motor Cycles

With the LE Velocette, use of waders or leggings proved unnecessary

or a below-walking-pace crawl. On corners and bends the machine may be heeled over to an angle that is limited only by the width across the base of the legshields.

Gear-changing on the LE is by means of a hand-operated lever on the right-hand side of the "body." The lever moves in a narrow gate and is extremely light in operation. Clean, sweet changes could be easily accomplished between any pair of gears, and the Velocette scheme of things has the advantage that neutral may be easily selected from any gear.

The clutch is very light, frees perfectly and instantly (so that bottom gear may be readily and noiselessly engaged when the machine is stationary with the engine idling) and it takes up the drive sweetly and without snatch.

When used seriously and in unison, the brakes provide stopping power that is far and away above the average. They have just the right "feel," being light to operate and giving just the desired degree of sensitivity. The braking figure of 26 feet is a mean of seven crash stops carried out in quick succession. No brake fade occurred and, though braking pressures are obviously high, no adjustment was required afterwards.

It has been mentioned that the machine was designed with the lay public in mind. The aim was to provide inexpensive, reliable transport, with easy starting and good weather protection as absolute "musts." All the aims behind the design have been achieved in an exceptionally high degree. To start the engine from cold it is necessary merely to switch on the ignition, pull out the starting control on the carburettor and give an upward pull on the starting handle. The first part of the movement of the lever raises the ingenious and quite fool-proof centre stand. If the engine does not fire on the first pull it will almost certainly do so on the second. The carburettor starting control, of course, is brought into use only when the engine is cold.

Engine idling was slow and reliable, and vibration almost totally absent. The pick-up throughout the entire throttle range was as clean-cut as could be wished. Acceleration more than matched that of normal city traffic without the need for high r.p.m. in the indirect gears. Pinking was never once apparent.

Weather protection was first-class and the use of waders unnecessary. The machine remained singularly clean, the deeply valanced mudguards, providing, in conjunction with the legshields, adequate defence against road filth and insects. Not the slightest trace of oil appeared outside the engine. On cold days the warm stream of air from the radiator proved most welcome. On the hottest days it passed unnoticed.

Both panniers were used frequently during the test—used to an extent, indeed, that caused one to wonder how they can possibly be considered by anyone to be "accessories." The glove-and-goggle compartment in the tank-top, too, was appreciated because of its convenience.

The LE is the perfect "lazy man's" motor cycle. To bring the centre stand into use it is only necessary to press it lightly downward with one foot. It is next to impossible for the machine to topple over when the stand is in use. The lighting and ignition switches are conveniently situated on top of the legshields. The very minimum of periodical maintenance is necessary, and even these tasks are designed to be easily carried out. Cleaning the LE is the work of five minutes.

That, then, is the new LE: a machine which, in terms of speed and power, is not to be confused with the original version. With its now adequate performance, smooth torque, freedom from vibration, silence, excellent weather protection, cleanliness and economy, it sets a new and most enviable standard in motor cycles.

The 192 c.c. LE Velocette

Information Panel

SPECIFICATION

ENGINE: 192 c.c. (50×49 mm), horizontally opposed twin-cylinder four-stroke, with side valves and water-cooling. Roller bearings at big-ends; ball and plain bearings supporting crankshaft. Light-alloy pistons and light-alloy cylinder heads; 10 mm sparking plugs. Wet-sump, pressure lubrication; sump capacity, 1¼ pints. Water system capacity, 2¼ pints.
CARBURETTOR: Special Amal multi-jet with butterfly-type throttle and petrol filter. Twistgrip throttle control. Air-filter.
TRANSMISSION: By shaft and bevel gears from engine-gear unit to rear wheel. Velocette three-speed gear box in unit with the engine. Hand gear-change with lever on right-hand side of frame pressing. Top 7.15 to 1, Second, 10.92 to 1, Bottom, 21 to 1. Two-plate clutch, operating dry, with control by handlebar lever. R.p.m. at 30 m.p.h. in top gear, 2,900 approx.
IGNITION: Battery and coil, with automatic-advance mechanism.
LIGHTING: B.T.-H. generator driven from crankshaft. 6in-diameter headlamp, with 24/24w twin-filament main bulb controlled by handlebar switch.
PETROL CAPACITY: 1¼ gallons.
TYRES: Dunlop 3×19in. Ribbed front tread, studded rear.
BRAKES: 5in × ¾in internal-expanding front and rear.
SUSPENSION: Telescopic front fork with coil springs. Pivot-fork rear suspension, with coil springs adjustable for load.
SADDLE: Velocette. Height 28in unladen.
GROUND CLEARANCE: 5¼in unladen. Wheelbase, 51¼in, machine normally loaded.
WEIGHT: 268lb, with one gallon of fuel and fully equipped.
PRICE: £133, plus Purchase Tax (in Great Britain only), £35 18s 3d.
ROAD TAX: £1 17s 6d a year; 10s 4d a quarter.
DESCRIPTION: *The Motor Cycle*, 9 November, 1950.

PERFORMANCE DATA

MEAN MAXIMUM SPEED: Bottom: 32 m.p.h.
Second: 44 m.p.h.
Top: 57 m.p.h.

ACCELERATION:

	10-20 m.p.h.	15-25 m.p.h.	20-30 m.p.h.
Bottom	2 secs	3 secs	3.2 secs
Second	2.6 secs	3.2 secs	3.4 secs
Top	5 secs	4.6 secs	4.4 secs

Mean speed at end of quarter-mile from rest (through gears): 49 m.p.h.
Mean time taken from rest to 30 m.p.h. (through gears): 6 secs.
PETROL CONSUMPTION: At 30 m.p.h., 119 m.p.g. At 40 m.p.h., 108 m.p.g. At 50 m.p.h., 100 m.p.g.
BRAKING: From 30 m.p.h. to rest: 26ft (surface, dry tarmacadam).
TURNING CIRCLE: 12 feet.
MINIMUM NON-SNATCH SPEED: 10 m.p.h. (top gear)
WEIGHT PER C.C.: 1.39 lb

First published 26 July 1951

497 c.c. Ariel Red

Famous Overhead-valve Sports Model Tested

FOR nearly twenty years Ariels have listed a 497 c.c. Red Hunter. Since the original two-valve model was introduced in 1933, very few changes in the engine design have taken place, though detail modifications such as total valve-gear enclosure and telescopic forks have become part of the general scheme of things to keep the model in step with current trends.

As all who study design practice well know, when few changes are made to any machine it means that (a) the manufacturer concerned is not suffering mechanical bothers, and (b) that

A straightforward and robust single— the Red Hunter Ariel

the model is proving popular with the public. And so far as the Ariel Red Hunter is concerned, the reasons behind these twin facts are simple ones: the design is straightforward and the construction robust; and, considered in its particular "type classification," the Red Hunter's all-round performance is most satisfying.

Cold or hot, engine starting was always easily accomplished: when cold on the second or third kick-starter depression, and when hot, invariably on the first. A certain cold start required only that the carburettor was flooded lightly, then, provided the throttle was barely open, the engine would fire, as has been mentioned, on the second or third prod on the kick-starter. With the exhaust-valve lifter operated in the approved manner, kick-starting called for no physical effort of any consequence. The air lever was at no time required during the test.

For the remaining starts after the first of the day, very light flooding was again sufficient to provide the required mixture strength. As soon as the engine had started, the twistgrip could be rolled right back against its closed stop with the certain assurance that a reliable tickover would result. At idling speeds, valve-gear and piston were audible if the ignition was fully advanced. On full retard, however, at which ignition setting the slowest and most reliable idling resulted, the piston was all but silent.

On the road with the Red Hunter, engine noises—piston slap chiefly—were apparent only as an undertone, which was barely heard above the sounds of the wind, and, at high engine r.p.m., the exhaust. Exhaust noise was not obtrusive in open country, but it was too reverberant when the machine was being driven in average-width city streets.

From idling speeds right up through the speed range the pick-up was clean-cut and brisk. Though the tendency to pinking was not particularly marked—even when the sidecar was fitted—it was necessary to use the ignition control in close conjunction with the throttle if the best results were to be obtained. Low-speed torque is particularly good; good to a degree, indeed, that gives one the initial impression that the engine falls into the "woofly" big-single class. Minimum non-snatch speed in top (solo) gear was 17 m.p.h., and the transmission at speeds above that was entirely free from harshness. Transmission smoothness, in fact, proved to be one of the Red Hunter's superior features.

Acceleration from 20 m.p.h. could be satisfactorily brisk in either top or third gears without fuss, provided the ignition control was used judiciously. However, if the right grip was twisted in earnest, and the full performance used in the indirect gears, the Red Hunter was transformed from a single definitely possessing those characteristics which are called "gentlemanly" into one in the famous big-single tradition: a tradition that will assuredly never die so long as there are motor cyclists.

In this case, acceleration was all that the majority of avid sports riders are ever likely to require. Peak r.p.m. in the indirect gears is achieved remarkably quickly. The gear change is utterly positive, and the pedal may be operated by pivoting the right foot in a short arc about the footrest. Snap changes could be made if desired, there being no doubt about certain engagement, though the change would be accompanied by a scrunch from the pinions. Snap upward gear changes, however, are rarely, if ever, required outside

Excellent low-speed torque was a feature of the 497 c.c. overhead-valve engine

Hunter Single
in Solo and Sidecar Forms

the sphere of competitive events, and the Red Hunter gear change was clean and sweet provided one caused the pedal to pause in mid-travel, or moved the pedal with a leisurely, deliberate movement. Pedal movement was pleasantly short and light. All the indirect gears were silent on both drive and overrun.

The clutch freed perfectly, and it was light in operation and sweet in its take-up of the drive. It required no adjustment or other attention throughout the test. As with all other hand-operated controls, that for the clutch was well placed in relation to its respective grip. The grips, in turn, go to provide, in conjunction with the footrest and saddle position, what is probably one of the most comfortable riding postures of the present day. The handlebar is of the flat, nearly straight pattern with the grips turned slightly to the rear.

Supreme comfort, however, was not the only attribute of the Ariel's riding position. In addition, it proved to be one which automatically sets the rider in a posture which means much in terms of maximum control—whether the speed be a traffic-crawl or a 70 m.p.h. bat on a fast dual-carriageway. Speeds in the 70 m.p.h. category were commonplace during the test, and were in no way considered excessive so far as the engine's capabilities were concerned. At 40 m.p.h. to 50 m.p.h. the engine was at its best, developing sufficient power to deal with steep gradients without a slackening in speed, and turning over with delightful smoothness. Above 60 m.p.h. there was high-frequency vibration which was not apparent lower down the scale.

If the machine had proved an attractive solo, it was found to be even more likeable as a sidecar mount. When fully laden with a complement of three males (scaling *in toto* some 30-stone), it would cruise quite comfortably at speeds in the region of 50-55 m.p.h. The speedometer fitted, incidentally, proved to have an error of rather more than 10 per cent. Acceleration was apparently little impaired by full loading, and neither was handling affected. Although there was sometimes, at high speeds on irregular surfaces, an impression of more than desired lightness in the fork and rear-springing characteristics, neither suspension was found to bottom even on cross-country going.

The Watsonian Albion coupé sidecar gave satisfaction in nearly every direction. Six-foot adults found it roomy, there being plenty of leg space whether the legs were stretched out or bent at the knees. A greater than average stature male—5ft 10in tall—could wear a hat inside and still have adequate clearance below the hood. But, in any case, the hood was seldom required—thanks to the adequate side panels, there are no draughts and all but the heaviest rain was deflected overhead.

The Watsonian Albion coupé sidecar was found to be roomy and comfortable

Information Panel

The 497 c.c. Ariel Red Hunter single

SPECIFICATION

ENGINE: 497 c.c. (81.8 × 95 mm) single-cylinder o.h.v. Fully-enclosed valve gear operated by push-rods from a single cam. Double-row roller bearing big-end. Roller and ball main bearings supporting drive-side of mainshaft, ball bearing on timing side. Compression ratio, 6.8 to 1. Dry-sump lubrication with double-plunger pump; tank capacity, 6 pints.
CARBURETTOR: Amal; twistgrip throttle control. Air slide operated by handlebar lever.
IGNITION and LIGHTING: Lucas Magdyno with manual ignition control. Long 3in 45w dynamo. 7½in headlamp, with 30/30w main bulb controlled by handlebar switch.
TRANSMISSION: Burman four-speed gear box with positive foot control. Bottom, 12.6 to 1. Second, 8 to 1. Third, 6 to 1. Top 4.7 to 1. Sidecar ratios: Bottom, 15.3 to 1. Second, 9.7 to 1. Third, 7.2 to 1. Top, 5.7 to 1. Multi-plate clutch with cork inserts. Primary chain, ⅝ × 0.305in in cast-aluminium oil-bath case. Secondary chain, ⅝ × ⅜in with guard over both runs.
FUEL CAPACITY: 3½ gallons.
TYRES: Dunlop. Front, 3.00 × 20in ribbed; rear, 3.25 × 19in studded.
BRAKES: Both 7in diameter × 1⅛in wide; fulcrum adjusters
SUSPENSION: Ariel telescopic front fork. Ariel link-type rear-springing, with springs for compression and rebound.
WHEELBASE: 56in. Ground clearance, 5in unladen.
SADDLE: Lycett. Unladen height, 30in.
WEIGHT: 385lb, with one gallon of fuel and fully equipped.
PRICE: £146; with Purchase Tax (in Britain only), £185 8s 5d. Spring-frame extra, £16; with P.T., £20 6s 5d.
ROAD TAX: Solo £3 15s a year; £1 0s 8d a quarter. Sidecar, £5 a year; £1 7s 7d a quarter.
MAKERS: Ariel Motors, Selly Oak, Birmingham, 29.
DESCRIPTION: *The Motor Cycle*, 28 November, 1950.

SIDECAR

MODEL: Watsonian Albion single-seater coupé.
CHASSIS: Tubular construction with Silentbloc wheel mounting. Silco-manganese, 1½in wide seven-leaf quarter-eliptic rear springs; eyes and shackles fitted with grease nipples. Front suspension by four coil springs. Taper-roller bearing wheel hubs. Wheel fitted with 3.25 × 19in tyre. Four-point chassis attachment with adjustable rise lug to allow correct fitting to different makes of machine.
WEIGHT: 90lb approx.

BODY: Ash framework panelled in sheet steel. Dimensions: Overall length, 85in; squab to nose, 54in; width inside at shoulder level, 21½in; height from cushion to roof, 34in; squab, 23in high × 21½in wide; seat, 20 × 20in; luggage boot, 15in deep × 22in wide × 29in long. Weight, approximately 110lb. Luggage grid and bumper bar standard.
PRICE: Complete, £57 10s 0d; with P.T. (in Britain only), £72 16s 8d.
DESCRIPTION: *The Motor Cycle*, 6 October, 1949; 9 November, 1950.

PERFORMANCE DATA
(Sidecar figures in brackets)

MEAN MAXIMUM SPEED: Bottom :* 40 (30) m.p.h.
Second :* 62 (49) m.p.h.
Third : 77 (62) m.p.h.
Top : 85 (63) m.p.h.
* Valve float occurring.

MEAN ACCELERATION:

	10-30 m.p.h.	20-40 m.p.h.	30-50 m.p.h.
Bottom	3.2 (3.8) secs	3.4 (—) secs	— (—) secs
Second	5.2 (5.8) secs	4 (7.2) secs	4 (7.4) secs
Third	— (—) secs	5.4 (8.4) secs	5.8 (9.4) secs
Top	— (—) secs	6.8 (11.4) secs	6.8 (13.4) secs

Mean speed at end of quarter mile from rest: 71 (54) m.p.h.
Mean time to cover standing quarter-mile: 13 (22.2) secs.
PETROL CONSUMPTION: At 30 m.p.h. 112 (70) m.p.g. At 40 m.p.h. 84 (53) m.p.g. At 50 m.p.h. 67 (40) m.p.g. At 60 m.p.h. 53 (32) m.p.g.
BRAKING: From 30 m.p.h. to rest, 29ft 6in (52ft) (surface, dry tar macadam).
TURNING CIRCLE: 14ft 4in.
MINIMUM NON-SNATCH SPEED: 16 (13) m.p.h. in top gear with ignition fully retarded.
WEIGHT Per C.C.: 0.77 (1.18) lb.

> First published 2 August 1951

249 c.c. Model

A De Luxe Two-fifty with Four-speed

THE smaller the engine, say the pundits, the larger should be the number of gears. The wisdom behind this is apparent to anyone who has had experience with small-capacity mounts fitted with three- and four-speed gear boxes. With four well-selected gear ratios, as opposed to a lesser number, it is easier to maintain the engine's "happiest" speed range under widely varying road conditions. The de luxe model 249 c.c. C11 B.S.A., which is fitted with a four-speed gear box, provides a most satisfactory all-round performance.

A two-fifty with a four-speed gear box—the C11 B.S.A.

It was on hills especially that the value of the extra gear was most appreciated. Indeed, the gear box as a whole gained many marks; the gear change was so good as to be classed as near perfect. Effortless gear changes could be made between any pair of gears. Between top and third, the operation could be likened to a hot wire passing through butter.

The gear pedal is short, it travels in a small arc about its pivot, and was relatively light in operation. Either upward or downward gear changes were accomplished by hingeing the right foot about the footrest. Certain, clean gear engagement was assured no matter how quickly or how negligently the controls were manipulated. There was at all times a satisfying "tautness" in the gear-selector mechanism. A certain amount of gear whine was audible when the machine was running in any of the indirect gears or on top. The clutch freed perfectly, allowing bottom gear or neutral to be selected quietly and with ease when the machine was at a standstill with the engine idling.

Average-light in operation, the clutch gave no indication of being overworked by the standing-start tests; it continued to free perfectly, and to take up the drive smoothly.

Engine starting was at all times commendably easy so far as muscular effort was concerned, and always achieved with a single depression of the kick-starter. Ignition is, of course, by battery and coil, with an automatic advance-and-retard mechanism incorporated with the contact-breaker. There is no air slide in the carburettor and no exhaust-valve lifter. Neither of these was required. Certain cold-starts demanded merely that the ignition was switched on, the carburettor flooded lightly, and the kick-starter depressed, this with the twistgrip turned just a fraction off its closed stop. With the exception of the fact that the carburettor did not require flooding, the drill was similar for starting the engine when it was warm.

As soon as it had started, the engine would settle down to an absolutely certain, perfectly even, and very slow tickover. The valve-gear, when the engine was idling, was audible as a faint rustling and piston slap could just be detected. Mechanical noises from the engine and transmission noise were apparent to the rider when the machine was being ridden on the road. The exhaust was commendably subdued and not considered to be sufficiently obtrusive to cause one to limit the C11's acceleration in towns and cities.

As a result of the additional gear ratio, acceleration was improved; and, what is probably even more important, adequately rapid acceleration could be achieved with an almost entire lack of fuss. In city traffic the machine could be started away from a standstill, and, without resort to obtrusive driving methods, was capable of more than matching other vehicle's acceleration. A criticism was that there was some transmission harshness at speeds below 30 m.p.h. Pinking was never experienced.

On the open road the B.S.A. would cruise with praiseworthy effortlessness at speeds a little in excess of 50 m.p.h. Vibration at high cruising speeds was slight and of high-frequency. It was most prevalent between 40 and 43 m.p.h. It all but disappeared between 50 and 55 m.p.h., and recurred only when the engine was revved excessively, or allowed to slog hard on gradients.

Throughout the test the engine, with its integral push-rod tunnel, remained entirely oil-tight. There was some seepage from the drive-side gear box mainshaft bearing, which soiled the left leg of the centre stand. The rear chain remained adequately lubricated throughout the test, yet the rear tyre and rim remained surprisingly clean.

The B.S.A. telescopic front fork and plunger-type rear-springing effectively damped out road shocks; handling on all types of road surface was excellent

C11 B.S.A.

Gear Box and Rear Springing

Coil ignition is employed, with automatic advance-and-retard mechanism incorporated with the contact-breaker

Both front- and rear-brake controls were well placed for ease of operation. Like that for the clutch, the front-brake lever is carried on a fixed pivot block welded to the handlebar. That the levers were not mounted on adjustable clamps was not found to have any apparent disadvantage. The handlebar was tried with the grips in two different (but each reasonably comfortable) positions, and the levers remained within sensible reach.

Both brakes were smooth in operation, but construed to be rather too spongy in operation. The braking figure of 34 feet is a mean of six crash stops, each of which returned a figure within one foot of the mean figure—a consistency seldom achieved, and proving that brake fade would never be experienced under normal riding conditions.

Riding Comfort

More than adequate comfort was provided by the combination of the really excellent B.S.A. telescopic front fork and the plunger-type rear-springing. Stone setts and other antiquated road surfaces could be traversed with serenity, road shocks being effectively damped and apparent to the rider only by the gentle rise and fall of the machine. On all the many different types of road surface encountered, the handling was exemplary. The B.S.A. could be heeled over on corners and bends stylishly and with equanimity. There was no drifting, no pitching, and no chopping or snaking—none of the faults which are evident in machines with indifferent handling properties.

The riding position was very compact: too compact, indeed, for maximum comfort. It was felt that there would have been an improvement had the saddle been slightly farther to the rear.

A centre stand is provided for parking purposes, or to hold either wheel clear of the ground during wheel removal. The stand is sturdy; it proved foolproof under most conditions, and easy to operate without excessive physical effort or knack.

The tank-mounted speedometer was for all practical purposes accurate throughout the machine's speed range. The ammeter, in the rear of the headlamp, was easy to read; it indicated that the full lamp and coil load was more than balanced by the dynamo output at 30 m.p.h. in top gear. The ignition switch is incorporated in the headlamp switch; thus it is in an excellently visible position and there is little likelihood of the rider parking the machine with the switch "on."

The test model was fitted with one of the new all-enamel tanks finished in blue and beige. The wheel rims were finished in matt-silver synthetic stoving enamel and had a blue medial strip. Exhaust pipe and handlebar were, of course, chromium-plated,

---

Information Panel

The 249 c.c. Model C11 B.S.A.

SPECIFICATION

ENGINE : 249 c.c. (63 × 80 mm) single-cylinder o.h.v. with fully enclosed valve-gear. Push-rods operated from single camshaft. Double-row, roller-bearing big-end. Ball bearing supporting drive side of crankshaft; plain bearing on timing side. Light-alloy piston. Dry-sump pressure lubrication—tank capacity, 4 pints. Gear type oil-pump. Compression ratio, 6.5 to 1.

CARBURETTOR : Amal ; twistgrip throttle control No air slide.

IGNITION and **LIGHTING :** By battery and coil, with auto-advance mechanism integral with contact-breaker. Lucas long-3in dynamo ; 7in headlamp with 30/30w main bulb controlled by handlebar switch.

TRANSMISSION : B.S.A. four-speed gear box. Top, 6.65 to 1 ; Third, 8.06 to 1 ; Second, 11.7 to 1. Bottom, 17.15 to 1. Single-plate clutch with cork inserts. Primary chain, ⅜ × 0.305in in pressed-steel oil-bath case. Rear, ½ × 0.305in with guard over top run. R.p.m. at 30 m.p.h. in top gear, 2,593 approx.

FUEL CAPACITY : 2½ gallons.

TYRES : Dunlop 3.00 × 20in front and rear.

BRAKES : 5½in diameter × 1in wide front and rear.

SUSPENSION : B.S.A. hydraulically damped telescopic front fork. Plunger-type rear-springing with coil springs for compression and rebound.

WHEELBASE : 52in. Ground clearance, 5in unladen.

SADDLE : Terry. Unladen height, 28½in.

WEIGHT : 309lb with fuel tank dry and fully equipped.

PRICE : £112 ; with Purchase Tax (in Great Britain only), £142 4s 10d.

ROAD TAX : £1 17s 6d a year ; 10s 4d a quarter.

MAKERS : B.S.A. Cycles, Ltd., Birmingham, 11.

DESCRIPTION : *The Motor Cycle*, 19 October, 1950.

PERFORMANCE DATA

MEAN MAXIMUM SPEED : Bottom :*27 m.p.h.
Second : *38 m.p.h.
Third : 55 m.p.h.
Top : 64 m.p.h.
*Valve float starting.

MEAN ACCELERATION :

	10-30 m.p.h.	20-40 m.p.h.	30-50 m.p.h
Bottom	—	—	—
Second	6.2 secs	—	—
Third	—	9.2 secs	10.2 secs
Top	—	11.8 secs	13 secs

Mean speed at end of quarter mile from rest : 59 m.p.h
Mean time to cover standing quarter-mile : 21.8 secs.

PETROL CONSUMPTION : At 30 m.p.h. 118 m.p.g. At 40 m.p.h. 94 m.p.g. At 50 m.p.h. 82 m.p.g. At 55-60 m.p.h. 70 m.p.g.

BRAKING : From 30 m.p.h. to rest, 34 feet (surface, dry tar-macadam).

TURNING CIRCLE : 12ft 6in.

MINIMUM NON-SNATCH SPEED : 20 m.p.h. in top gear.

WEIGHT PER C.C. : 1.26 lb.

First published 9 August 1951

The 98 c.c. Two-

A New and Thoroughly Practical Lightweight

WITH its rich maroon finish, relieved by chromium plating, the 98 c.c. Bown is possibly one of the most attractive-looking lightweight motor cycles available today. Careful planning of the machine as a whole results in the rider gaining an impression of sitting on a much larger model, and each of those on the Staff who rode the Bown remarked upon the ease with which one could accommodate oneself to the machine.

The only available adjustment to the riding position is that afforded by the bicycle-type mounting of the handlebar, but the machine tested

Although of only 98 c.c., the Bown provides a big-machine "feel"

proved to have just the right proportions for riders varying from 5ft 8in to almost 6ft. The saddle height of 27½in and well-placed footrests ensured that the rider's legs were not cramped at an acute angle; with this and the sit-up handlebar, an extremely comfortable posture resulted.

Starting was simple and certain in all circumstances provided that, from cold, the carburettor was liberally flooded, the strangler control closed and the throttle about one-third open. Two, or sometimes three, digs at the kickstarter invariably started the engine, and almost immediately the strangler could be fully opened and ignored until the next cold-start was made. It was necessary to use the toe-portion of the foot to start the engine; otherwise the foot would foul the footrest. If, on the machine tested, the full travel was used, the kickstarter crank was held in the "down" position owing to a protruding footrest hanger bolt. The effort required to start the engine was negligible; the kickstarter could even be operated successfully by hand.

To select bottom gear quietly by means of the handlebar control it was necessary to ease the machine forward slightly; silent engagement was then certain. The clutch, which could be operated by one finger, was sweet and positive in its action. Even after the fierce standing-start tests had been completed, no adjustment was required.

Except during a restart on a steep hill, the clutch could be fully engaged in the first foot or two of motion without any transmission snatch being apparent. At approximately 14 m.p.h., top gear would be engaged by a slow movement of the handlebar lever and the machine could then be left in this gear except when traffic conditions reduced progress to a crawl.

Downward changes could be made silently and positively by leaving the throttle open, withdrawing the clutch to its fullest extent and pushing the gear lever right home. Although there is no positive stop for "neutral," no difficulties were experienced over finding this position; the "neutral" marked on the top portion of the gear-change proved to be slightly out of place.

Both the steering and the general handling of the Bown were excellent. Even on wet wood blocks and tramlines there was no feeling of instability; the machine was remarkable in that an exceptionally high degree of confidence was conveyed under adverse conditions. On corners any selected line could be held without the slightest trace of "wander."

A girder-type front fork is fitted. This absorbed most road shocks, although on very poor cobbled surfaces there were occasions when the spring clashed—apparently on rebound.

At 30 m.p.h. the Bown was at its best maximum cruising speed; much above this speed the engine would start to fuss and the raucous exhaust note, besides attracting unwelcome attention from other road-users, was tiring to the rider. By the time the machine had covered some 400 miles, the exhaust was only slightly less obtrusive. More effective silencing was greatly desired.

At no time during the test was there any engine-fading. After a full-throttle burst lasting over three miles, the engine was only sufficiently hot to prevent the rider holding a hand on the fins. The brakes, although inclined to "shriek" in the earlier stages of the test, were very efficient; the rear-brake pedal could, with advantage, be cranked out from its present position near the frame so that it comes more directly below the rider's foot.

This point, which was mentioned when the machine was taken over, was stated to have been attended to and would automatically be rectified in the next batch of machines. The front mudguard proved effective. Even after a run in heavy rain it was found that scarcely any dirt had been thrown on the frame or engine, and little or none reached the rider's legs—a most excellent and all-too-rare feature. The rear mudguard was found to be equally good.

On the whole, the engine and gear box

A large-capacity and highly ingenious toolbox is fitted on the seat tube

speed Bown

with Appealing Characteristics

were commendably oil-tight. Merely faint traces of oil became apparent on the exterior of the gear box. Oil was reaching the rear chain from the gear box and some of this was thrown on to the centre stand and rear wheel. As a result the rider's shoe was liable to become oily when the stand was operated.

An ingenious, large-capacity, cylindrical toolbox is fitted on the seat tube and is thus placed so that the tools suffer a minimum from road shocks. To a certain extent the box is tamper-proof. In spite of a close-fitting lid with some 3/16in overlap, during a storm of unusual violence some water managed to find its way inside. During the test the only time the comprehensive toolkit was used was to adjust the rear chain after 400 miles had been covered. This operation proved to be extremely simple and took only five minutes to complete.

Dual-purpose Stand

The high-lift centre stand was reasonably easy to operate. It could be a little more accessible to the toes. The machine would rest on either the front or rear wheel; it was merely a question of pressing down one end of the machine or the other—no weight was necessary to hold the machine down. The speedometer lighting cable proved to be too short and pulled out when the machine was placed on the stand.

The Villiers direct-lighting set gave a light sufficient for the maintenance of daytime speeds. Full power, it seemed, was obtained from the headlight almost as soon as the machine was under way, and even at very low engine speeds there was sufficient light for such jobs as manoeuvring into a garage.

Two-stroking, in general, was good. As usual, on the overrun and when the machine was running lightly, four- and sometimes eight-stroking was marked. Hill-climbing capabilities were excellent. All the main-road inclines encountered in the 500 miles were tackled in top gear with the speedometer needle rarely falling below 25 m.p.h. During the test a hill with a gradient of 1 in 9 with a short section of 1 in 6 was tackled and the Bown climbed this at about 12 m.p.h. in bottom gear. Restarts on the 1 in 9 section were just possible, although the clutch was abused to some extent.

Unusual with a 98 c.c. mount, the machine has a duplex-cradle frame

Mechanical noise from the engine was negligible and could only be heard when the machine was stationary and the engine merely ticking over.

In thick traffic the Bown was a delight. It was possible to ride to a standstill and balance, for seconds, with the feet on the rests. The nippy acceleration ensured that the rider could hold his own with the usual run of vehicles.

Throughout the period of the test, the rear brake was adjusted once and, as mentioned earlier, the rear chain had its initial slack taken up; apart from this, no attention was needed at any time, and at the end of the test there were no indications that further adjustments were desirable.

To sum up, the Bown is an excellent machine for the rider who wants to combine general utility riding with modest touring—this at the lowest cost consistent with comfort and efficiency.

98 c.c. two-speed Bown

Information Panel

SPECIFICATION

ENGINE: Villiers 98 c.c. (47 × 57 mm) single-cylinder two-stroke with two-speed gear in unit. Roller bearing big-end; ball bearings supporting mainshafts. Flat-crown die-cast, aluminium-alloy piston. Detachable light-alloy cylinder head. Petroil lubrication.

CARBURETTOR: Villiers "Junior" single-lever type with air filter and strangler. Twistgrip throttle control.

TRANSMISSION: Villiers two-speed in unit with the engine; gear change operated by handlebar lever through control cable. Top, 8.47 to 1. Bottom, 13.05 to 1. Cork-insert clutch running in oil. Primary chain $\frac{3}{8}$ × 0.225in in oil-bath case. Rear, $\frac{1}{2}$ × 0.305in with guard over top run.

IGNITION: Villiers flywheel magneto.

LIGHTING: Villiers direct. Twin-filament 12/12 w main bulb. Dry battery in headlamp for parking.

PETROIL CAPACITY: 1$\frac{1}{4}$ gallons.

TYRES: Dunlop studded, 19 × 2.50in, front and rear.

BRAKES: 4in internal-expanding, front and rear.

SUSPENSION: Bown link-type front fork with central compression spring.

WHEELBASE: 48in.

SADDLE: Wright. Unladen height, 27$\frac{1}{2}$in.

WEIGHT: 138 lb with approx. $\frac{1}{4}$ gallon of petrol.

PRICE: £59 16s 5d; with Purchase Tax (in Britain only), £75 19s 6d.

ROAD TAX: 17s 6d a year; 4s 10d a quarter.

MAKERS: Bown Cycle Co. Ltd., Tonypandy, Glamorgan.

PERFORMANCE DATA

MAXIMUM SPEED: Bottom: 29 m.p.h.
Top: 38 m.p.h.

ACCELERATION:

	10-20 m.p.h	15-25 m.p.h	20-30 m.p.h
Bottom	3.2 secs	4.8 secs	—
Top	4.4 secs	5.2 secs	6.2 secs

Mean speed at end of quarter-mile from rest: 38 m.p.h.
Time taken from rest to 30 m.p.h.: 13.2 secs.

PETROIL CONSUMPTION: At 20 m.p.h., 151 m.p.g. At 30 m.p.h., 128 m.p.g.

BRAKING: From 30 m.p.h. to rest, 30ft (surface, dry, coarse-granite chippings set in tar).

TURNING CIRCLE: 11ft.

MINIMUM NON-SNATCH SPEED: 11 m.p.h. in top gear.

WEIGHT PER C.C.: 1.4 lb.

499 c.c. J2

First published 23 August 1951

Exceptional Low-speed Torque

A first-class touring outfit—the Royal Enfield with Blacknell Derby sidecar

NUMEROUS older enthusiasts of the present day look back on the 1920's with regret. Many of the characteristics which chiefly endeared the machines of that time to them, they maintain, have been lost in the cry for speed—and still more speed. Among the features for which they pine are good low-speed torque and sweetness of power-delivery at low engine r.p.m. It is in these particular respects above all others that the 499 c.c. J2 Royal Enfield pre-eminently excels.

The machine tested was fitted with a Blacknell Derby coupé, single-seater sidecar. As may be observed from the information panel, the minimum non-snatch speed of the outfit, on its 5.95 to 1 top gear, was 11 m.p.h. At any speed in excess of this figure, transmission smoothness was exemplary. There was no trace of snatch at 13 m.p.h., even if the ignition was fully advanced. So good was the engine's low-speed torque that, normally, the ignition control was not required. There was complete freedom from pinking—thanks to the relatively low (5½ to 1) compression ratio.

For average requirements third gear was seldom needed at speeds above 20 m.p.h. Power on hills was so good that the machine would climb in top gear, in traffic queues, gradients which at similar low speeds would call for second gear from nearly every other 500 c.c. sidecar machine of the present day. After a get-away from a standstill, top gear could be in engagement in a few seconds—when only, say, seven or eight yards had been covered. There was never, in any circumstances, the need to rev the engine noisily in order to obtain the best results. For all practical purposes, acceleration was as brisk in top gear between 20 and 30 m.p.h. as it was in third.

On first acquaintance, this exceptional low-speed torque came as a surprise, and the natural tendency was to use the gear box much more than was strictly necessary. It took time to realize that the engine would respond to the throttle being opened—even indiscriminately—at very low speeds.

Engine starting was at all times effortless. The cold-starting drill required merely that the throttle be opened fractionally before the kickstarter was depressed. Neither flooding of the carburettor nor closing of the air lever was found necessary nor, indeed, desirable. The ignition lever was best left in the fully advanced position. Starting was certain at the first or second kick. No particular physical effort or knack was required provided, of course, that the engine was turned over compression with the exhaust valve raised.

Immediately the engine fired the throttle could be rolled right back against its closed stop without risk of the engine's stalling. Idling was slow and even and quite reliable with the ignition on full advance. It became even better with roughly one-quarter retard—but it was so good on full advance that during the course of the test the ignition was retarded only for experimental purposes. At idling speeds, piston-slap predominated over other engine noises whether the engine was cold or hot. The valve gear remained notably quiet throughout the test. By virtue of the large air-cleaner, induction hiss was totally absent. Reasonably quiet at low engine r.p.m., the exhaust was considered at normal cruising speeds to be too noisy, though the low-frequency "metallic" note was not unpleasant.

Short Movement

Gear changing was smooth and slick between any pair of gears. The pedal has a commendably short movement through which it may be moved without pause or "feel." It was literally impossible to miss a gear or to make a noisy gear change. If any criticism could be applied to the selection mechanism it was that it could have been lighter in operation. By means of the over-riding gear box control, neutral could be easily obtained from second or third gears. The control was awkwardly placed for use from top gear. The clutch on the test machine was inclined to drag—which probably accounts for the slightly heavy gear change. In operation, too, the clutch was slightly heavy, but so sweetly did it take up the drive that it was by no means unpleasant to use.

All controls were well placed, notably that for the rear brake which has an adjustable stop, allowing it to be positioned to perfection in relation to the left footrest. Handlebar levers are of the "solid" type which have a smooth movement and no tendency to flapping. The riding position is conventional, allowing the rider to adopt an "arms loosely-straight" posture which proved comfortable on long or short journeys for a driver of average stature.

Since the J2 with its good low-speed power, is so well suited to sidecar work, it is available with a sidecar fork (which has stronger springs and gives reduced trail) and fitted with a steering damper.

Low-speed steering is commendably light and the steering damper required to be just biting. The test outfit was imperfectly lined-up with the result that there was a slight tendency for it to pull to the left. A relatively soft movement around the static-load position of the front fork allowed it to iron out admirably small road irregularities or pot holes, at high or low speeds.

It was impossible to overdrive the Royal Enfield.

Power unit is a lusty twin-port o.h.v. Note the neat air-filter

Royal Enfield and Sidecar

and Transmission Smoothness the Outstanding Features

During a particularly prolonged test, during the course of which the outfit was used as a hack in the Isle of Man during the T.T. period, no adjustments of any kind were made to the engine. There were no traces of abuse when the performance figures were taken although the machine did eight consecutive runs on full bore over a 1¼-mile stretch. Third gear was used on the first four runs (and top on the second four) and the engine speed in third gear was verging on the valve-float range.

The only traces of oil which showed externally were from two of the timing-chest screws. One exhaust pipe discoloured slightly, the other hardly at all. Engine balance was good and vibration chiefly apparent at between 35 and 45 m.p.h. in top gear. Cruising speeds of between 45 and 50 m.p.h. were frequently held for long periods without physical discomfort to the driver.

Both brakes were smooth and surprisingly powerful in operation. They did not fade under conditions of regular severe application; nor did they require frequent adjustment. Mudguards on the J2 are of deep section and provide average protection against road filth. The driving beam provided by the Lucas headlamp was satisfactory for cruising speeds of 45 m.p.h. on main roads. Full lamp-load was balanced by the generator output at a speed of 30 m.p.h. in top gear.

The Blacknell sidecar gained nearly full marks. It was roomy and comfortable for passengers of average build and there was next to complete freedom from draughts. Both the cushion and

The Blacknell sidecar was found to have comfortable upholstery and good springing

squab were well sprung. Road shocks were adequately damped by the leaf springing. It was felt that for maximum comfort for average-stature passengers when the hood was raised, slightly more height would have been an advantage. The tank of the machine is smartly finished in black; it is neatly gold-lined, and the exhaust pipes, handlebar and wheel rims are chromium-plated. The sidecar, too, is finished in black.

Information Panel

SPECIFICATION

ENGINE: 499 c.c. (84 × 90 mm) single-cylinder, with overhead valves and fully enclosed valve gear. Roller bearings supporting mainshafts. Plain bearing (floating-bush type) big-end. Light-alloy connecting rod. Compression ratio, 5½ to 1. Dry-sump lubrication. Oil compartment integral with crankcase: capacity 4 pints.

CARBURETTOR: Amal. Twistgrip throttle control. Air lever on handlebar. Air cleaner mounted on seat pillar.

IGNITION AND LIGHTING: Lucas Magdyno, with manual ignition control. Long 3in dynamo. 7in. headlamp with 30/30w twin-filament main bulb.

TRANSMISSION: Separate four-speed gear box with positive foot control, and over-riding control for selecting neutral. Bottom, 16.6 to 1. Second, 10.7 to 1. Third, 7.7 to 1. Top, 5.95 to 1. Rear wheel incorporates rubber vane-type shock absorber. Multi-plate clutch with cork and Ferodo inserts. Primary chain, ½ × 0.305in in pressed-steel oil bath case. Rear chain, ⅝ × ⅜in with guard over top run. R.p.m. at 30 m.p.h. in top gear, 2,320 approx.

PETROL CAPACITY: 2¾ gallons.

TYRES: Dunlop, 3.25 × 19in ribbed front; 3.50 × 19in Universal rear.

BRAKES: 6in × 1in front and 7in × 1in rear; finger adjusters.

SUSPENSION: Royal Enfield telescopic front fork with two-rate springs for compression and hydraulic control.

WHEELBASE: 54¼in. Ground clearance, 4¾in unladen.

SADDLE: Terry. Unladen height, 28½in.

WEIGHT: Complete Sidecar outfit, 588lb with one gallon of fuel and full equipment.

PRICE: Machine only, £140; with Purchase Tax (in Great Britain only), £177 16s 0d. Sidecar fork, sidecar gears and steering damper, £3 3s 0d extra, with P.T., £3 19 11d.

ROAD TAX: £5 a year; £1 7s 7d a quarter.

MAKERS: The Enfield Cycle Company, Ltd., Redditch, Worcs

DESCRIPTION: *The Motor Cycle*, 8 November, 1945.

SIDECAR

MODEL Blacknell Derby single-seater coupé.

CHASSIS: Blacknell Safety. Tubular construction. Body suspension by means of quarter-elliptic springs at rear and bonded rubber blocks at front. Weight, 117lb approx.

PRICE: £34 15s 4d, with P.T., £44 0s 9d.

BODY: Ash framework panelled in sheet aluminium when available (otherwise sides are in "fabric.") Celluloid windows. Black-twill, roll-up hood.

PRICE: £41 10s 0d; with P.T., £52 11s 4d.

DESCRIPTION: *The Motor Cycle*, 7 December, 1950.

Royal Enfield J2 and Blacknell Derby coupé sidecar

PERFORMANCE DATA

MEAN MAXIMUM SPEED: Bottom: 24 m.p.h.*
Second: 36 m.p.h.*
Third: 49 m.p.h.
Top: 56 m.p.h.

* Valve float occurring.

MEAN ACCELERATION:

	10–30 m.p.h	20–40 m.p.h	30–50 m.p.h
Bottom	—		
Second	5.4 secs	—	
Third	7.2 secs	8.2 secs	—
Top	—	10.2 secs	12.8 secs

Mean speed at end of quarter-mile from rest (through gears): 50 m.p.h.
Mean time to cover standing quarter-mile: 24.2 secs.

PETROL CONSUMPTION: At 30 m.p.h., 77 m.p.g. At 40 m.p.h., 66 m.p.g. At 50 m.p.h., 43 m.p.g.

BRAKING: From 30 m.p.h. to rest, 49ft 6in (surface, dry tar macadam).

TURNING CIRCLE: 13ft 2in.

MINIMUM NON-SNATCH SPEED: 11 m.p.h. in top gear with ignition fully retarded.

WEIGHT PER C.C.: 1.18lb.

> First published 27 December 1951

646 c.c. B.S.A. Golden

A Pulse-stirring Vertical Twin Tested Solo

AFTER the war a spate of vertical twins appeared on the British market. These at first were limited to 500 c.c. capacity and there ensued a widespread demand for larger engines, especially from oversea riders and from those requiring machines for sidecar work. The 646 c.c. B.S.A. A10, or Golden Flash, was introduced to meet this demand. It was an immediate success, and in terms of all-round engine performance generally, and in its good torque at medium engine r.p.m. particularly, it far exceeded popular expectations.

The compactness of the engine and gear box—which are wedded on semi-unit-construction lines—makes it difficult to realize that the capacity is as much as 646 c.c. Indeed, the entire machine is clean and trim and, bearing in mind its 425 lb weight, it presents no special difficulties in wheeling it in and out of garages. An idea of its degree of compactness may be judged from the wheelbase, which is less than 55in.

An admirable riding position is provided by the relationship between the seat, footrests and handlebar. The new B.S.A. dual-seat is of ample dimensions and nicely shaped for the maximum comfort of both rider and pillion passenger. Well judged for persons of average stature, the height of the seat furnishes a comfortable knee angle and does not prove unduly high on the occasions when the machine is straddled while at rest, or is being kick-started. Handlebar angle and the height of the footrests are adjustable.

Starting, so far as the test machine was concerned, was not at first as easy as could be desired. Considerable muscular effort was required to rotate the engine, and the mixture strength was weak at smallish throttle openings. The impression was that a throttle slide with rather less cut-away was desirable.

When the engine was cold the starting drill was to flood the carburettor, close the air lever and open the throttle fractionally. Four digs on the kick-starter were the maximum required during the test. When the engine had been running for perhaps a minute, or when, say, a quarter of a mile had been covered, the air slide could be opened fully. Idling had to be on the fast side to be satisfactorily reliable, this because of the patchiness of the carburation mentioned earlier.

Mechanical Quietness

With the engine idling, mechanical noises were all but absent. Piston slap was just audible when the engine was cold, and slight rustling from the overhead-valve rockers could also be heard. In short, however, mechanical quietness is of an extremely high order. Exhaust silencing is most effective and commendably subdued throughout the entire speed range. It is good enough, indeed, to place the Golden Flash right in the front rank in this respect. Induction hiss is completely eliminated by the built-in air filter.

Bottom gear could be engaged noiselessly with the engine idling and the machine stationary. Slightly heavy in operation, the clutch freed perfectly on all occasions, and it was smooth and sweet in taking up the drive. The gear change was well-nigh perfect. Clean and entirely positive upward changes could be made with an easy movement of the right toes. Pedal movement is light and creditably short, and no deliberate slowness in pedal travel was necessary to ensure noiseless gear engagement.

Although driven at high speeds throughout the test, the engine unit remained entirely free from oil leaks

The 646 c.c. Golden Flash is a compact machine—its wheelbase is less than 55in. Riding position and dual-seat comfort were both found to be excellent

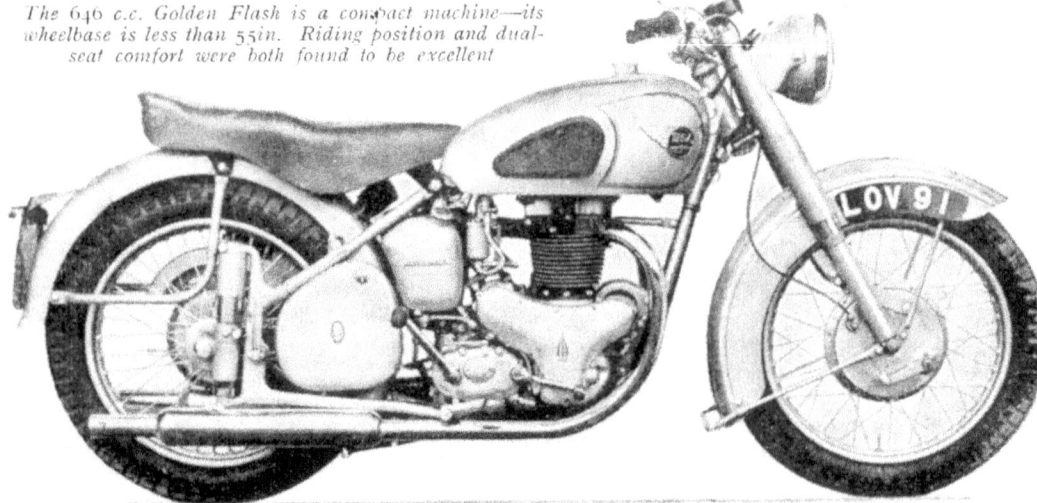

A criticism is that there was considerable gear whine in the indirect ratios, particularly in third. Clean, sweet downward changes could be executed between any pairs of gears just as rapidly as the controls could be operated.

Generally speaking, a small, light machine possessing nippy acceleration forms the most attractive type

Flash

and with Sidecar

Best cruising speed with the B.S.A. single-seat sidecar fitted was judged to be between 55 and 65 m.p.h.

for use in towns and cities. But the A10, though no lightweight, has perfect city manners. Low-speed handling and manœuvrability are first class; so good, in fact, as to make one forget that the machine is a six-fifty. Low-speed torque is exceptional and the transmission is smooth at low r.p.m. The tendency to pinking was not unduly pronounced, and the response to opening the throttle was full-blooded. Not least important is that the full performance in the indirect gears could be used without fuss from the engine, transmission or exhaust.

But if the Golden Flash has traits which make it attractive in towns and cities, it really comes into its own when being ridden at speed on the open road. Exceptionally high average speeds could be achieved with the minimum of effort on the part of the rider. This was so, not so much because of the machine's over-95 m.p.h. maximum speed, but because of the engine's high mechanical efficiency, even at speeds in excess of those normally used, and its excellent torque at medium revs.

At speeds over 70 m.p.h. there was no marked impression of deliberate hard riding. Only slight increase in throttle opening was necessary to compensate for head-winds or up-gradients. With such colossal engine performance the rider's chosen cruising speed was almost instantaneously regained after a slow-up made necessary by adverse road conditions or traffic. Although consistently high speeds were used throughout the test, the engine remained free from the slightest oil leak. Further, though Pool petrol was used, "running-on" after really hard riding was never experienced. The timing-side exhaust pipe discoloured only faintly, the drive-side one considerably, betraying some degree of carburettor bias.

Handling was very good indeed under all conditions, and the degree of comfort afforded was distinctly outstanding, even judged by the highest present-day standards. The B.S.A. telescopic fork has a long, soft movement which not only absorbs road shocks satisfactorily but, in conjunction with the duplex frame, furnishes, in addition, precise, hair-

Information Panel

SPECIFICATION

ENGINE : 646 c.c. (70 x 84 mm) o.h.v. vertical twin. Fully enclosed valve gear operated by push rods from a single camshaft. Plain bearing big-ends. Mainshafts supported by roller and plain bearings. Compression ratio, 6.5 to 1. Dry-sump lubrication ; oil-tank capacity, 4 pints.
CARBURETTOR : Amal ; twistgrip throttle control ; air-slide operated by handlebar lever. Built-in air-cleaner.
IGNITION AND LIGHTING : Lucas magneto with auto-advance. Separate 45w Lucas dynamo. 7in head lamp. 30/30w head lamp bulb.
TRANSMISSION : B.S.A. four-speed gear box with positive-stop foot control. Solo ratios : Bottom, 11.41 to 1. Second, 7.77 to 1. Third, 5.36 to 1. Top, 4.42 to 1. Sidecar ratios : Bottom, 13.3 to 1. Second, 9.06 to 1. Third, 6.26 to 1. Top, 5.16 to 1. Multi-plate clutch with fabric inserts. Primary chain, $\frac{3}{8}$in duplex in cast-aluminium case. Secondary chain, $\frac{5}{8}$ x $\frac{3}{8}$in. R.p.m. at 30 m.p.h. on solo top gear, 1,723 ; sidecar, 2,012 approx.
FUEL CAPACITY : 4$\frac{1}{4}$ gallons.
TYRES : Dunlop. Front, 3.25 x 19in. Rear, 3.50 x 19in., both studded tread.
BRAKES : 7 x 1$\frac{1}{8}$in rear ; 8 x 1$\frac{1}{8}$in front ; finger adjusters.
SUSPENSION : B.S.A. telescopic front fork with hydraulic damping. B.S.A. plunger-type rear springing.
WHEELBASE : 54$\frac{3}{4}$in. Ground clearance, 4$\frac{1}{2}$in unladen.
SEAT : B.S.A. dual-seat.
WEIGHT : 425 lb fully equipped and with one gallon of fuel. Complete outfit, 660 lb fully equipped and with one gallon of fuel.
PRICE : Machine only, £175, with Purchase Tax (in Britain only), £223 12s 3d. Extras : Dual-seat, £3 ; beige finish, £3 (P.T., 16s 8d extra in each case) ; prop-stand, 15s (P.T., 4s 2d).
ROAD TAX : Solo, £3 15s a year ; £1 0s 8d a quarter. Sidecar, £5 a year, £1 7s 7d a quarter.
MAKERS : B.S.A. Cycles, Ltd., Small Heath, Birmingham, 11.
DESCRIPTION : *The Motor Cycle*, 6 October, 1949, and 19 October, 1950.

SIDECAR

MODEL : B.S.A. 22/47.
CHASSIS : Triangular, with quarter-elliptic springs at rear and twin compression coil springs at front. Four-point attachment.
BODY : Coachbuilt (timber frame, steel panels). Celluloid screen. Folding twill hood. Locker at rear.
PRICE : £61, with Purchase Tax (in Britain only), £77 18s. Beige finish, £3 extra (P.T., 16s 8d extra).

646 c.c. B.S.A. Golden Flash.

PERFORMANCE DATA
(Sidecar figures in brackets)

MEAN MAXIMUM SPEED : Bottom : *42 (*36) m.p.h.
　　　　　　　　　　　　Second : *61 (*51) m.p.h.
　　　　　　　　　　　　Third : 89 (69) m.p.h.
　　　　　　　　　　　　Top : 96 (70) m.p.h.
　　* Valve float starting.

MEAN ACCELERATION :

	10-30 m.p.h.	20-40 m.p.h.	30-50 m.p.h.
Bottom	2.6 (3.5) secs	3 (—) secs	—
Second	4 (4.8) secs	3.2 (4.2) secs	3.6 (4.1) secs
Third	—	5.2 (6.8) secs	5 (6.4) secs
Top	—	— (9.3) secs	6.8 (9) secs

Mean speed at end of quarter-mile from rest : 84 (64) m.p.h.
Mean time to cover standing quarter-mile : 16.8 (20) secs.
PETROL CONSUMPTION : At 30 m.p.h., 72 (50) m.p.g. At 40 m.p.h., 69 (47) m.p.g. At 50 m.p.h., 65 (42) m.p.g. At 60 m.p.h., 59 (37) m.p.g.
BRAKING : From 30 m.p.h. to rest, 29ft (44ft 6in). Surface in each case, dry tar macadam.
TURNING CIRCLE : 12ft 9in.
MINIMUM NON-SNATCH SPEED : 21 (20) m.p.h. in top gear.
WEIGHT PER C.C. : 0.66 lb (1.02 lb).

646 c.c. B.S.A. Golden Flash

line steering. Uncertainty was never felt, no matter how greasy the road surface or how tricky the conditions. On one occasion, indeed, when an attempt was made to take the maximum speed figures, the road was distinctly greasy and there was a strong, gusty cross-wind.

As will be seen from the information panel, the mean maximum speed is given as 96 m.p.h. That figure was obtained at the M.I.R.A. Proving Ground and represents a mean of runs in opposite directions. Average wind speed was 14 m.p.h., with gusts up to 20 m.p.h. The maximum speed recorded down wind—with the air filter connected—was 102.75 m.p.h. and, with it disconnected, 104.5 m.p.h. Maximum speeds up-wind were 86.7 and 87.5 m.p.h. respectively with, and without, the air filter.

Control Positions

When these figures were taken the steering damper was just biting, and the handling was exemplary. Light although the fork movement is, there was no pitching, and there remained a direct "tautness" about the steering that was most satisfying.

In delivery tune, the twistgrip was unduly heavy in operation and a replacement throttle cable and twistgrip had to be fitted to effect a cure. In the main, the controls were well placed for ease of operation, but a criticism in this respect is that it was not possible to set the brake pedal so that the pad lay in the desired position relative to the left footrest.

Used in unison, the brakes provided adequate stopping power even for a machine in the A10's performance class. During the course of the solo test, which included over 500 miles of hard riding, the brakes inevitably came in for severe usage, yet no adjustment was required throughout. Both brakes possessed just the right amount of sponginess to permit hard application. Braking from speed was smooth and progressive, and not the slightest indication of fade, nor any loss of power whatever, was experienced at any time.

At the end of the solo part of the test, the Golden Flash was returned to the factory, where it was fitted with a B.S.A. single-seat sidecar. Alterations to the machine included changing the 42-tooth rear wheel sprocket for one of 49 teeth, and fitting heavier fork springs. At this time, too, the standard 6/4 throttle slide was replaced by a 6/3 (which has ⅛in less cutaway) in order to enrich the mixture at smallish throttle openings.

The result was that patchiness at low speeds disappeared entirely; starting became first-kick instead of third or fourth; acceleration was better than before; and the pick-up was as clean and brisk as could be desired by the most critical enthusiast.

Some 400 miles were covered during the sidecar test. For the greater part of this mileage a 10½-stone passenger was carried and for the remainder of the time the sidecar was empty. In either case the outfit handled magnificently, steering hands-off (with the steering damper just biting) and sweeping round corners with the utmost facility. No more than slight steering-damper friction was required at either high or low speeds. Owing in part to this, the steering was light enough for there to be no driving fatigue, even after a full day in the saddle.

Sidecar Cruising Speed

Best maximum cruising speed with the sidecar fitted appeared to be anything between 55 and 65 m.p.h. At the lower end of the scale the outfit would trickle along in top gear without snatch at speeds of just over 20 m.p.h. Careful handling of the throttle was necessary if, with Pool-quality fuel, pinking was to be avoided during acceleration from this speed. But, bearing in mind the excellent exhaust silencing and the effortless gear change, it was, of course, advisable to make use of the indirect ratios when accelerating from inordinately low speeds.

There was at no time any external indication of over-driving, even though on several occasions the outfit was driven for mile after mile with the throttle against the stop. The riding position for sidecar work was excellent, and no change was required either in footrest position or angle of the grips from the settings used earlier in the test.

Some high-powered machines of the past have been criticized when fitted with sidecars because the brakes have not provided adequate stopping power. No such criticism could be levelled at the B.S.A., however. On the contrary, the sidecar braking figure of 44ft 6in is well above average and would be difficult to better.

The sidecar itself earned all but full marks. The suspension absorbed road shocks satisfactorily and provided an extremely high degree of comfort for the passenger. Seat and squab are at comfortable angles to one another, and when the hood was raised the interior was cosy and unusually free from draughts. Of the folding type, with a pivoting frame, the hood stows away in a twill envelope when not in use but can be erected in a matter of seconds. A criticism is that during the unusually cold weather prevailing when the test was carried out, the screen provided rather insufficient side protection.

Both the machine and the sidecar were luxuriously finished in polychromatic beige. The tank finish was fully polychromatic, with no chromium plating, and with red lining on the top and side surfaces. The quality of the Golden Flash finish as a whole was unusually high for any class of road vehicle. It is a machine which will undoubtedly do as much to enhance the reputation of the marque as any other B.S.A produced in the last 20 years.

The 646 c.c. engine, neat and well-proportioned, appears to be no larger than the average five-hundred unit

> First published
> 24 January 1952

197 c.c. D.M.W.

Lightweight with Rectangular-section Frame

WHEN the present range of D.M.W. lightweights was announced in September, 1950, it aroused widespread interest by a major, unusual feature: rectangular-section tubing replaced the round tubes used formerly for the frames of the de luxe models. The D.M.W. engineers claimed that practical tests had proved that square-section tube, as opposed to round, gave greater lateral rigidity for less weight of material, and also that frame whip, especially at the rear of a machine

The 197 c.c. D.M.W. is a true lightweight; weight is under 200lb

employing plunger-type rear-springing, was materially overcome. As if to prove this, the weight of the new frame was 3lb lighter than that of the round-tube frame although, in order to increase the resistance to sideways bending, the weight of the rear part of the frame had been increased by no less than 22 per cent.

The machine tested was a 197 c.c. de luxe model incorporating the rectangular-tube frame, M.P. front fork and rear-springing, and a D.M.W. dual-seat. Total weight of this model is under 200lb—a fact which impresses itself immediately the machine is manhandled. It is one of the easiest machines to wheel; and the centre stand fitted is among the easiest to operate of any stand of this particular type. This stand is equipped with an extension on the left side so that it can be readily depressed. Only light backward and upward pressure on the underside of the dual-seat is required to park the machine.

When straddling the machine while at rest, one is immediately impressed by the excellence of the riding position. The seat height of 28¾in is fixed, and it is a good average height for riders of all but inordinately tall stature. A comfortable knee angle, and a leg position which allows one to poise readily on the footrests, is provided by the relative positions of the footrests and seat. The seat, incidentally, has a foam-rubber interior, and it is covered by a smart, beige-coloured hide.

Carried in a pair of split clamps on the top fork lug, the handlebar is adjustable for angle of the grips. It was found that the position when the machine was delivered— grips almost horizontal—was as near perfect as might be for a 5ft 7in rider. The solid-type front-brake and clutch levers are fitted on fixed pivot blocks, a feature which appeared to have no disadvantage. Brake and gear-change pedals were perfectly positioned in relation to their respective footrests.

As would be expected in Britain in January, vile road conditions were the rule rather than the exception for the D.M.W. test period. In spite of that the machine never gave the slightest cause for concern. Stability was good at extremely low speeds, and it was equally good when the machine was being ridden in the upper fifties. Wet, greasy wood blocks, and cobbles with stretches of sunken tram track, were crossed with impunity. Ice, too, was encountered during the test. Here again, however, the D.M.W. scored heavily. The ease with which it could be ridden on slippery surfaces—especially in comparison with bigger machines—was most marked. Reasonable freedom from road shocks was provided by the telescopic fork and rear-springing. It was considered, however, that the fork movement could, with advantage, have been softer, especially around the position of static load.

Cruising speeds in the region of 45-50 m.p.h. were commonplace when the machine was ridden on the open road. On up-gradients, and against gusty head-winds, the D.M.W. would maintain those speeds in the most praiseworthy style. Full throttle could be used, apparently to an unlimited degree, without external indication of overdriving becoming apparent. Indeed, the cylinder and head never became really hot during the test. Oil leaks were never apparent from the engine, though there was slight seepage from the joints of the built-up silencer.

Engine starting from cold was extremely easy. The "preparation" called for no skill or knack, and merely required that the mixture control be pulled to the rear and the carburettor lightly flooded. Assuming a throttle opening of roughly one-third, the engine would generally respond at the second depression of the kick-starter. Starting when the engine was hot was, in nine cases out of ten, accomplished on the

No matter how hard the machine was driven, the cylinder and head were never found to get really hot

De Luxe
and Rear-Springing

first kick. However, for no apparent reason the engine was, on odd occasions, a capricious starter when hot.

After a cold start, the mixture control could be moved forward to its normal-running position as soon as, say, 200 yards had been covered. After this, engine idling was reasonably slow and reliable, although firing on light load was, as with all orthodox two-strokes, irregular. The test engine was reasonably quiet mechanically. But it was felt to be a shade below the usual production standard in that piston slap was more clearly audible than is generally the case with Villiers engines. This is a criticism, however, that would be voiced only by an owner who was fastidious mechanically, since the noises were slight, and not audible to a normally seated rider. At speeds of over 30 m.p.h., wind and exhaust sounds superseded all others. The exhaust, incidentally, was as well silenced as most other British two-strokes, though even better silencing would have been appreciated.

Two-stroking of the engine was moderate by contemporary standards. At above approximately 25 m.p.h. in top gear, the engine would two-stroke happily under very light loading.

As is usual with new Villiers units the gear change was heavy in the early stages and feeding-in bottom gear required some muscular effort. This condition was aggravated slightly by the fact that the clutch barely freed when the operating lever was pulled right up to the grip. As the test progressed, however, the gear-change operating mechanism freed considerably, and after 250 miles it was as light as desired. Neutral was easily located from bottom or second gears. Clean, upward gear changes called for a somewhat slow movement of the gear pedal. However, snap changes could be made if required; in these instances, there was an audible "click" as the pinions engaged.

Braking power was all that was necessary from a machine in the D.M.W.'s performance class. Both brakes were equally powerful, and both were smooth and progressive when applied earnestly from high speed. Since the machine was driven consistently at speeds near the maximum during the test, the brakes inevitably came in for hard usage. But in spite of this they required adjusting on only one occasion—just after the performance figures had been taken. Slight fade was experienced when the brake tests were made, but, of course, the circumstances were much more severe than those likely to be encountered by the average rider.

The tool-box is under the dual-seat; the triangular-shape box encloses the battery

Lighting is by battery and rectifier, the circuit incorporating the latest Villiers, four-position switch (on the fourth position the total dynamo output is passed direct to the head-lamp bulb —whereas on the third position the bulb is fed from the battery; the other position on the switch are "off" and "pilot"). It was felt that, except under favourable conditions, the driving beam when the switch was on the "fourth" position was not up to the desired standard

Delivery tune of the D.M.W. was well-nigh perfect and good enough, indeed, to merit a special word of praise. In every respect, the machine gave the impression of having been carefully planned and carefully assembled. Production is relatively small, of course, and the machines are individually built. Standard of the finish is extremely high. The colours are turquoise blue for the tank and mudguards, silver for the frame, fork and rear-springing plunger units, and chromium plate for the handlebar, handlebar controls and the exhaust system. Only the head lamp and the number plates are black.

Information Panel

The 197 c.c. D.M.W. de luxe

SPECIFICATION

ENGINE: Villiers 197 c.c. (59 × 77 mm) single-cylinder two-stroke with three-speed gear in unit. Roller-bearing big-end; ball bearings supporting mainshafts. Flat-crown, die-cast aluminium-alloy piston. Detachable, light-alloy cylinder head with hemispherical combustion chamber. Petroil lubrication.

CARBURETTOR: Villiers "Middleweight," with twistgrip throttle control and separate mixture control operated by handlebar lever. Air filter standard.

TRANSMISSION: Villiers three-speed in unit with the engine. Gear ratios: Bottom, 15.6 to 1. Second, 8.2 to 1. Top, 5.9 to 1. Primary drive by ¾ × 0.225in chain in oil-bath case. Secondary, ½ × 0.225in chain with guard over top run.

IGNITION and LIGHTING: Villiers flywheel magneto with lighting coils. Westinghouse rectifier and Lucas 6-volt, 5-amp accumulator. Twin filament 24 w main bulb.

PETROIL CAPACITY: 2½ gallons.

TYRES: Dunlop, 3.00 × 19in front and rear, both studded tread.

BRAKES: 5in × ⅞in internal expanding front and rear; finger adjusters.

SUSPENSION: Metal Profiles telescopic front fork and Metal Profiles plunger-type rear-springing, both employing coil springs for impact and rebound.

WHEELBASE: 47in. Ground clearance, 7in.

SEAT: D.M.W. Latex. Height, 28½in unladen.

WEIGHT: 197lb, fully equipped and with ¼-gallon of fuel.

PRICE: £103, with Purchase Tax (in Great Britain only), £131 12s 3d.

ROAD TAX: £1 17s 6d a year; 10s 4d a quarter.

MAKERS: D.M.W. Motor Cycles (Wolverhampton), Ltd., Valley Road Works, Sedgley, Dudley, Worcs.

DESCRIPTION: The Motor Cycle, 20 September, 1951.

PERFORMANCE DATA

MEAN MAXIMUM SPEED: Bottom : 28 m.p.h.
Second : 51 m.p.h.
Top : 58 m.p.h.

MEAN ACCELERATION:

	10-20 m.p.h.	15-25 m.p.h.	20-30 m.p.h.
Bottom	2.2 sec	3 sec	—
Second	3.6 sec	3.6 sec	3.2 sec
Top	—	5 sec	5 sec

Mean speed at end of quarter-mile from rest : 55 m.p.h.
Mean time taken from 0-30 m.p.h. : 5.8 sec.

PETROIL CONSUMPTION: At 30 m.p.h., 112 m.p.g. At 40 m.p.h., 101 m.p.g. At 50 m.p.h., 88 m.p.g.

BRAKING: From 30 m.p.h. to rest, 30ft 6in (surface, dry tar macadam).

TURNING CIRCLE: 11ft 6in.

MINIMUM NON-SNATCH SPEED: 19 m.p.h. in top gear.

WEIGHT Per C.C.: 1.0 lb.

498 c.c. Ariel Twin

An Outfit Providing Excellent All-round Performance

First published 14 February 1952

Excellent handling was a feature of the Ariel outfit

AS a solo, the Ariel Red Hunter Twin has come steadily to the fore since its introduction in 1947. Just over a year ago (in September, 1950), flywheel weight was increased by 20 per cent, indicating that the machine's performance with a sidecar would be enhanced, especially at low and medium engine revolutions. This has, indeed, proved to be the case, and the all-round performance now leaves little to be desired, bearing in mind the engine capacity of 498 c.c.

Low-speed torque with the machine tested was of an extremely high order. But good low-speed torque is not in itself an indication that the machine's low-speed performance is satisfactory. Allied with it must be freedom from all forms of transmission roughness. And, in this respect, the Ariel gained nearly full marks. The engine-shaft shock-absorber was more than up to its job; snatch, when it did occur at inordinately low revolutions, was perceptibly cushioned. There was no snatch at speeds upward of 17 m.p.h. in top gear. The Ariel would accelerate from this speed to absolute maximum with freedom from chain thrash, except for a very slight period at 30 m.p.h.

Extremely cold weather prevailed throughout the test period, and quite often the outfit stood outside overnight. Notwithstanding these conditions, however, starting from cold was generally certain at the second or third kick-starter depression. It was never found necessary to close the carburettor air slide. Starting when the engine was warm was generally accomplished with an easy half-swing on the kick-starter. Ignition advance and retard is automatic; at no time was it felt that manual control would be an advantage.

Judged by contemporary standards—and, indeed, by recognized Ariel standards—the engine of the test machine was mechanically noisy. There was distinct slap from the timing-side piston, and the valve gear was clearly audible.

The test model was fitted with a Burman B52 gear box—the new gear box fully described in *The Motor Cycle* for 30 August, 1951. At present, some production Ariels are being fitted with this gear box, and eventually it will supersede the BA type on all models. The gear change was well-nigh perfect; it was extremely light in operation, and the pedal required only a short movement. Clean and positive upward or downward changes could be made without lag in pedal travel. So easily did the pinions engage that no special skill was required to make clutchless gear changes.

The clutch was light enough to permit single-finger operation. It freed perfectly throughout the test period and took up the drive smoothly and sweetly. Bottom gear could be quickly and noiselessly engaged from neutral when the machine was at a standstill with the engine idling. Neutral was easily selected from bottom or second gears. In short, the new gear box was good enough to be classed among the very best.

Engine idling was reliable, though rather faster than some would prefer. It was not found to be possible to slow it to "demonstration" standards without loss of reliability. The pick-up from idling to, say, a quarter throttle, was marred by a flat spot just off the pilot jet.

Freedom from Pinking

Low-speed performance, as has been mentioned, was most satisfying. Gear ratios were perfectly matched to engine characteristics. Acceleration was satisfactorily lively without the necessity for high revolutions in the indirect gears. There was all but complete freedom from pinking on Pool petrol.

Normal main-road gradients were taken in the Ariel's stride. At the top end of the scale, cruising speeds of 50-55 m.p.h. could be used indefinitely, up hill and down dale, against head winds, and with a fully laden sidecar. Given reasonable conditions, 40 m.p.h. averages could be achieved without the driver's using the engine performance to the full, or having recourse to inconsiderate driving methods. On one occasion, with a tail wind judged to have a speed in the region of 20 m.p.h., the outfit covered 33 miles with the speedometer needle hovering between 65 and 70 m.p.h. wherever possible. (The instrument, incidentally, read 2 m.p.h. fast at 30 m.p.h., 3½ m.p.h. fast at 40 m.p.h., and 5 m.p.h. fast at 50 m.p.h.)

No matter how hard the machine was driven there were never any signs of overheating. The drive-side exhaust pipe discoloured close to the port, the other remained unblemished. There were no real oil leaks, though a faint trace of oil did appear on the fins below the cylinder-head joint. There was freedom from vibration except when in the engine's "period," which could be felt at speedometer speeds of 20, 33, 44 and 60 m.p.h. in bottom, second, third and top gears respectively.

Both brakes, and the front one especially, were smooth and progressive, and powerful in action. Such indeed was the potency of the front brake that its full power could be used only when the road surface was quite dry. Although frequently used really hard during the test, it was adjusted on only one occasion. As shown in the performance data, the noteworthy figure of 33 feet from 30 m.p.h. was achieved.

As would be expected, the Ariel front fork earned full marks. It provides a long, soft movement with adequate build-up. It was never felt to bottom on either depression or rebound. Road shocks, however severe, were adequately absorbed. The fork characteristics also mated in well with those of the link-type rear-springing

Characteristics of the front suspension mated in well with the link-type rear-springing

and Sidecar
and a High Standard of Comfort

(which is designed with a view to constant chain tension over its approximately 1½in of movement). There was no pitching, whether the sidecar was laden or empty. No chain adjustment was required throughout and the rear chain remained nicely lubricated, yet did not become so "wet" as to fling excess oil on to the rear mudguard stays, lifting handle and number plate.

Handling of the outfit left nothing to be desired. Steering was light and positive, and there was an almost entire absence of sideways front-wheel movement at low speeds. The steering damper was kept slackened right off at all times. Excellent machine and sidecar rigidity was provided by the Swallow chassis. Straight-ahead steering was hands-off, whether the sidecar was laden or empty. Driving fatigue after a full day's hard driving was negligible.

Contributory reasons for this high degree of comfort were the excellence of the riding position and the lightness and near-perfect positioning of the controls. The Ariel handlebar is carried in inverted U-type clamps forward of the steering axis, and it has the grips swept back slightly to provide a sensible wrist angle. Relationship between the grips and the saddle permits the adoption of an arms-loosely-straight posture. An angle of less than 90deg was formed at the knees of an average-stature rider with the footrest hangers in their horizontal-rear position.

An adequate driving beam was provided by the Lucas headlamp. Full lamp load was balanced by the generator at rather less than 30 m.p.h. in top gear. The toolbox was sufficiently large to carry the complete tool kit and a repair outfit. Throttle and clutch cable outer casings are provided with sensibly accessible adjusters.

The Swallow Commando sidecar, with its body panelled in light alloy, is one of the lightest available today. It is also one of the most comfortable, since both the seat and squab

The power unit provided lively acceleration, as well as good low-speed torque

are fully sprung, and the squab height is sufficient to provide support for the passenger's shoulders. In addition to this, the rubber suspension proved most satisfactory. There is adequate headroom for a passenger of average height when the hood is raised. The celluloid screen is of ample proportions. When the hood was raised, slight draughts could be felt.

To sum up, it may be said that the Red Hunter Twin and Swallow Commando form an admirable outfit, which provides good all-round performance, and a high standard of comfort for both driver and passenger.

Information Panel

SPECIFICATION

ENGINE : Ariel 498 c.c. (63 × 80 mm) twin-cylinder o.h.v. Separate cylinder heads each with cast-in rocker box. Forged, one-piece crankshaft ; roller bearing on drive side, and plain, white-metal bearing on timing side. Light-alloy connecting rods, with shell, white-metal, big-end bearings. Compression ratio, 6.8 to 1. Dry-sump lubrication ; oil-tank capacity, 5 pints.
CARBURETTOR : Amal : twistgrip throttle ; air valve operated by plunger on top of mixing chamber.
TRANSMISSION : Burman B52 four-speed gear box with positive-stop foot control. Gear ratios (sidecar) : bottom, 15.15 ; second, 9.72 ; third, 7.50; top, 5.72 to 1. Multi-plate clutch. Primary chain, ½ × 0.305in in oil-bath case. Secondary chain, ⅝ × ⅜in. lubricated by bleed from primary case and by crankcase breather. R.p.m. at 30 m.p.h. in top gear, 2,210.
IGNITION AND LIGHTING : Lucas or B.T.-H. magneto with auto-advance. Separate Lucas dynamo ; 7½in diameter head lamp.
FUEL CAPACITY : 3¾ gallons. Reserve taps.
TYRES : Dunlop. Front, 3.25 × 20in ribbed. Rear, 3.50 × 19in studded.
BRAKES : Ariel, 7 × 1⅛in, front and rear. Fulcrum adjusters.
SUSPENSION : Ariel telescopic front fork with hydraulic damping. Ariel link-type rear-wheel springing.
WHEELBASE : 56in. Ground clearance, 5½in unladen.
SADDLE : Terry. Unladen height, 28in.
WEIGHT : Complete outfit, 602lb fully equipped and with one gallon of fuel.
PRICE : Machine only, £174, with Purchase Tax (in Great Britain only), £222 6s 8d. Spring-frame extra, £16 ; with P.T., £20 8s 11d.
ROAD TAX : £5 a year ; £1 7s 7d a quarter.
MAKERS : Ariel Motors, Ltd., Selly Oak, Birmingham, 29.
DESCRIPTION : *The Motor Cycle*, 27 November, 1947 and 25 October, 1951.

SIDECAR

MODEL : Swallow Commando single-seater.
CHASSIS : Swallow "Velvet" supporting body through bonded-rubber-controlled pivoted arms at the rear and hinged pivots at the front. Resilient wheel mounting.
BODY : Constructed from hardwood frame, panelled in light alloy. Folding scuttle, and door on nearside. Celluloid windscreen. Stowaway hood. Fully sprung seat and squab. Luggage compartment behind squab.

498 c.c. Ariel twin and sidecar

PRICE : £57 4s 6d ; with Purchase Tax, £72 9s 8d.
MAKERS : Swallow Coachbuilding Co. (1935), Ltd., The Airport, Walsall; Staffs.
DESCRIPTION : *The Motor Cycle*, 25 October, 1951.

PERFORMANCE DATA

MEAN MAXIMUM SPEED : Bottom :* 31 m.p.h.
  Second :* 42 m.p.h.
  Third : 60 m.p.h.
  Top : 64 m.p.h.
  * Valve float starting.

MEAN ACCELERATION :

	10-30 m.p.h.	20-40 m.p.h.	30-50 m.p.h.
Bottom	4.2 secs	—	—
Second	6.2 secs	5.6 secs	—
Third	9.6 secs	9.2 secs	9.4 secs
Top	—	11.2 secs	13.6 secs

Mean speed at end of quarter-mile from rest : 55 m.p.h.
Mean time to cover standing quarter-mile : 22 secs.
PETROL CONSUMPTION : At 30 m.p.h., 60 m.p.g. At 40 m.p.h., 55.2 m.p.g. At 50 m.p.h., 47 m.p.g. At 60 m.p.h., 42 m.p.g.
BRAKING : From 30 m.p.h. to rest, 33 feet (surface, dry tar macadam).
TURNING CIRCLE : 14ft 4in.
MINIMUM NON-SNATCH SPEED : 16 m.p.h. in top gear.
WEIGHT PER C.C. : 1.2lb.

> First published 13 March 1952

The 125 c.c. RE Royal

An Attractive Two-stroke Machine in the Front Rank Among

NUMEROUS features of the 125 c.c. Royal Enfield model RE place it among the foremost of modern lightweights. First, there is an engine-gear unit that is designed as a clean, homogeneous whole and encased in smooth, light-alloy, pressure die-castings. Secondly, the total weight is a mere 143lb. Thirdly, the engine is a very potent one—hence power-to-weight ratio is favourable and good all-round performance results.

Announced in November, 1950, the current model is one

A combination of low weight and a powerful little engine results in a nippy performance

which, in nearly every respect, gives the impression of having been capably manufactured and subject to close attention to detail. As an example of this, the handlebar levers are beautiful, polished light-alloy pressings which have just the necessary side play at their pivots to permit silky operation and yet eliminate end flap. They are the sort of levers one expects to find on a luxury roadster.

In addition to those already quoted, there are other features of the RE which earned it full marks. The chief of these, possibly, was the notable quietness of the exhaust. When the

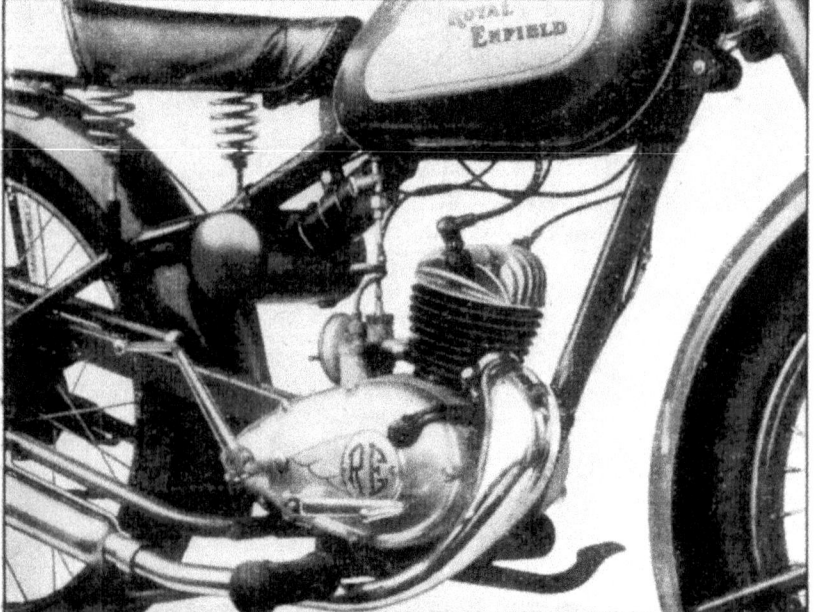

engine was idling and, therefore, four-stroking, the individual "pops" were naturally audible. But to a rider in the saddle, the exhaust was just barely distinct, both when the engine was running light and under load. At speed, the exhaust was apparent only as a mild and pleasant whirr, mingling in roughly equal volume with the sound of the rush of air.

Engine starting was at all times easy. When cold, it was necessary merely to flood the carburettor slightly, close the strangler, and open the throttle rather more than one-third before depressing the kick-starter. The strangler could be operated easily by a normally seated rider. Immediately the engine had fired, the strangler could be opened fractionally and a few second later, opened fully. Starting when the engine was warm could be accomplished on quite small throttle openings. More than two kick-starter depressions were never required for either cold or hot starts. Mechanical quietness of the engine was of an extremely high order, and piston slap could only just be detected when the engine was cold.

Gear changing on the latest RE is by means of a foot control through a positive-stop mechanism. The gear change is light and decisive, but the combination of an engine-speed clutch and the widely spaced gear ratios (22, 12.3 and 7.55 to 1 respectively), demand that care be taken to ensure silent engagement of the pinions. In order to achieve noiseless upward changes, the pedal needs to be moved with an uncommonly slow and deliberate movement, and silent downward changes were certain only at very low speeds.

If desired, rapid gear changes could be made—and there was no difficulty should engine-speed not match up with road speed as the gears were engaged; what happened in these instances was that there was a distinct "click" as the pinions slid home. The single-plate clutch freed perfectly and gave no trace of slipping. It was smooth, sweet, and light in operation, and required no adjustment throughout the test.

Whether the engine was idling or under load, the pick-up was clean and brisk. Acceleration was pleasantly lively throughout the speed range—a feature resulting from the good power-to-weight ratio. There was almost complete freedom from vibration, an attribute which, in common with the excellent exhaust silencing, made the highest comfortable cruising speed difficult to determine. During the test, the speedometer needle was generally kept hovering between 40-45 m.p.h. and, under favourable conditions, 47 m.p.h. The true mean maximum speed was exceeded for considerable mileages.

With this treatment, there was slight fuss from the engine, but no signs of abuse; nor were there any when the maximum speed figures were taken. Below these speeds, say, at 40 m.p.h., there was always an impression of high mechanical efficiency and the certainty that the engine was working well within its limits. Fuel consumption at a maintained 40 m.p.h. was 116 m.p.g., and barely less when the machine was driven flat out.

The use of smooth, light-alloy die-castings gives the engine a neat appearance

Enfield

Lightweights

The combination of nippy acceleration, light weight, good exhaust silencing and easy starting, made the RE an excellent proposition for town riding. Another contributory factor in this respect was the machine's high degree of stability on greasy surfaces. No matter how fearsome road conditions appeared, the RE at no time gave cause for concern.

The telescopic fork has the desired characteristics of light movement round the static load position—so that the smallest of road irregularities are absorbed—and a build-up that prevents bottoming on either compression or rebound. At high speeds, the RE could be swept round corners and bends with exhilarating verve and great facility. Steering is light and positive, and the machine could be ridden hands-off at 10 m.p.h. with the engine barely pulling.

A compact riding position is provided by the relative positions of the saddle, handlebar and footrests. The position was entirely comfortable for riders of somewhat below average male height, but tall riders would prefer a saddle position slightly farther to the rear. Footrests are adjustable for fore and aft position. The gear pedal is adjustable for height, though it could not be set so that gear changing could be carried out without lifting the right foot from the footrest.

Stopping Power

The pad of the brake pedal lay just below the rider's left foot and was perfectly located for ease of operation. Carried in inverted U-type clamps forward of the steering axis, the handlebar is adjustable for angle of the grips. Though the degree of adjustment is limited because the brake and clutch levers are on fixed pivots, there was no difficulty in obtaining the desired angle.

Used together, the brakes provided stopping power that was in keeping with the machine's speed performance. The braking figure of 31ft 6in is the mean of five crash stops in quick succession from 30 m.p.h. No fade resulted from this treatment and, indeed, it was noted that the brake drums did not become unduly hot.

Mudguards on the RE are 4¼in wide and they are carried on

Footrests are adjustable for fore or aft position. Use of the sturdy centre stand required little effort

sensibly sturdy stays which eliminate blade flutter. The ignition coil, which is energized directly from the A.C. generator, is mounted to the underside of the top frame tube, where it is out of reach of spray and road dirt. To the rear of the coil is a cylindrical tool-box across the frame. The box is too small to house a full tool kit and a repair outfit as well. The carrier on the rear mudguard proved a commendable fitting and was in use each time the machine was ridden.

A sturdy centre stand, so designed that it will raise either wheel clear of the ground, is provided for parking purposes; its use required negligible muscular effort.

The machine is finished in grey, and chromium plating is used for the handlebar, exhaust pipe and headlamp rim. Wheel rims are enamelled grey and relieved with thin gold lines. The tank panel is in silver enamel, and the name "Royal Enfield" is lettered in red.

The 125 c.c. RE Royal Enfield

Information Panel

SPECIFICATION

ENGINE: Royal Enfield 125 c.c. (53.79 × 55 mm), single-cylinder two-stroke with three-speed gear box in unit. Roller-bearing big-end; four ball-bearings supporting mainshafts. Semi-dome top silicon-alloy piston, with two compression rings. Detachable aluminium-alloy cylinder head. Petroil lubrication.

CARBURETTOR: Amal needle-jet type with twistgrip throttle; strangler for cold starting. Air filter.

IGNITION and LIGHTING: Miller 40-watt A.C. generator and coil. Twin-filament 24-watt main bulb. Parking battery in head lamp.

TRANSMISSION: Royal Enfield three-speed gear box with positive foot control. Bottom, 22 to 1. Second, 12.3 to 1. Top, 7.55 to 1. Single-plate clutch with cork inserts. Primary chain, ⅜in × 0.225in in oil-bath case. Secondary chain, ½in × 0.205in with guard over top run. R.p.m. at 30 m.p.h. in top gear, 3,150.

FUEL CAPACITY: 1¾ gallons. Oil measure with filler cap.

TYRES: Dunlop 2.75 × 19in, studded tread.

BRAKES: 5in diameter front and rear, finger adjusters.

SUSPENSION: Royal Enfield lightweight telescopic front fork, containing oil for lubricating bushes.

WHEELBASE: 48in. Ground clearance, 5¾in unladen.

SADDLE: Mansfield; unladen height, 28in.

WEIGHT: 143lb, fully equipped and with fuel tank dry.

ROAD TAX: 17s 6d a year; 4s 10d a quarter.

PRICE: £72, with Purchase Tax (in Great Britain only), £92.

DESCRIPTION: *The Motor Cycle* dated 16 November, 1950.

MAKERS: The Enfield Cycle Company, Ltd., Redditch, Worcs.

PERFORMANCE DATA

MEAN MAXIMUM SPEED: Bottom: 20 m.p.h
Second: 34 m.p.h.
Top: 47 m.p.h.

MEAN ACCELERATION:

	10-20 m.p.h	15-25 m.p.h	20-30 m.p.h.
Bottom	3.4 secs		
Second	3.6 secs	3.8 secs	4.8 secs
Top	6.2 secs	6 secs	6.4 secs

Mean speed at end of quarter mile from rest: 44 m.p.h.
Mean time from rest to 30 m.p.h.: 8.2 secs.

PETROIL CONSUMPTION: At 20 m.p.h., 160 m.p.g. At 30 m.p.h., 152 m.p.g. At 40 m.p.h., 116 m.p.g.

BRAKING: From 30 m.p.h. to rest, 31ft 6in (surface, dry tar macadam).

TURNING CIRCLE: 10ft 8in.

MINIMUM NON-SNATCH SPEED: 12 m.p.h. in top gear.

WEIGHT Per C.C.: 1.14lb.

First published 17 April 1952

497 c.c. B.S.A.

High-performance Model in the Best

ZESTFUL acceleration, excellent road holding, and the ability to devour the miles in unobtrusive fashion, are but a few of the attributes of the 497 c.c. B.S.A. Star Twin. Fitted with the compact, semi-unit construction B.S.A. engine and gear box, the machine is the sports version of the now celebrated A7. A redesigned engine was employed for 1951. Good as the pre-1951 Star Twin was, the present model is decidedly better. There is now only one carburettor instead

The Star Twin now has a single carburettor and an 8in-diameter front brake

of two; and carburation, once the engine is warm, is as clean as could be desired. With the present B.S.A. gear box, the gear-change is among the best encountered on present-day machines.

A sports machine in the true tradition, the Star Twin requires "knowing" if it is to give of its best on Pool-quality fuel. The throttle must be used intelligently in conjunction with the manual ignition control; engine revolutions must be maintained in the higher ranges; in short, there must be knowledgeable understanding of the engine's characteristics. These requirements fulfilled, the Star Twin has few equals as a machine for sustained, high-speed road work.

Used to the full in conjunction with the indirect gear ratios, the twin-cylinder engine provides acceleration of no mean order. In bottom and second gears the speed can be stepped up with exhilarating rapidity; and even in third or top gears the build-up from medium to peak r.p.m. is shatteringly quick. At 70 m.p.h. in top gear, the machine noticeably surged forward in response to a tweak of the twistgrip. Vibration was negligible. No matter how hard the engine was driven or for how long, there was at no time any indication that it was being over-driven.

During the test, cruising speeds in the seventies were used as often as road conditions permitted; 70 m.p.h., indeed, was felt to be the machine's happiest cruising speed. The engine turned over smoothly and sweetly, and with no more fuss than there was in the fifties. That it would cruise without being over-driven at higher speeds, say, 75-80 m.p.h., there is little doubt; but, at speeds of over 70 m.p.h., wind pressure became tiring to the rider's arms. At a true road speed of 65 m.p.h., the speedometer registered approximately 5 m.p.h. fast.

An idea of the Star Twin's performance may be gained from the fact that on several (admittedly favourable) occasions during the course of the 700-mile test, 20 miles were covered in as many minutes. Notwithstanding such usage, no engine oil leaks were apparent at the end of the test. A small seepage of oil appeared at the oil-tank filler-cap, and some messiness resulted through excessive oil issuing from the oil-tank breather if the tank was overfilled.

Engine performance is but one of the ultimate factors in the attainment of high road averages. Steering and road-holding are equally important; as far as the B.S.A. was concerned, these characteristics were fully up to desirable standards. The long, soft action of the B.S.A. telescopic front fork dealt adequately with every type of going encountered. Steering was of the hairline variety. A steering damper is fitted; during most of the test it was set just barely biting.

The action of the plunger-type rear springing was pleasantly soft around the static-load position and it proved to be equally effective whether the machine was ridden one- or two-up. A criticism is that the suspension clashed on the occasions when deep road irregularities (such as sunken manhole covers) were encountered. Steering was good whether the machine was on greasy city surfaces, or ridden at speed on the open road.

For a person of average height, the riding position could hardly be bettered. Seat height is 30in—a height which permitted a comfortable knee angle while allowing easy straddling of the machine for kick-starting. The position of the brake-pedal pad was such that the brake could be applied without the foot being taken off the rest; an adjustable brake-pedal stop—a new feature—allows the pedal to be set in the optimum position relative to the footrest. Some discomfort to the rider's knees resulted from contact with the angular edge of the tank kneegrips.

That the Star Twin is a sports machine has been amply illustrated, and it might be thought

Though endowed with zestful performance characteristics, the 497 c.c. engine was found to be pleasantly flexible

Star Twin

Sporting Tradition

A picture showing the compactness of the semi-unit construction of engine and gear box

from this that the engine would prove intractable under slow-running conditions. Yet the reverse is true. During town riding the machine proved to be pleasantly flexible. As intimated earlier, knowledgeable handling of the ignition control was called for; the long ignition lever fitted to the left handlebar is pleasant to use and, because of its length, greatly facilitates accurate settings.

Upward or downward gear changes could be effortlessly achieved by lightly pivoting the right foot on the footrest. Pedal movement was short and feather-light, and clean, precise upward or downward gear changes called for no special care. Racing-type upward gear changes were accompanied by a slight click from the gear box as the pinions engaged—a click which could be heard rather than felt. Clean, noiseless downward changes could be made as rapidly as the clutch and gear pedal could be operated.

Both front and rear brakes were smooth and progressive and, applied in unison, provided satisfactory stopping power, even for a machine in the Star Twin's performance class. The 8in front brake was very good, yet did not provide quite all the power of which this type of brake is known to be capable. During the course of several hundred miles of fast road work, both brakes came in for hard usage. In spite of this, no fade was experienced, and only slight adjustment was called for.

Little effort was required to operate the kick-starter. With the temperature below freezing point, the engine would start from cold at the second or third kick—this provided that the carburettor was lightly flooded and normal cold-starting procedure followed. The air lever could be fully opened after the engine had been running for about a minute.

The degree of exhaust and mechanical quietness was commendably high. With the machine stationary and the engine idling on full retard, no individual source of mechanical noise could be identified. Slight piston-slap could just be detected when the ignition was set at full advance. Induction hiss is eliminated by the built-in air-cleaner. Effective at all speeds, the silencers produced a pleasant yet unobtrusive exhaust note.

Mudguarding on the Star Twin was only reasonably effective. Operation of the centre-stand called for a fair amount of muscular effort until the knack had been mastered. Its use is facilitated by the lifting handle on the left side and, a curved, "roll-on" extension piece on the left leg of the stand. Adjustment of the primary chain is by moving the slipper-tensioner inside the chain case; the adjusting screw protrudes through the bottom of the case. Another commendable feature is that the guard for the rear chain has a deep back plate which effectively shields the chain from much of the road grit shed by the rear tyre. Other notable features are the B.S.A. really quickly detachable wheels; and the use of heavy-gauge clutch and front brake control cables. A comprehensive set of tools is provided.

The standard of finish on the Star Twin is extremely high. A general colour scheme of black and silver is employed; the tank is finished in matt-silver, lined in red, and it bears a handsome "Star Twin" insignia.

Information Panel

The 497 c.c. B.S.A. Star Twin

SPECIFICATION

ENGINE: 497 c.c. (66 x 72.6 mm) o.h.v. vertical twin. Fully enclosed valve gear operated by push-rods from a single camshaft. Plain-bearing big-ends. Mainshaft supported by roller and plain bearings. Compression ratio, 7.2 to 1. Dry-sump lubrication; tank capacity, 4 pints.

CARBURETTOR: Amal; twistgrip throttle control; air-slide operated by handlebar lever. Built-in air cleaner.

IGNITION and LIGHTING: Lucas magneto with manual ignition control on left side of handlebar. Separate, 3in diameter Lucas dynamo; 7in headlamp; 30/24w headlamp bulb.

TRANSMISSION: B.S.A. four-speed gear box with positive-stop foot control. Bottom, 12.9 to 1. Second, 8.8 to 1. Third, 6.05 to 1. Top, 5.0 to 1. Multi-plate clutch with fabric inserts. Primary chain, ⅜in duplex running in cast-aluminium, oil-bath case. Rear chain, ⅝ x ⅜in. lubricated by breather from oil tank. R.p.m. at 30 m.p.h. in top gear, approximately 1,950.

FUEL CAPACITY: 3½ gallons.

TYRES: Dunlop; front 3.25 x 19in; rear, 3.50 x 19in; both studded tread.

BRAKES: 8in diameter front, 7in diameter rear; finger-operated adjusters.

SUSPENSION: B.S.A. telescopic front fork with hydraulic damping; plunger-type rear springing.

WHEELBASE: 54½in. Ground clearance, 4½in. unladen.

SEAT: B.S.A. dual-seat. Unladen height, 30in.

WEIGHT: 423 lb fully equipped and with one gallon of fuel.

PRICE: £174, with Purchase Tax (in Great Britain only), £222 6s 8d. Extras: dual-seat in lieu of saddle, £3 (P.T., 16s 8d); prop-stand, 15s (P.T., 4s 2d).

ROAD TAX: £3 15s a year; £1 0s 8d a quarter.

DESCRIPTION: *The Motor Cycle*, 19 October, 1950.

MAKERS: B.S.A. Cycles, Ltd., Small Heath, Birmingham, 11.

PERFORMANCE DATA

MEAN MAXIMUM SPEED: Bottom: 37 m.p.h.*
Second: 55 m.p.h.*
Third: 86 m.p.h.
Top: 92 m.p.h.
* Valve float just starting.

MEAN ACCELERATION:

	10-30 m.p.h.	20-40 m.p.h.	30-50 m.p.h.
Bottom	3 secs	2.4 secs	—
Second	4.2 secs	3.2 secs	3.2 secs
Third	6 secs	5.4 secs	4.8 secs
Top	—	7.2 secs	6.8 secs

Mean speed at end of quarter-mile from rest: 84 m.p.h.
Mean time to cover standing quarter-mile: 16.8 secs.

PETROL CONSUMPTION: At 30 m.p.h., 89 m.p.g. At 40 m.p.h., 75 m.p.g. At 50 m.p.h., 70 m.p.g. At 60 m.p.h., 64 m.p.g.

BRAKING: From 30 m.p.h. to rest, 30ft 6in (surface, dry tar macadam)

TURNING CIRCLE: 13ft 6in.

MINIMUM NON-SNATCH SPEED: 22 m.p.h. in top gear.

WEIGHT per C.C.: 0.73 lb.

First published 1 May 1952

197 c.c. Francis-Barnett

Attractive Lightweight Which Sets a High Standard

GOOD suspension, excellent finish and handsome appearance are outstanding features of the 197 c.c. Francis-Barnett Falcon 58. First impressions were very good, and these were fully substantiated during the test. It is an acknowledged fact that the 197 c.c. Villiers two-stroke engine is an extremely potent performer in its class; the installation of this unit in the new Francis-Barnett pivoted-fork spring frame has resulted in a machine which can only enhance the already elevated reputation of the makers.

Extremely comfortable riding results from the highly efficient suspension of the front and rear wheels

The spring frame gained full marks in defiance of almost every type of road surface encountered. Under normal conditions, maximum engine performance could be used with impunity. Irregularly surfaced country lanes were traversed at speeds which would normally be expected to cause the wheels to start hopping; with the Francis-Barnett all that was felt was an easy rising and falling of the machine on its suspension—this without any pitching—while both wheels hugged the road. There is total possible movement of 5in on the telescopic front fork, and 4in at the rear-wheel spindle. Pleasantly light around the static-load position, the movement is progressively resisted. At no time was bottoming or "topping" of the rear spring units apparent. However, on steep, very badly surfaced descents, which were taken fast, application of the front brake caused the front fork to bottom.

The long, soft action of the front fork furnished hair-line steering. Bend swinging at speeds in the fifties was sheer delight, and any chosen line could be held irrespective of undulations in the road surface. Handling at low speeds was equally good, and stability on treacherous surfaces was of a very high order.

An admirable feature of the Francis-Barnett is that the saddle is adjustable for height. The highest setting furnished what was considered to be a comfortable knee angle for a rider of average height. A loose, straight-arms posture which gave absolute control under all conditions and was not tiring over long distances, was provided by the reach between the saddle and handlebar. For some, the footrest position was judged to be too far to the rear, with the result that there was a tendency for the rider to sit rather far back on the saddle, a position in which the metal frame of the saddle could be felt. When the footrests were moved to their lower, forward position, the brake pedal pad, which is not adjustable for height, lay too high in relation to the rest. No knee-grips are fitted.

Hand and foot controls, in delivery trim, were well positioned, and the minimum of effort was required for their operation. The handlebar is adjustable for angle of the grips; clutch and front-brake lever mountings are welded to the bar. Though this gives a clean appearance to the bar, no lever adjustment is, of course, available. The gear-change pedal is mounted on a serrated shaft and is fully adjustable for height.

With such a high degree of comfort as that afforded by the suspension, high speeds were often indulged in for long periods. Yet signs of overdriving were never evident. The cylinder barrel and head remained remarkably cool throughout. No oil leaks from the engine were apparent during the 500-mile test. Except for a little messiness round the carburettor—as a result of over-flooding—the engine maintained a high degree of external cleanliness. With the fuel tank full, no petroil seepage occurred from the tank filler-cap.

The engine was a glutton for work; it turned over smoothly, effortlessly and not unduly fast at road speeds in the region of 45-50 m.p.h. This was felt to be the ideal cruising speed for the Falcon 58. When the machine was driven flat-out, vibration could be felt at the handlebar, but there was no vibration at normal cruising speeds.

Engine starting after hard driving was always accomplished with one light prod on the kick-starter, provided that the carburettor was not allowed to become even slightly flooded. This was guarded against by turn-

Details of the frame construction and pivoted-fork rear springing are clearly shown in this illustration

Falcon 58

in Comfort, Steering and Stability

ing off the petrol tap immediately the machine was stopped. With a cold engine, starting was invariably accomplished at the second kick, assuming the carburettor was flooded, the handlebar mixture control set to rich, and the throttle set about one-quarter open. After the engine had been running for a minute or two the mixture control could be set at approximately the halfway position and left there. When the engine was pulling hard at relatively high speeds in top gear, it was found to be an advantage to move the control to the three-quarter rich position. Idling, with a warm engine and the throttle a fraction open, was reasonably slow and reliable, but, as with most two-strokes, it was irregular. Two-stroking with the engine under load was good. Pick-up was clean and positive throughout the throttle range.

The engine was extremely quiet mechanically. Even when it was cold, there was no trace of piston slap or any other positively identifiable noise. Some "two-stroke rattle" was apparent when the machine was at speed, such as when running downhill on small throttle openings. The exhaust note manifested itself at speeds of 30-40 m.p.h. in top gear only as a pleasantly subdued purr. Under brisk acceleration the exhaust note was much more distinctive but was never so loud as to put a limit on the desired performance.

Light in operation, the clutch was smooth and progressive in taking up the drive. Upward gear changes were initially stiff, and a certain amount of effort was required to engage bottom gear from neutral. During the test, however, the gear change became progressively easier. Clean and positive upward or downward changes could be made provided that the gear pedal was moved with deliberation. Snap changes could be equally positive, but in this case there was an audible click as the gear pinions meshed. Oil seepage occurred at the gear box inner end-cover joint; however, a reading of the dip-stick indicated that the box was overfilled with oil.

Braking was well up to standard in relation to the performance of the machine. Both front and rear brakes were equally effective; after hard usage, slight adjustment was made on the finger-operated adjusters. The front brake developed a squeak when it was applied hard. During a ride through torrential rain, the rear brake was affected slightly by water; the front brake retained full efficiency.

Close-up of the Villiers 6E engine-gear unit. Note also the neat tool-box which is provided internally with two compartments

When the headlamp switch was placed in the direct-lighting position, the driving beam obtained was sufficient to allow the full cruising speed to be used at night on the open road. In towns and cities the "battery" switch position was employed; there was ample illumination and the battery retained its charge.

The centre stand fitted to the Francis-Barnett was easy to operate; it has an extension piece projecting clear of the silencer to facilitate its use. Two small bags of tools are provided; the tool box is of robust construction, roomy and divided into two compartments. Mudguarding is efficient—the deeply valanced rear mudguard especially so. The rear chain guard has a deep back plate which shields the chain from much of the road grit whirled round by the rear tyre. There was a tendency for the chain to foul the guard. A Smiths 80 m.p.h. trip speedometer is fitted to the machine; this registered approximately 2½ m.p.h. fast at 30 m.p.h. and 3½ m.p.h. fast at 50 m.p.h.

As mentioned earlier, the finish of the machine sets a high standard and is extremely attractive. On the model tested, the colour scheme was black, with chromium-plated fittings and a gold-lined tank. A blue colour scheme is also available.

Information Panel

The 197 c.c. Francis-Barnett Falcon 58

SPECIFICATION

ENGINE : Villiers 197 c.c. (59 × 77 mm) single-cylinder two-stroke, with three-speed gear in unit. Roller-bearing big-end ; ball bearings supporting mainshafts. Flat-crown, die-cast, aluminium-alloy piston. Detachable, light-alloy cylinder head with hemispherical combustion chamber. Petroil lubrication.

CARBURETTOR : Villiers Middleweight, with twistgrip throttle control and separate mixture control operated by handlebar lever. Air filter.

TRANSMISSION : Villiers three-speed gear box in unit with the engine. Gear ratios : Bottom, 15.6 to 1. Second, 8.2 to 1. Top 5.9 to 1. Primary drive by ⅜ × 0.225in pre-stretched chain in oil-bath case. Secondary, ½ × 0.205in chain with guard over top run.

IGNITION and LIGHTING : Villiers flywheel magneto with lighting coils. Westinghouse rectifier and Exide 6-volt, 13-amp-hr accumulator. Twin-filament 24/24-watt main bulb, AC/DC headlamp switch.

TANK CAPACITY : 2¼ gallons.

TYRES : Dunlop, 3.00 × 19in ; ribbed front, studded rear.

BRAKES : 5in diameter front and rear, with finger-operated adjusters.

SUSPENSION : Telescopic front fork employing coil springs ; pivoted-fork rear springing, hydraulically damped, with rubber rebound buffer mounted below pivot lug.

WHEELBASE : 49½in. Ground clearance, 5in.

SADDLE : Lycett, adjustable for height from 28 to 29in.

WEIGHT : 224 lb fully equipped with one gallon of fuel.

PRICE : £99 10s. With Purchase Tax (in Britain only), £127 2s 10d.

ROAD TAX : £1 17s 6d a year ; 10s 4d a quarter.

DESCRIPTION : *The Motor Cycle*, 30 August, 1951.

MAKERS : Francis and Barnett, Ltd., Lower Ford Street, Coventry.

PERFORMANCE DATA

MEAN MAXIMUM SPEED : Bottom : 29 m.p.h.
Second : 47 m.p.h.
Top : 57 m.p.h.

MEAN ACCELERATION :

	10-20 m.p.h.	15-25 m.p.h.	20-30 m.p.h.
Bottom	2.4 secs	2.7 secs	—
Second	3.6 secs	3.4 secs	3.2 secs
Top	—	5 secs	5.4 secs

Mean speed at end of quarter-mile from rest : 53 m.p.h.
Mean time taken from 0-30 m.p.h. : 5.7 secs.

PETROIL CONSUMPTION : At 30 m.p.h., 130 m.p.g. At 40 m.p.h., 107 m.p.g. At 50 m.p.h., 72 m.p.g.

BRAKING : From 30 m.p.h. to rest, 32ft (surface, dry tar macadam)

TURNING CIRCLE : 12ft 2in.

MINIMUM NON-SNATCH SPEED : 21 m.p.h. in top gear.

WEIGHT Per C.C. : 1.13lb.

487 c.c. S7 Sunbeam

First published 5 June 1952

Luxurious Touring Twin With Shaft-drive Provides

ALTHOUGH introduced six years ago, the 487 c.c. S7 Sunbeam continues to be regarded as a novelty. Wherever the road-test outfit was parked, lay public and motor cyclists alike, paused in tribute to its clean design and flowing lines. Since production began, no major changes have been made to the basic layout which includes such intriguing features as unit construction and shaft drive, overhead camshaft operation of the valves, and squish-type combustion chambers.

Finish of the road-test outfit was mist green for machine and sidecar

There is a hydraulically-controlled telescopic fork, plunger-type rear springing, 4.50 and 4.75in section tyres front and rear respectively, and a large saddle which pivots vertically from its nose. As a luxury, touring solo, the S7 excels for its smoothness, mechanical and exhaust quietness, and its high degree of comfort. As a sidecar mount it is equally attractive, and perhaps even more so, bearing in mind that few other machines on the British market have frames as suitable as the Sunbeam's for dealing with the loads imposed by a sidecar.

Irrespective of weather conditions, every outing with the road-test sidecar outfit gave so much æsthetic pleasure that it was certain to remain long in the memory. When the outfit was at speed on the road, the engine was so smooth as to make most others—irrespective of make or capacity—seem rough by comparison. It was flexible and thrived on revs. The faster it was revved the smoother it became. No matter how hard it was driven, the engine remained oil-tight with the exception of a modest seep from the oil-indicator unit. Only slight exhaust pipe discoloration appeared; that was at the junction of the pipes below the right footrest.

Engine starting from cold demanded so little physical effort that it could be accomplished by hand. One kickstarter depression was generally all that was needed. The procedure was to switch on the ignition, flood the carburettor, open the throttle fractionally, and give a light prod on the kickstarter. As soon as the engine became warm, the twistgrip could be rolled back to its stop. Idling from then on was so slow that the induction strokes could almost be counted, yet it was reliable to the nth degree.

Provided a momentary pause was made after freeing the engine-speed clutch, bottom gear could be engaged easily and quietly when the machine was stationary with the engine idling. Neutral could be effortlessly selected from either bottom or second gears. The gear change was lighter than average—so light that the pedal could barely be felt under a bewildered foot. Clean and positive upward changes were certain between any pair of gears, provided a longer-than-usual pause was made in pedal travel. Slick, racing-type changes were entirely positive, but accompanied by a distinct "clonk" as the pinions engaged. No harm resulted from this treatment, however, and racing changes were the rule when the performance figures were taken. The gear pedal is mounted on a serrated shaft and could be perfectly positioned relative to the right footrest.

With the exception of a very slight flat-spot at the bottom of the throttle range, the pick-up was clean and brisk. Pinking on current British pool petrol was decidedly marked and occurred even if the throttle was blipped when the gear was in neutral. The tendency to pinking was sufficient to put a limit on the maximum acceleration performance. But under normal driving conditions it was not so marked as to cause annoyance.

After the performance figures and other data had been obtained there was an opportunity to try the machine on 80-octane spirit. The improvement in the anti-knock value was sufficient to transform the performance. It became impossible to make the engine pink, even by using

In-line o.h.c. engine with unit-construction gear box and shaft drive are prominent features of the Sunbeam design

with Sidecar

Excellent Sidecar Performance

full throttle at such low speeds in top gear that the engine "choked." Low-speed pulling was immeasurably improved, and the machine, therefore, was more pleasant to drive.

When the engine was idling it rocked perceptibly on its rubber mountings. The rocking increased during the get-away period, and was present on all occasions when the engine was under load at low speeds. This rocking was transmitted to the handlebars and footrests in the form of only mild vibration, and was never considered objectionable. As the engine speed was increased, the rocking disappeared, and the engine gave that impression of delightful smoothness mentioned earlier.

Both mechanically and on the exhaust, the engine was notably quiet. When it was idling, faint rustling could be heard from the pistons and valve gear, but these were inaudible to a rider in the saddle when the machine was on the move. At any speed of which the machine was capable the exhaust was no more than a pleasant, subdued purr. Maximum acceleration, if desired, could be used in built-up areas, without fear of the exhaust being considered objectionable by pedestrians.

High Cruising Speed

Cruising speed could be anything between 30 m.p.h. and maximum. Since its inception, the Sunbeam, with its unique luxury features, has come to be regarded in some quarters as a touring mount of mediocre speed capabilities. Yet the performance with a sidecar was as satisfying as that of many a so-called sports machine. The high degree of smoothness and silence were ever impressive. At 50 m.p.h. there was no more fuss than there was at 40 m.p.h. During much of the test a 12-stone passenger was carried in the sidecar. Cruising speeds were generally in the region of 50-55 m.p.h. wherever possible, and the engine was given no quarter during acceleration. As a rule, the outfit would be accelerated to 50 m.p.h. in third gear. The head-lamp mounted speedometer recorded 9 per cent fast. One of the reasons for such high speeds being used in third gear was that the test outfit was slightly overgeared. The maximum speed figures of 64 m.p.h. in third and 62 m.p.h. in top bear this out. But overgearing is no disadvantage on a touring mount. Rather it is the reverse, since engine r.p.m. are lower for a given speed on top gear; this fuel consumption is reduced and greater engine longevity results.

Road shocks were adequately insulated from the rider by the large-section tyres and the soft suspension. At high speeds or low, the riding position was most satisfactory. The relationship between the saddle and footrests provided a knee angle that was comfortable for tall or short riders. Both saddle and footrests are adjustable for height—and the footrests for fore and aft position also.

For sidecar work, a handlebar with a more backward sweep to the grips would have been considered an advantage since, with solo fork trail, the steering was slightly heavy. Controls for the clutch, throttle and front brake were heavier than usual in operation. Both brakes were extremely powerful, though both required heavy pressure if their full retarding effort was to be obtained. Only slight fade resulted under conditions of use far more severe than are ever likely to be encountered during normal driving.

Ignition on the Sunbeam is by battery and coil. The coil is fully protected from the elements yet accessibly housed in a metal container, along with the lighting and ignition switch, the ammeter and the automatic voltage-control regulator. In another metal container on the opposite side of the frame, the battery is concealed, though it was not too accessible because of the sidecar. The tool box is also mounted on the nearside of the machine, by the side of the gear box.

A driving light that was fully adequate for the Sunbeam's performance was provided by the 8in headlamp. The twin-filament bulb is controlled by an orthodox handlebar switch mounted close to the left grip. The fact that the headlamp switch is situated on the side of the machine, below the saddle, was found to be no disadvantage.

The sidecar fitted was a Sunbeam de Luxe Tourer. It was sufficiently roomy for a six-foot passenger and adequately comfortable during days on which over 300 miles were covered. The celluloid windscreen is of ample dimensions and there is very little back-draught. When not in use the folding twill hood stows neatly into a twill envelope. The hood could be erected without effort in less than a minute. Both machine and sidecar were luxuriously finished in mist green.

Information Panel

487 c.c. Sunbeam and sidecar

SPECIFICATION

ENGINE: 487 c.c. (70 × 63.5 mm) in-line twin with chain-driven overhead camshaft; valves set in single row at 22½ deg to vertical; squish-type combustion chambers; one-piece aluminium-alloy cylinder head; crankcase and cylinder block in one-piece aluminium-alloy casting; light-alloy connecting rods with indium-flash, lead-bronze big-ends. Wet-sump lubrication; sump capacity, 3½ pints. Compression ratio 6.5 to 1.
CARBURETTOR: Amal; twistgrip throttle control; air control on carburettor.
TRANSMISSION: Sunbeam four-speed gear box in unit with engine; positive-stop foot control. Sidecar ratios: Bottom 16.6 to 1. Second 10.3 to 1. Third 7.4 to 1. Top 6.13 to 1. Single-plate clutch. Final drive by shaft and underslung worm. R.p.m. in top gear at 30 m.p.h., 2,600 approx.
IGNITION AND LIGHTING: Lucas 60 watt, pancake-type generator at front end of crankshaft. Coil ignition with auto-advance. 8in diameter headlamp.
FUEL CAPACITY: 3½ gallons.
TYRES: Dunlop. Front, 4.50 × 16in Ribbed; rear, 4.75 × 16in Universal.
BRAKES: 8in diameter front and rear; fulcrum adjusters.
SUSPENSION: Sunbeam telescopic front fork with hydraulic damping. Plunger-type rear springing.
WHEELBASE: 57in. Ground clearance, 4½in unladen.
SADDLE: Terry, with single compression spring in top frame tube; unladen height, 30½in.
WEIGHT: Complete outfit, 648 lb fully equipped and with one gallon of fuel.
PRICE: Machine only, £220; with Purchase Tax (in Great Britain only), £281 2s 3d.
ROAD TAX: £5 a year, £1 7s 6d a quarter.
MAKERS: Sunbeam Cycles, Ltd., Birmingham, 11.
DESCRIPTION: *The Motor Cycle*, 7 March, 1946; 14 July, 1949.

SIDECAR

MODEL: Sunbeam, S22/50.
CHASSIS: Triangulated with quarter-elliptic springs at rear and coil springs at front. Four-point attachment.
BODY: Coachbuilt (timber frame, steel panels). Celluloid screen. Folding twill hood. Locker at rear. Weight 209 lb.
PRICE: £64 10s, with Purchase Tax (in Britain only), £81 14s.

PERFORMANCE DATA

MEAN MAXIMUM SPEED: Bottom :* 29 m.p.h.
Second :* 47 m.p.h.
Third : 64 m.p.h.
Top : 62 m.p.h.
* valve float occurring.

MEAN ACCELERATION:

	10-30 m.p.h.	20-40 m.p.h.	30-50 m.p.h.
Bottom	4 secs	—	—
Second	5.7 secs	5.8 secs	6.9 secs
Third	10.5 secs	9.2 secs	10.1 secs
Top	—	14.7 secs	15.7 secs

Mean speed at end of quarter-mile from rest: 58 m.p.h.
Mean time to cover standing quarter-mile: 22.3 secs.
PETROL CONSUMPTION: At 30 m.p.h., 55 m.p.g. At 40 m.p.h., 48 m.p.g. At 50 m.p.h., 43 m.p.g.
BRAKING: From 30 m.p.h. to rest, 47ft (surface, dry tar macadam).
TURNING CIRCLE: 16ft (to left).
MINIMUM NON-SNATCH SPEED: 16 m.p.h. on top gear.
WEIGHT PER C.C.: 1.33 lb.

> First published 17 July 1952

244 c.c. Excelsior

A Vertical Twin Two-stroke Lightweight with

SINCE its introduction late in 1949, the 244 c.c. Excelsior parallel twin two-stroke, the Talisman, has achieved no small measure of popularity. The Talisman Sports, which made its bow at last year's London Show and which recently came into production, embodies modifications that are mainly

Luxury features include plunger-type rear springing, twin carburettors and a special twin-seat adjustable for height

in the nature of "gilding the lily"—except that the "gilding" process has included functional as well as ornamental features. Among the refinements are twin Amal carburettors. As a result, increased maximum speed has been obtained.

Salient characteristics of the twin two-stroke engine are its "four-cylinder" torque and well-nigh perfect balance. Almost throughout the entire speed range the engine delivers its power in a turbine-like flow, without fuss or vibration. Only at one small period (a period bracketed by a bare 2 m.p.h.) could the slightest of vibration tremors be detected; this was at 40-42 m.p.h. in top gear. No palpable vibration was apparent at the handlebars.

Like most two-strokes, the Excelsior would not fire evenly with the engine on light load. For instance, at a steady 30 m.p.h. along a level road, with no headwind, the twistgrip had to be eased off fractionally, then opened again if a tendency to four-stroking was to be avoided. Under such conditions, the minimum speed in top gear (on a fixed throttle opening) required to avoid four-stroking was approximately 34 m.p.h. This does not mean, of course, that there was not good two-stroking at low speeds. On the contrary, due to the exceptionally good low-speed torque, the engine was so flexible that it would pull evenly away from speeds as low as 12 m.p.h. in top gear. At any speed between 15 and 50 m.p.h. in top gear, the throttle could be wound open without any protest from the engine, and immediate results were forthcoming.

Acceleration through the indirect ratios, as well as in top gear, was extremely lively for a 250 c.c. machine. A comfortable cruising speed for both engine and rider was adjudged to be 50 m.p.h., though even when the engine was held on full throttle for long periods, it gave the impression that it would hum on tirelessly for as long as the rider wished. Under these conditions there was not the slightest sign of overheating; the cylinder head and barrel fins remained relatively cool, and the exhaust pipes did not become even slightly discoloured. The power unit remained absolutely oil-tight, but burnt oil leaked from the joint between silencer and exhaust pipe.

When the maximum speed, acceleration and fuel consumption figures were taken, a stiffish breeze was blowing which had some adverse effect. It should be mentioned that the engine just failed to reach its ultimate peak revs in second gear, because of a period of four-stroking occurring high up in the r.p.m. range. When the engine was held on full throttle in bottom gear, the revs climbed slowly through, and clear of, this four-stroking period and attained absolute maximum.

It is an axiom that the smaller the engine, the greater should be the number of gears. In hilly country, four carefully chosen gear ratios enable a small-capacity engine to be kept turning over happily, as distinct from slogging hard or over-revving. However, such was the flexibility of the Excelsior that it tended to make the four-speed gear box appear something of a luxury rather than a necessity. There were occasions, of course, such as when overtaking slower traffic on hills, on which the four-speed gear box was a valuable asset.

Only slight effort was required to operate the gear-change pedal, which has a short arc of travel. Quick-action gear changes, both upward and downward, could be made without fear of "scrunching." Some deliberation had to be exercised when engaging neutral; otherwise there was a tendency to overshoot the neutral position.

It was felt that the gear pedal was a little too low, in relation to the most desirable footrest position, for maximum ease of operation when making downward gear changes, i.e., moving the pedal upward. Though the pedal is located on serrations, and is therefore adjustable, its adjustment for height is limited by the position of the mag-generator case. The clutch was exceptionally light to operate; it was smooth and progressive in taking up the drive.

Starting the engine from cold, even after it had been standing all night, was invariably accomplished

Impressive twin power unit. Note also the pivoted crank of the kick-starter pedal and the rectifier mounted below the tank

Talisman Sports

an Attractive Performance

Both exhaust pipes are led into one pipe which feeds into a silencer on the left side of the machine

first kick provided the following simple preliminaries were observed: the float chamber tickler was depressed until the fuel just began to appear at the base of the mixing chambers; the air lever was fully closed and the twistgrip was set one-third open. After the engine had been running for a few minutes, the air control could be opened fully. Starting with the engine warm could usually be effected by a leisurely prod on the kick-starter, with the throttle set one-third open. The kick-starter crank is mounted concentrically with the gear pedal; if the ball of the foot was used when operating the kick-starter, the crank could be moved through its full arc of travel without the foot-rest obstructing it.

For its exhaust silencing and quiet running, the Excelsior gained full marks. Even under conditions of brisk acceleration, the exhaust note was little more than an unobtrusive buzz. At cruising speeds on the open road, especially when there was a slight breeze, the rider could not hear a sound from the machine unless his head was turned sideways—then the pleasant thrum of the exhaust could be heard, but no more. At maximum speed, very slight piston rattle ("two-stroke rattle") was audible.

Both steering and road-holding are first class. The machine could be whistled round bends and corners without deviating a fraction from the desired line. Handling was equally good at high or low speeds. All road shocks were cushioned, and an appreciated degree of comfort was provided by the telescopic front fork and the plunger-type rear springing. It was felt that a softer action of the front fork would have further enhanced the riding comfort.

An excellent riding position is furnished by the relationship between dual-seat (adjustable for height), handlebar and foot-rests. The split handlebar is accommodated in sockets which lie one on each side of the top fork bridge. By swivelling the bars in their sockets, adjustment for both height and angle of the grips is obtainable. The handlebar control levers are of the clip-on type and are therefore adjustable; they fell easily to hand. The twin-rotor twistgrip throttle control for the two carburettors was inordinately stiff in operation, and no amount of lubrication of the cables resulted in much improvement.

Perfectly positioned in relation to the footrest, the brake pedal pad could be depressed merely by swivelling the foot lightly on the rest. An adjustable stop for the brake pedal is provided. Though subjected to hard usage, both front and rear brakes retained their efficiency. Applied in unison, they provided commendable stopping power.

The driving light provided by the Lucas pre-focus lamp unit was considered adequate for the full performance of the machine to be used at night. The total lamp load was balanced on the ammeter at 38-40 m.p.h. in top gear. Mounted on top of the fork bridge, the speedometer was easily read by day or by night; it registered accurately at 30 m.p.h. and was 2½ m.p.h. fast at 50 m.p.h.

Parking equipment consists of a spring-up central stand; even after much practice this proved difficult to operate. Embodied in the gear box is a dip-stick; an excellent feature in itself, it nevertheless proved awkward to read as, during extraction, it fouled the right-hand carburettor. Two spacious tool boxes provide good facilities for carrying tool-kit, repair outfit and spares. The Talisman Sports is finished in beige enamel, with the fuel tank lined red and bearing the Excelsior motif.

Information Panel

The 244 c.c. Excelsior Talisman Sports

SPECIFICATION

ENGINE: 244 c.c. (50 x 62 mm) two-stroke parallel twin. Separate cast-iron cylinder barrels and light-alloy heads; crank throws at 180 deg; crankshaft supported on four ball bearings and one roller bearing; roller-bearing big-ends; aluminium-alloy, flat-top pistons. Compression ratio 7.8 to 1. Petroil lubrication.

CARBURETTORS: Amal; twistgrip throttle control; air-slides operated by handlebar lever.

IGNITION AND LIGHTING: Wico-Pacy flywheel mag-generator, with rectifier and battery. 7in headlamp with pre-focus light unit. 24/24 w headlamp bulb.

TRANSMISSION: Four-speed gear box with positive-stop foot control. Bottom, 17.78 to 1. Second, 10.86 to 1. Third, 9.22 to 1. Top, 6.09 to 1. Two-plate cork-insert clutch running in oil. Shock absorber incorporated in clutch. Primary chain, duplex ⅜ x 3/16 in cast-aluminium case. Rear chain, ½ x ¼ in with guard over top run. Engine r.p.m. at 30 m.p.h. in top gear, 2,380.

FUEL CAPACITY: 2¾ gallons.

TYRES: Dunlop, 3.00 x 19in front and rear.

BRAKES: 5in-diameter front, 6in rear.

SUSPENSION: Excelsior undamped telescopic front fork. Plunger-type rear springing.

WHEELBASE: 50½in. Ground clearance, 5in unladen.

SEAT: Excelsior twin seat. Unladen height, 30in.

WEIGHT: 250lb fully equipped and with one gallon of fuel.

PRICE: £136, plus Purchase Tax (in Britain only), £173 15s 7d.

ROAD TAX: £1 17s 6d a year; 10s 4d a quarter.

MAKERS: Excelsior Motor Co., Ltd., King's Road, Tyseley, Birmingham, 11.

DESCRIPTION: *The Motor Cycle*, 15 November, 1951.

PERFORMANCE DATA

MEAN MAXIMUM SPEED: Bottom: 30 m.p.h.
Second: 45 m.p.h.
Third: 55 m.p.h.
Top: 64 m.p.h.

MEAN ACCELERATION:

	10-30 m.p.h.	20-40 m.p.h.	30-50 m.p.h.
Second	4.6 secs	5.4 secs	—
Third	5.6 secs	6.4 secs	9.0 secs
Top	8.2 secs	7.6 secs	10.0 secs

Mean Speed at end of quarter-mile from rest: 57 m.p.h.
Mean time to cover standing quarter-mile: 23 secs.

PETROIL CONSUMPTION: At 30 m.p.h., 96 m.p.g. At 40 m.p.h., 88 m.p.g. At 50 m.p.h., 67 m.p.g. At 55-60 m.p.h., 60 m.p.g.

BRAKING: From 30 m.p.h. to rest, 29ft 11in (surface, dry tar macadam).

TURNING CIRCLE: 13ft.

MINIMUM NON-SNATCH SPEED: 12 m.p.h. in top gear.

WEIGHT PER C.C.: 1.02 lb.

> First published 14 August 1952

498 c.c. Triumph

Outstanding Sports Twin with a Scintillating Performance

FOR a number of years the 498 c.c. Triumph Tiger 100 has enjoyed an enviable reputation as a super-sports mount with a Jekyll and Hyde personality, docile and gentle when the occasion demands, such as in heavy traffic, yet possessed of truly tigerish characteristics when given its head on the open road. In 1951 its appeal was widened by the introduction of a light-alloy cylinder block and head and, as an extra, a conversion kit for transforming the model into a pukka racing machine. The model's success in the competition sphere was recently underlined by victory in the 1952 Senior Clubman's T.T.

Finish of the Tiger 100 is silver, black and chromium

It is on the open road, as "Mr. Hyde," that the Tiger 100 really comes into its own. Acceleration up to speeds in the seventies is vivid yet smooth. The engine seems to revel in the continued use of full throttle, and high average speeds are not difficult to maintain. The rapidity with which the speedometer needle could be sent round to the 80 m.p.h. mark in third gear, and held between 80 and 85 m.p.h. in top for as long as road and traffic conditions permitted, made averages of over 50 m.p.h. commonplace.

Twice in one day the 102-mile journey between the Midlands and a London suburb was covered in an hour and three-quarters, in spite of the usual volume of week-day traffic. On these trips the speedometer frequently read 87 m.p.h. for some miles, though the rider was normally seated and clad in a stormcoat and waders. Long main road hills pulled the needle back no farther than the 80 m.p.h. mark. Checked electrically, the speedometer was found to register 2½ m.p.h. fast at 30 m.p.h. and approximately 5 m.p.h. fast at all speeds between 40 and 80 m.p.h.

In spite of the hardest of driving methods, there was never the slightest sign of engine tiredness, nor was there any tendency for the engine to "run on" when the ignition cut-out was operated after prolonged use of the maximum speed performance. At the conclusion of one particular day's riding, which comprised some 300 miles—many of them on full throttle—the only visible signs of hard riding were discoloration of the exhaust pipes for a few inches from the ports, an oil leak from the cylinder head joint, a faint smear at the base of the push-rod tubes and a slight oil deposit on the rear-wheel rim.

Except at high engine r.p.m. there was no vibration. At no speed, indeed, was vibration sufficient to warrant criticism. Provided normal use was made of the gear box and manual ignition control, there was no undue tendency for the engine to pink, even though the fuel employed throughout the test was the usual low-octane Pool petrol.

The exhaust note was pleasant and inoffensive whether the Tiger 100 was trickling through towns and villages or being driven hard. Mechanically, as is to be expected with light-alloy cylinders and heads, the engine was slightly noisy, though this ceased to be apparent to the rider when the road speed rose above 35 m.p.h. Most of the mechanical noise was from the pistons, and it was emphasized mainly by the complete absence of induction noise; responsible for this last condition is a large Vokes air filter incorporated as a standard fitting.

Top gear maximum speed figures were taken, on a 1,650-yard straight, both with and without the air filter. Downwind speeds were identical (97.06 m.p.h.) in each case; upwind, without the filter and using the same 170 main jet, there was a speed increase of 1.79 m.p.h. compared with that obtained with the filter in position.

Engine starting, whether the unit was hot or cold, was invariably accomplished at the first kick. The air control, which is situated beneath the left-hand side of the twinseat, was never required during the course of the test. When the engine was cold, the only pre-starting drill was flooding of the carburettor. Provided a small throttle opening was used, there was no need to retard the ignition. As would be expected, the tick-over was rather "lumpy" on full advance, but the idling was improved when the ignition was one-third retarded; however, for complete reliability, the tick-over had to be set faster than some consider desirable.

As to "Dr. Jekyll," though a certain amount of docility and low-speed flexibility is inevitably sacrificed in the interests of top-end performance, the Tiger 100 is nevertheless very well-mannered.

The high-efficiency power unit has impressive and pleasing lines

Tiger 100

for Fast Road Work or Racing

It could be driven unobtrusively at speeds in the region of 30 m.p.h. in top gear. Fuel consumption under these conditions was markedly good. Oil consumption was negligible throughout the test.

The relationship between the handlebar, with its distinctive, rearward sweep, the footrests and the twinseat provided a comfortable riding position for all normal conditions. For prolonged, ultra high-speed work, a slightly more rearward footrest mounting or a raised support on the twinseat would have been appreciated—these solely to relieve the arms of tension caused by wind pressure. Much appreciated was the slenderness of that part of the tank which lies between the rider's knees; the width was just right for maximum comfort and controllability.

Located on a serrated shaft, the gear pedal was adjustable to a position which gave easy operation without removing the foot from its rest. The rear brake pedal came conveniently under the ball of the left foot. The reach from the handlebar to the clutch and front-brake levers was felt to be a trifle too great. Horn button and dipswitch were excellently positioned for left and right thumb operation respectively. The twistgrip, which incorporates a knurled, self-locking friction adjuster, was slightly heavy in operation. The pillion footrests were well positioned for passenger comfort and the twinseat provided comfortable accommodation for two. Riders of large build, dressed for long-distance travel, might desire slightly greater length in the seat.

Pleasantly close, top and third gear ratios are well-chosen in relation to engine characteristics; in fact, the gear change between them was so slick as to encourage more frequent changes than was necessary—just for the sheer pleasure of it. In order to achieve silent changes between bottom and second, and second and third gears, a leisurely movement of the pedal was called for. Owing to slight clutch drag on the machine tested, bottom gear could not be engaged silently when the machine was stationary with the engine idling. Neutral selection was easy from either bottom or second gears. The clutch was delightfully sweet in taking up the drive. It was light in operation and appeared to be impervious to abuse.

Both brakes were smooth, reasonably powerful, and progressive

The light-alloy cylinders and heads are die-cast and are characterized by their close-pitch fins

in action. The front brake by itself was good but required somewhat heavy pressure. Rear-brake pedal travel was rather too long to permit maximum braking effort.

The Triumph front fork has a soft action around the static-load position; it absorbed road shocks in an exemplary manner. Occasionally, with the added weight of a pillion passenger, it was made to bottom under conditions of heavy braking. The sprung rear hub provided reasonable comfort at touring speeds but rather more movement would have been preferred at high speeds.

On corners and bends the Tiger 100 could be heeled over confidently and stylishly. On very bumpy bends taken at speed there was a slight tendency to roll. Straight-ahead steering was first class. Bumpy surfaces and gusty winds produced an impression of lightness, which could be curbed by a turn of the steering-damper knob.

With its fine blending of silver, black and chromium, the finish of the machine is a credit to the manufacturers. To sum up, the Tiger 100 is a thoroughbred sporting five-hundred, calculated to inspire pride of ownership both on account of its magnificent all-round performance and its handsome appearance.

Information Panel

498 c.c. Triumph Tiger 100

SPECIFICATION

ENGINE: 498 c.c. (63 × 80 mm) vertical twin o.h.v.; fully enclosed valve gear. Die-cast aluminium-alloy cylinder block and head; Hiduminium alloy connecting rods; Duralumin push rods; plain bearing big-ends; mainshafts mounted on ball and roller bearings. Dry-sump lubrication: oil tank capacity, 6 pints.

CARBURETTOR: Amal; twistgrip throttle control; air slide operated by Bowden cable with lever situated under seat. Large Vokes air filter included.

TRANSMISSION: Triumph four-speed gear box with positive-stop foot control. Bottom, 12.2 to 1. Second, 8.45 to 1. Third, 5.95 to 1. Top, 5. to 1. Multi-plate clutch with cork inserts operating in oil. Primary chain ⅜ × 0.305in, in oil-bath case. Rear chain, ⅝ × ⅜in, lubricated by bleed from primary chain case. Guards over both runs of rear chain. R.p.m. at 30 m.p.h. in top gear, 1,938.

IGNITION AND LIGHTING: Lucas magneto with manual control. Separate Lucas 60-watt dynamo. 7in-diameter headlamp.

FUEL CAPACITY: 4 gallons.

TYRES: Dunlop. Front, 3.25 × 19in ribbed. Rear, 3.50 × 19in Universal.

BRAKES: Triumph 6⅞ × 1⅛in front; 8 × 1⅛in rear; hand adjusters.

SUSPENSION: Triumph telescopic front fork with hydraulic damping. Triumph spring hub in rear wheel.

WHEELBASE: 55in. Ground clearance, 6in unladen.

SADDLE: Triumph Twinseat; unladen height, 31in.

WEIGHT: 383 lb with approximately one gallon of fuel, full oil tank, and fully equipped (including pillion footrests and prop stand).

PRICE: £175, plus Purchase Tax (in Britain), £48 12s 3d. Spring hub extra, £16, plus £4 8s 11d P.T. Pillion footrests and prop stand extra.

MAKERS: Triumph Engineering Co. Ltd., Meriden Works, Allesley, Coventry.

DESCRIPTION: *The Motor Cycle*, 9 November, 1950.

PERFORMANCE DATA

MEAN MAXIMUM SPEED: Bottom: *41 m.p.h.
Second: *60 m.p.h.
Third: 85 m.p.h.
Top: 92 m.p.h.
* Valve float occurring.

MEAN ACCELERATION:

	10-30 m.p.h.	20-40 m.p.h.	30-50 m.p.h.
Bottom	2.3 secs	2.2 secs	—
Second	3.0 secs	3.0 secs	2.6 secs
Third	—	4.6 secs	4.6 secs
Top	—	5.6 secs	5.8 secs

Mean speed at end of quarter-mile from rest: 79 m.p.h.
Mean time to cover standing quarter-mile: 16.6 secs.

PETROL CONSUMPTION: At 30 m.p.h., 101.6 m.p.g. At 40 m.p.h., 83.2 m.p.g. At 50 m.p.h., 70.4 m.p.g. At 60 m.p.h., 59.2 m.p.g.

BRAKING: From 30 to rest 28ft 6in (surface, dry tar macadam).

TURNING CIRCLE: 16ft.

MINIMUM NON-SNATCH SPEED: 17 m.p.h. in top gear.

WEIGHT PER C.C.: 0.8 lb.

First published 21 August 1952

The 122 c.c. Tourist

A Lively, Comfortable, Two-stroke Lightweight with Excellent

INTRODUCTION of the new Tourist Trophy model to the Bown range of lightweights marks a worthy addition to the ranks of one-two-fives. Powered by the 122 c.c. Villiers engine-gear unit, the new Bown belies its small size, for it has a comfortable riding position and a lively performance. The rear of the saddle is provided with an ample range of adjustment, and the handlebar can be swivelled in its mounting. With these two items individually adjusted, the riding position was found to be comfortable

The Bown incorporates a 122 c.c. Villiers engine-gear unit and Metal Profiles telescopic front fork

for long periods; allied to light weight and positive steering, it provided the maximum degree of control at all times.

The gear pedal is adjustable for height by virtue of its serrated mounting. It was positioned so that both upward and downward gear changes could be made without removing the right foot from its footrest. The rear brake pedal was slightly too high and too tucked in for the easiest of manipulation.

Of braced, duplex cradle layout, the frame proved to be extremely rigid laterally; undoubtedly this contributes to the machine's excellent handling characteristics. Bends and corners of all types were a joy to negotiate on the Bown, so accurate was the steering. Even when severe road bumps caused the machine to hop on bends taken at top speed, there was not the slightest tendency for the front wheel to stray from its appointed direction. At the other end of the scale, when traffic conditions made it necessary, the Bown could be ridden at well below walking speed with the front wheel pointing straight ahead and both feet on the rests.

Indeed, the machine could even be brought to a halt and moved off again immediately without putting down a foot and without employing any delicate balancing technique.

Initially, the low-speed steering was found to be stiff and there was a marked tendency for it to roll. The trouble, however, was traced to an over-tightened steering head adjustment; this was quickly rectified. The action of the telescopic fork was unduly short and stiff.

Both brakes were potent yet smooth in operation; and although they were used hard during the 1,000-mile test, they required little adjustment. There was complete absence of sponginess in brake operation, and in both cases rather more than average pressure was required to obtain the best results. Either brake would evoke a squeal of protest from its tyre; applied together, they provided safe and efficient retardation.

The engine-gear unit was new when the machine was taken over for the test. Consequently, the gear change was stiff in the early stages, but it freed considerably as the mileage mounted, and was firm and positive to operate. Quiet upward changes at low engine r.p.m. were best accomplished with a deliberate movement of the pedal. At higher speeds, noiseless and rapid changes were the order of the day. Quick and clean downward charges could be made at all appropriate speeds. Neutral was easy to locate from either bottom or second gears. The clutch freed perfectly and was smooth and positive in its take-up of the drive. No amount of hard work was too much for it. An excellent feature is the readily accessible, self-locking fulcrum adjustment for the operating lever; the adjustment could be carried out from the saddle.

First-kick starting was invariably achieved throughout the test. On most occasions it was necessary only to flood the carburetter and set the throttle approximately one-third open. On the few occasions when the temperature was low, the strangler was closed for starting with the engine cold. After the engine had fired, the strangler was set half

Very sturdy frame construction, giving excellent steering, is a feature of the Bown

Trophy Bown

Handling and Steering Characteristics

Neat arrangement of the handlebar controls, speedometer and horn

open for the first hundred yards or so. The folding crank on the kick-starter was appreciated. Also appreciated was the footrest position, which in no way interfered with the swing of the kick-starter.

Very effective at all speeds and throttle openings was the Burgess silencer. When the machine was driven on full throttle, the exhaust note was a pleasant but by no means offensive hum. Careful setting of the throttle produced a slow, reliable tick-over, though, of course, the firing was irregular in the usual two-stroke manner. Except when the engine was running light at very small throttle openings, two-stroking was excellent. Mechanical quietness, too, was of a high order, there being only a little "two-stroke rattle" at high r.p.m. and slight transmission whine on the overrun.

Acceleration was distinctly lively for a one-two-five. The engine displays good flywheel effect and good balance. It is thus smooth in operation and holds its speed on gradients. A period of roughness was perceptible at 38 m.p.h. in top gear—mainly through the saddle and handlebar. At similar r.p.m. in second gear a slight hesitation was apparent when the engine was warm.

Comfortable Cruising

It was impossible to make the engine pink—even by the most drastic use of the throttle. Forty miles an hour was a happy cruising speed, which could be held indefinitely; indeed, once the engine was fully run-in, any speed between 20 m.p.h. and maximum could be regarded as comfortable for cruising. The speedometer was found to register 2 m.p.h. fast at 30 m.p.h. and 4 m.p.h. fast at 40 m.p.h.

A bulb horn is mounted transversely on the handlebar, well positioned for convenient operation by the left hand. It proved surprisingly effective. A slight amount of oil leaked from the vicinity of the gear box final-drive sprocket and discoloured the exhaust pipe. Other messiness resulted from a seep from the petroil filler cap, which has no internal baffle, and the carburettor became messy externally as a result of flooding for starting purposes. A neat, cylindrical tool box, containing a comprehensive kit, is housed beneath the saddle. On the model tested, there was a persistent tendency for the knurled retaining nut of the tool-box lid to work loose.

Centrally placed is a sturdy stand. It was easy to operate, and it enables either wheel to remain clear of the ground without the use of any additional weight. A small extension on the left side of the stand would obviate the possibility of the rider's shoe becoming fouled on the underside of the silencer.

In appearance, as well as in performance, the Bown is distinctly attractive. It is finished throughout in maroon, with gold lines on the wheel rims, and gold-lined, blue-grey panels on the tank sides.

Information Panel

The 122 c.c. Tourist Trophy Bown

SPECIFICATION

ENGINE: Villiers 122 c.c. Mark 10D (50 × 62 mm) single-cylinder two-stroke, with three-speed gear box in unit. Flat crown, die-cast, aluminium-alloy piston. Roller bearing big-end; mainshaft supported on three ball races. Detachable, light-alloy cylinder head. Petroil lubrication.

CARBURETTOR: Villiers Single Lever, with twistgrip throttle control. Air filter, incorporating strangler.

TRANSMISSION: Villiers three-speed foot-change gear box in unit with engine. Gear ratios: Bottom, 20.1 to 1. Second, 10.51 to 1. Top, 7.55 to 1. Primary chain, ⅜ × 0.225in in oil-bath case. Rear chain, ½ × 0.205in with guard over top run. R.p.m. at 30 m.p.h. in top gear, 3,090.

IGNITION AND LIGHTING: Villiers flywheel magneto incorporating lighting coils. Twin-filament 30-watt main bulb. Dry battery in headlamp for parking.

PETROIL CAPACITY: 2¼ gallons.

TYRES: Dunlop, 3.00 × 19in front and rear.

BRAKES: 5in diameter internal expanding front and rear.

SUSPENSION: Metal Profiles undamped telescopic front fork.

WHEELBASE: 46in.

GROUND CLEARANCE: 6in.

SADDLE: Lycett. Height, 29in.

WEIGHT: 172 lb fully equipped and with ⅜ gallon of petrol.

PRICE: £80 12s 2d, plus Purchase Tax (in Britain only), £22 7s 10d.

ROAD TAX: 17s 6d a year; 4s 10d a quarter.

MAKERS: Bown Cycle Co., Ltd., Tonypandy, Glamorgan.

PERFORMANCE DATA

MEAN MAXIMUM SPEED: Bottom: 17 m.p.h.
Second: 36 m.p.h.
Top: 45 m.p.h.

MEAN ACCELERATION:

	10-20 m.p.h.	15-25 m.p.h.	20-30 m.p.h.
Second	3.2 secs	2.6 secs	3.2 secs
Top	—	4.8 secs	4.6 secs

Mean speed at end of quarter-mile from rest: maximum.
Mean time taken from 0-30 m.p.h.: 7.9 secs

PETROIL CONSUMPTION: At 20 m.p.h., 176 m.p.g. At 30 m.p.h., 128 m.p.g. At 40 m.p.h., 80 m.p.g.

BRAKING: From 30 m.p.h. to rest, 29ft (surface, dry tar macadam).

TURNING CIRCLE: 12ft 6in.

MINIMUM NON-SNATCH SPEED: 13 m.p.h. in top gear.

WEIGHT PER C.C.: 1.409 lb

First published 22 January 1953

197 c.c. Norman

A de Luxe Lightweight Equipped with

IN the post-war expansion of the Norman range of lightweight machines, a 197 c.c. model was introduced in 1950. For 1953, this model can be obtained with the added refinement of pivoted-fork rear springing. It is available in Standard and de Luxe forms; the latter incorporates rectifier-and-battery lighting. The machine tested was of de Luxe specification—

Rear suspension is unorthodox in appearance. The Feridax Lightweight Dualseat and the deeply valanced mudguards will be noted

the B2S/DL model—and it was found to furnish the rider with a fascinating and tireless engine performance allied to excellent handling qualities.

The rear sub-frame is of unusually robust design for a lightweight machine and is of somewhat unorthodox appearance. Twin tubes extend rearward from the top of the seat tube, form a support for the Feridax Dualseat, then turn downward and forward to a lug near the base of the seat tube. The rear fork pivots in a lug at the lower end of the seat tube and is cross-braced behind the pivot. Telescopic spring units are fitted between lugs at the rear of the fork arms and at the upper end of the seat tube. This rear springing layout provides a reasonably comfortable ride and a high degree of rear-wheel adhesion.

Action of the telescopic front fork was unduly short and stiff. It was considered that a greater degree of insulation from shocks would result from the use of coil springs of lesser poundage, thus allowing greater deflection of the front wheel.

The relationship of handlebar, seat and footrests provided a riding position which was felt to be too compact, even for a rider of no more than average stature. Runs of a hundred miles or more were prone to produce cramp in thighs and back. A fine adjustment of the footrests is available by reason of their serrated mounting. It was not practicable to fit them as low as was desired for comfort since no corresponding adjustment is provided for the rear-brake pedal. The gear pedal could be ideally positioned in relation to the right-side footrest. The handlebar, mounted in 3in extension brackets on the fork-crown lug, was a few inches too far rearward and, with an overall width of 29in, afforded rather too much leverage over the delightfully light steering.

Handling and steering of the Norman were exemplary under all road conditions. Straight-ahead steering was positive at all speeds and was unaffected by road bumps. No steering damper was fitted or was even remotely desired. For test purposes, the rider's hands could be removed from the handlebar with every confidence at any speed above 10 m.p.h. Initially, a low-speed roll was perceptible. This disappeared immediately the over-tightened steering head bearings were adjusted.

Cornering was equally delightful. Whether a bend was fast or slow, it was necessary only lightly to heel over the Norman, when the front wheel automatically turned inward by just the right amount. The machine could be banked over to a considerable extent without there being any tendency for it to drift, or for footrests or other components to touch the ground. Rapid changes of lock when negotiating S-bends could be made with unusually little effort. On greasy surfaces, the model's inherent stability and low build engendered a high degree of confidence.

The all-round performance of the power unit lived up to the best Villiers traditions. In practically every respect it was a joy to use. With the engine cold, a second-kick start could be guaranteed by moving the mixture control lever to full rich, depressing the carburettor tickler until fuel issued from the float chamber, and opening the throttle about one-third. When the engine was warm, one kick brought it to life without any preliminary drill, save for slightly opening the throttle.

As soon as the engine fired, the mixture control could be moved towards the weak position. To obtain the best carburation in all circumstances it was advantageous to vary the setting of the mixture lever according to

The apparently tireless Villiers engine-gear unit provides a creditable performance

Two-stroke

Pivoted-fork Rear Springing

Handlebar layout: all controls are adjustable for position

running conditions. However, to avoid frequent manipulation of the lever, it was found that a good all-round compromise was to run with the lever set one-half to two-thirds weak. As might be expected of a two-stroke, the engine, when idling, fired erratically, though careful throttle setting ensured that the tick-over was reliable. Much better results in this connection were obtained with the new high-octane petrol which was used for a part of the test.

At all engine speeds from tick-over to maximum, the unit was turbine-like in its power delivery. No vibration period was perceptible throughout the range. Response to the throttle was unhesitant at all speeds, and the torque characteristics endowed the engine with considerable flexibility. Not the least of its charms was its utter tirelessness.

Main road averages of 45 m.p.h. were achieved. Frequently 60 m.p.h. was held for miles at a stretch, and downhill the indicator could be made to go "off the clock." An accurate check showed the speedometer to be 3 per cent fast at 30 m.p.h. and 5 per cent fast at 40 and 50 m.p.h. The only audible engine noise was an indefinable whine. The exhaust was reasonably subdued except when idling.

The Norman was equally delightful to ride in town. The engine pulled smoothly almost regardless of its rotational speed, and the transmission was free from snatch except at very low speeds. Consequently, the machine was smooth and pleasant to drive at 30 m.p.h. in top gear, and would accelerate sweetly from that speed. Short of deliberate misuse, it was virtually impossible to cause the engine to pink. Provided that the engine was pulling, even lightly, two-stroking was good right down to idling speed. Equally smooth, though livelier, acceleration in town could be obtained by the use of second gear. By virtue of the machine's excellent handling qualities, negotiation of dense traffic was child's play.

In spite of the weight of the robustly constructed frame and cycle parts, acceleration was first class. The three gear ratios are excellently chosen for normal road use. Rapid and almost noiseless changes were easily made both upward and downward. Neutral was easily located from bottom or second gear. With the engine idling, bottom gear could be engaged noiselessly from neutral; it was sometimes necessary to release the clutch partially to effect this engagement. Clutch operation was light and its take-up of the drive was sweet and positive.

At the conclusion of the test, a certain amount of oil had found its way on to the cylinder fins—apparently by way of the compression release valve. It was not found necessary to use this control during the test. Further messiness was in evidence around the carburettor. Both mudguards are well valanced and reasonably effective.

The efficiency of the brakes was not in keeping with the performance of the machine. The front brake in particular was lacking in power and had a tendency to fade. Owing to the strength of the pull-off spring fitted to the rear brake rod, considerable pedal pressure was required to produce results; it was possible to lock the rear wheel, however. Heavy pressure was also needed on the front-brake lever.

Driving light provided by the Villiers headlamp was adequate for cruising up to 50 m.p.h. on unlit roads. Full lamp load was never balanced by the flywheel generator, but a drain on the accumulator could be avoided by use of the direct lighting position of the headlamp switch.

Initially, trouble was experienced with a choked petroil pipe after refuelling unless the fluids were pre-mixed. Subsequent fitting of a reserve-type tap, incorporating a gauze filter, overcame this shortcoming.

Information Panel

The 197 c.c. Norman B2S/DL

SPECIFICATION

ENGINE: Villiers 197 c.c. Mark 6E (59×77 mm) single-cylinder two-stroke. Roller-bearing big-end; ball bearings supporting mainshaft. Flat-crown, die-cast, aluminium-alloy piston. Detachable light-alloy cylinder head with hemispherical combustion chamber. Petroil lubrication.

CARBURETTOR: Villiers type 4/5, with twistgrip throttle control and separate mixture control operated by handlebar lever. Air filter.

TRANSMISSION: Villiers three-speed gear box in unit with the engine. Gear ratios: Bottom, 15.6 to 1. Second, 8.2 to 1. Top, 5.9 to 1. Primary chain, $\frac{1}{2} \times 0.205$in. in oil-bath case. Secondary chain, $\frac{1}{2} \times 0.205$in with guard over top run.

IGNITION AND LIGHTING: Villiers flywheel magneto with lighting coils. Westinghouse rectifier and Lucas 6-volt, 10 ampere-hour accumulator. Twin-filament, 24/24-watt main bulb; A.C./D.C. headlamp switch.

TANK CAPACITY: 2¾ gallons.

TYRES: Dunlop, 3.00×19in studded front and rear.

BRAKES: 5in diameter front and rear; finger-operated adjusters.

SUSPENSION: Telescopic front fork and pivoted-fork rear springing, both employing undamped, two-rate coil springs.

WHEELBASE: 51in. Ground clearance, 5in.

SEAT: Feridax Lightweight Dualseat. Height, 29in. unladen.

WEIGHT: 244lb fully equipped and with half a gallon of fuel.

PRICE: £108 7s 6d. With Purchase Tax (in Gt. Britain only), £138 9s 7d.

ROAD TAX: £1 17s 6d a year; 10s 4d a quarter.

DESCRIPTION: *The Motor Cycle*, 21 February 1952.

MAKERS: Norman Cycles Ltd., Beaver Road, Ashford, Kent.

PERFORMANCE DATA

MEAN MAXIMUM SPEED: Bottom: 27 m.p.h.
Second: 50 m.p.h.
Top: 60 m.p.h.

MEAN ACCELERATION:

	10-20 m.p.h.	15-25 m.p.h.	20-30 m.p.h.
Bottom	2.4 secs	2.2 secs	—
Second	3 secs	3 secs	4 secs
Top	—	—	5 secs

Mean speed at end of quarter-mile from rest: 55 m.p.h.
Mean time taken from 0-30 m.p.h.: 6.2 secs.

PETROIL CONSUMPTION: At 30 m.p.h., 110 m.p.g. At 40 m.p.h., 96 m.p.g. At 50 m.p.h., 64 m.p.g.

BRAKING: From 30 m.p.h. to rest, 42ft (surface, damp tar macadam).

TURNING CIRCLE: 12ft 6in.

MINIMUM NON-SNATCH SPEED: 17 m.p.h. in top gear.

WEIGHT PER C.C.: 1.22lb.

First published 29 January 1953

490 c.c. Model
All-purpose Overhead-valve Single Capable

IT is over a quarter of a century since the Model ES2 was introduced into the Norton range. Throughout that time it has retained its basic design characteristics and has achieved popularity as a reliable, pushrod-operated, overhead-valve, single-cylinder five-hundred with a full cradle frame. Now, with the adoption of pivoted-fork rear springing in addition to its telescopic front fork, it combines the traditional performance of the long-stroke big single with modern trends in wheel suspension.

In appearance the ES2 is well proportioned. Engine and gear box remained commendably oiltight

The riding position is good, though the reach from seat to handlebar is long for a rider of average build. The resultant extended-arm posture caused the rider's shoulders to ache on a long run. The most comfortable leg angle was achieved with the footrest hangers mounted one serration below the horizontal position. When the machine carried a pillion passenger, the rider's footrests could be made to ground fairly easily at this setting. Both brake and gear pedals could be ideally adjusted to suit the footrest position.

A standard fitment, the 25in-long dual-seat was comfortable and very well placed on the machine. It was found that the rider's natural seating position was at the front of the seat; hence there was ample room for rider and passenger, both wearing bulky winter riding kit. Owing to the combination of front-brake and air levers and clutch and ignition levers, it was not possible to arrange the horn button and dipswitch as closely to the grips as was desired for convenient operation. The speedometer registered four to five per cent fast throughout its range; both mileage recorders were inconsistent.

Engine starting from cold was normally effected at the first kick, provided that care was taken to depress the carburettor tickler only momentarily, and the throttle was opened no more than a sixteenth of an inch. An accessible throttle-stop adjuster on the carburettor obviates the need for fine judgment in this respect. When hot, the engine was more sensitive to fuel level and throttle opening. If it failed to respond at the second kick, a wide-open throttle could be relied upon to evoke a start. The tick-over was completely reliable, and retarding the ignition one-third eliminated a slight tendency for it to be erratic.

At the lower end of the r.p.m. scale, the engine responds to an unusual degree to the use of the ignition control. By this means considerable flexibility under traffic conditions could be achieved. There was no undue tendency to pinking, even on Pool petrol. Thus the use of 80-octane fuel produced no marked difference in acceleration and speed performance unless the engine was deliberately abused. Compression ratio of the model tested was 6.16 to 1. Piston slap was pronounced when the engine was cold; otherwise the engine was reasonably quiet mechanically.

In town, the Norton would tick along smoothly at 30 m.p.h. in top gear on full advance, though lusty acceleration from that speed necessitated use of the ignition control if some pinking was not to be heard. The charm of the engine lay in its lusty pulling power at low and moderate r.p.m., and its immediate response to throttle opening. Because of these characteristics, allied to its high gearing and the positive manner in which the clutch takes up the drive, the ES2's getaway is deceptively good.

It is difficult to define the most comfortable top-gear cruising speed. At 50 m.p.h. the machine lopes along lazily at a fast tick-over; at sixty, the engine still turns over freely and effortlessly. It is not until 70 m.p.h. is reached that the engine appears to be really working. This speed can be maintained indefinitely; indeed, the Norton never showed the slightest objection to the prolonged use of maximum performance. Engine vibration was negligible in the lower and middle speed ranges, but became more noticeable from just below 70 m.p.h. to the maximum, and was the chief factor in determining the highest indefinite cruising speed.

A characteristic which contributed to the achievement of 50 m.p.h. averages is the way in which the engine maintains a set cruising speed up long gradients without an increase in throttle

Latest ES2 rear suspension layout. Noteworthy features are the lifting handle and wide mudguard

ES2 Norton

of Effortless High-speed Cruising

The lusty long-stroke power unit is notable for its good low-speed pulling characteristics

opening. Power reserve is exemplified by the fact that maximum speed figures achieved by runs in opposite directions differed only by little over one m.p.h. The exhaust note was pleasant at moderate engine speeds but was obtrusive at large throttle openings.

It was a simple matter to effect clean gear changes. When changing up at low r.p.m. it was sometimes necessary to feel in the gears by engaging the clutch before pressure was removed from the gear pedal. At higher engine speeds, however, silent changes could be made, upward or downward, as quickly as the controls could be operated. Indeed, the more quickly and lightly the controls were manipulated, the sweeter was the gear change. Third and top gear ratios are pleasantly close. Neutral could be located easily from either bottom or second gear. With the engine idling, engagement of bottom gear from neutral was noiseless. The gear box was quiet in the indirect ratios.

Steering and cornering were first class. At no time was the steering damper required. In fact, its use, even lightly, tended to spoil low-speed cornering. Straight-ahead steering was positive and unaffected by road bumps provided that the rider resisted a subconscious tendency to pull on the handlebar owing to the long reach from the seat. Rippled surfaces produced a slight tendency for the machine to wriggle. Negotiation of slippery city streets showed excellent stability. If either wheel was locked at low speed, it skidded in a straight line. On slow corners or fast bends, the Norton could be heeled well over with complete confidence. Any desired line could easily be held on a bend.

Both front and rear springing were hard and could not be made to bottom. Normal movement of the rear wheel with the machine ridden solo was approximately one and a half inches, though the potential maximum movement permitted by the layout is 3½in. Road holding at high speeds was good.

Both brakes were smooth and reasonably powerful. Considerable pressure was needed on the front-brake lever to obtain good results. The heavy Bowdenex control cable gave a very solid feel to this lever; there was an entire absence of sponginess. The movement of the rear brake pedal necessary for full application of the brake was too long for comfort.

The main headlamp beam enabled the machine's maximum performance to be used at night; the pilot light was felt to be insufficiently conspicuous. Full lamp load was balanced by the dynamo at 30 m.p.h. in top gear. During the test, the dynamo ceased to charge; a replacement instrument, fitted by the dynamo makers' service department, proved satisfactory.

By means of the convenient side lifting handles, the machine could be easily placed on its excellent centre stand. The propstand fitted to the front of the engine cradle is efficient but proved inaccessible with the footrests set in the preferred position. The toolbox thumbscrew earned full marks for convenience.

Particularly effective was the 7½in-wide rear mudguard. A criticism can be levelled at the chromium plating of the exhaust pipe, which showed rust inside a week during which the machine was exposed to the elements; conversely, handlebar and tank were not similarly affected.

The 490 c.c Norton ES2

Information Panel

SPECIFICATION

ENGINE: 490 c.c. (79 × 100 mm) single-cylinder o.h.v. Fully enclosed valve gear. Ball and roller bearings supporting mainshafts. Compression ratio 6.16 to 1. Dry sump lubrication; oil-tank capacity, 4 pints.

CARBURETTOR: Amal, with lever-operated throttle-stop for easy starting. Twistgrip throttle control. Gauze air filter in intake.

IGNITION AND LIGHTING: Lucas Magdyno with manual ignition advance and retard control. 7in-diameter headlamp.

TRANSMISSION: Norton four-speed gear box with positive-stop foot control. Bottom, 14.2 to 1. Second, 8.4 to 1. Third, 5.75 to 1. Top, 4.75 to 1. Multi-plate clutch with Ferodo inserts. Primary chain, ½in. × 0.305in in pressed-steel oil-bath case. Secondary chain, ⅜in × ¼in. R.p.m. at 30 m.p.h. in top gear, 1,900.

FUEL CAPACITY: 3½ gallons.

TYRES: 3.25 × 19in Avon studded front and rear.

BRAKES: Both 7in diameter × 1¼in wide; hand adjusters.

SUSPENSION: Norton Roadholder telescopic front fork with hydraulic damping. Pivoted-fork rear springing employing coil springs and hydraulic damping.

WHEELBASE: 56½in unladen. Ground clearance, 5¼in unladen.

SEAT: Norton dual-seat. Unladen height, 30½in.

WEIGHT: 406 lb fully equipped and with approximately one gallon of fuel.

PRICE: £164. With Purchase Tax (in Britain only), £209 11s 1d.

ROAD TAX: £3 15s a year; £1 0s 8d a quarter.

MAKERS: Norton Motors, Ltd., Bracebridge Street, Birmingham, 6.

DESCRIPTION: *The Motor Cycle*, 2 October 1952.

PERFORMANCE DATA

MEAN MAXIMUM SPEED: Bottom :* 28 m.p.h.
Second :* 48 m.p.h.
Third :* 70 m.p.h.
Top : 79 m.p.h.
* Valve float occurring.

MEAN ACCELERATION:

	10-30 m.p.h.	20-40 m.p.h.	30-50 m.p.h.
Bottom	—	—	—
Second	4.2 secs	4 secs	—
Third	—	6.4 secs	6 secs
Top	—	8 secs	8 secs

Speed at end of quarter-mile from rest: 68 m.p.h.
Time to cover standing quarter-mile: 18.8 secs.

PETROL CONSUMPTION: At 30 m.p.h., 96 m.p.g. At 40 m.p.h., 77 m.p.g. At 50 m.p.h., 65 m.p.g. At 60 m.p.h., 50 m.p.g.

BRAKING: From 30 m.p.h. to rest, 33ft (surface, damp tar macadam).

TURNING CIRCLE: 16ft 6in.

MINIMUM NON-SNATCH SPEED: 20 m.p.h. in top gear, with ignition fully retarded.

WEIGHT PER C.C.: 0.81 lb.

498 c.c. Triumph

First published 12 March 1953

A Silk-smooth, A.C. Generator-equipped Tourer With Brisk

FORERUNNER of the vertical-twin vogue, the Triumph Speed Twin, in its 1953 form, is fitted with an alternating-current generator which supplies current for both lighting and coil ignition, thus superseding the separate dynamo and magneto. One of the traditional bugbears of motor cycle coil ignition—reliance on battery condition for engine starting—is eliminated by the incorporation of an emergency ignition circuit whereby the full generator can be fed direct to the coil, should the battery be in a discharged condition.

With its finish of amaranth red enamel and chromium plating, the Speed Twin is distinctly handsome

This change still further enhances the appeal of the 5T as an excellently mannered, de-luxe, medium-capacity touring machine. The absence of separate drives for magneto and dynamo certainly makes a contribution to quietness of operation of the engine and, as mentioned later in this report, the engine starts whether the battery is in circuit or not. Sweetness, in all aspects of the performance, is an outstanding characteristic. Power delivery is smooth and the transmission silky. Acceleration was zestful, yet gentlemanly. All controls operated with an easy lightness which made the machine a delight to ride, alike in town and on the open road.

Such is the flexibility and even torque of the engine that, within the limits of available performance, cruising speed is dependent solely upon the mood of the rider. One may go through the gears without exceeding the speed limit in built-up areas, or one may make upward changes at 30, 50 and 65 m.p.h. One may cruise at 40 m.p.h. or at 70—always there is the same cultured and unobtrusive performance, accompanied by a pleasant hum from the silencers, and no more than a rustle from the engine. Response to the throttle, from idling speeds upward, was immediate, yet devoid of any trace of harshness. With the exception of a slightly rich spot just off the pilot jet, carburation was commendably clean throughout the range. A new and effective rubber transmission shock absorber is incorporated in the clutch; this change was made necessary because the engine drive-side mainshaft now carries the alternator rotor.

It would be difficult to conceive an easier and more certain starter than the 5T engine. The first depression of the kickstarter invariably brought a healthy response assuming light flooding of the carburettor and a small opening of the throttle. The air lever, mounted under the seat, required to be closed only when the engine was started under cold conditions. Once the engine was warm, it settled down to a remarkably slow and reliable tickover when the throttle was closed. Piston slap was audible when the engine was cold, but at normal running temperatures mechanical noise was unobtrusive; new cam contours incorporating quietening ramps contribute largely toward the quietness of the valve gear.

Engagement of bottom gear from neutral with the machine stationary and the engine running was slightly audible, though this noise could be reduced to an almost negligible degree by utilizing the engine's excellent tickover. The achievement of completely silent upward gear changes required a slight pause in pedal movement. However, if desired, clean downward changes could be made as rapidly as the controls could be operated. Gear-pedal movement was very light. Neutral selection was positive from either first or second gear. The gear ratios are excellently chosen for all normal conditions of use; the clutch was very smooth in its take-up of the drive and was light to operate.

A comfortable and natural riding position adds much to the pleasure of riding the Triumph. The relationship of handlebar, seat and footrests is excellent for all normal cruising speeds, and the twinseat is well upholstered. Accommodation for the pillionist was reasonably comfortable, though long journeys with both

The distributor is driven from the rear of the timing case; above it is mounted the ignition coil

Speed Twin

Performance and Excellent Road Manners

rider and passenger heavily clad indicated that slightly greater length of the seat would have been an advantage.

Rear-brake and gear pedals could be ideally adjusted relative to the footrests. Operation of the clutch and front-brake levers, however, required what was considered a large hand span, and for the test, improvised stops were fitted and found advantageous. Full marks are due for the excellent positioning of the horn button and dipswitch alongside the left and right handlebar grips respectively.

Further aids to rider and passenger comfort are the front- and rear-wheel suspensions. The telescopic fork absorbed road shocks with a soft, progressive action, and was adequately damped. Bottoming could be provoked only by braking hard on a bumpy surface when carrying a passenger. The spring hub largely eliminated shocks from the rear wheel, though its comparatively short travel meant that severe bumps at high speeds were not completely absorbed.

Straight-ahead steering of the Triumph was positive on all road surfaces, and the steering damper was never brought into use. On bends and corners, the model could be heeled over stylishly with every confidence; in fact, it was characteristic of the steering that a generous degree of banking was required for cornering. In keeping with the general sweetness of the machine's performance, both brakes were smooth, progressive and powerful in action.

For experimental purposes, the Lucas alternator was subjected to a drastic test which provided impressive evidence of its capabilities. The 6-volt accumulator was completely discharged immediately before a 150-mile night journey. Not only did the engine respond to the first depression of the kick-starter (with the ignition switch turned to the emergency position), but full intensity of the head-lamp beam was maintained throughout the journey regardless of engine speed. Additionally, a steady 6-amp charge was recorded on the ammeter, and the battery was found to be com-

Grouping of controls and instruments is neat and functional

pletely re-charged at the end of the long night journey.

Output of the alternator is automatically regulated by the demand made upon it. At 55-60 m.p.h. in top gear, the ammeter showed a 1½-amp charge with the headlamp switch in the off position, a 3-amp charge with the pilot, rear and speedometer lights on, and a full 6-amp input with the main headlamp bulb in use.

The sealed-beam light unit provided a wide spread of light which was entirely adequate for speeds in the seventies on straight roads after dark. On bends, however, the shallow depth of the beam resulted in a shortening of its range which could be disconcerting. An accurate check of the speedometer showed the instrument to read approximately ten per cent fast at all speeds.

The connoisseur will appreciate several rider's points. These include the fuel-tank capacity of four gallons plus; the offset filler cap, permitting an easy visual check of the fuel level; the tank-top parcels grid; and the eminently sensible extension which enables the prop stand to be operated easily with the foot. Added to these features, the very handsome appearance and the excellent amaranth red and chromium-plated finish, inspire pride of ownership.

Information Panel

498 c.c. Triumph Speed Twin

SPECIFICATION

ENGINE: 498 c.c. (63 x 80 mm) vertical twin o.h.v.; fully enclosed valve gear; Hiduminium alloy connecting rods; plain-bearing big-ends; mainshafts mounted on ball and roller bearings. Dry-sump lubrication; oil-tank capacity, 6 pints.

CARBURETTOR: Amal; twistgrip throttle control; air slide operated by cable with lever situated under seat. Vokes air filter.

TRANSMISSION: Triumph four-speed gear box with positive-stop foot control. Bottom, 12.2 to 1. Second, 8.45 to 1. Third, 5.95 to 1. Top, 5 to 1. Multi-plate clutch with cork inserts operating in oil. Primary chain, ½ x 0.305in, in oil-bath case. Rear chain, ⅝ x ⅜in, lubricated by bleed from primary chaincase. Guards over both runs of rear chain. R.p.m. at 30 m.p.h. in top gear, 1,950.

IGNITION and LIGHTING: Coil ignition with automatic advance and retard. Lucas RM12 alternator mounted on drive-side mainshaft and supplying current via Westinghouse rectifier to 6-volt, 13-amp-hour battery. 7in-diameter headlamp with sealed-beam light unit.

FUEL CAPACITY: 4 gallons.

TYRES: Dunlop. Front, 3.25 x 19in ribbed. Rear, 3.50 x 19in Universal.

BRAKES: Triumph 7 x 1⅛in front; 8 x 1⅛in rear; hand adjusters.

SUSPENSION: Triumph telescopic front fork with hydraulic damping. Triumph spring hub in rear wheel.

WHEELBASE: 55½in unladen. Ground clearance, 4½in unladen.

SADDLE: Triumph Twinseat; unladen height, 30½in.

WEIGHT: 364 lb with no fuel, full oil tank, and fully equipped (including pillion footrests and prop stand).

PRICE: £159; with purchase tax (in Britain only), £203 3s 4d. Spring hub extra, £16, plus £4 8s 11d purchase tax. Twinseat, pillion footrests and prop stand extra.

MAKERS: Triumph Engineering Co., Ltd., Meriden Works, Allesley, Coventry.

DESCRIPTION: *The Motor Cycle*, 11 September, 1952.

PERFORMANCE DATA

MEAN MAXIMUM SPEED: Bottom: 40 m.p.h.
Second: 60 m.p.h.
Third: 76 m.p.h.
Top: 83 m.p.h.

MEAN ACCELERATION:

	10-30 m.p.h.	20-40 m.p.h.	30-50 m.p.h.
Bottom	2.8 secs	2.6 secs	—
Second	4 secs	3.6 secs	3.6 secs
Third	—	6.4 secs	5.8 secs
Top	—	7.6 secs	7.6 secs

Mean speed at end of quarter-mile from rest: 74 m.p.h.
Mean time to cover standing quarter-mile: 17.4 secs.

PETROL CONSUMPTION: At 30 m.p.h., 95 m.p.g. At 40 m.p.h., 75 m.p.g. At 50 m.p.h., 62 m.p.g. At 60 m.p.h., 51 m.p.g.

BRAKING: From 30 m.p.h. to rest, 30ft (surface, dry tar macadam).

TURNING CIRCLE: 15ft 6in.

MINIMUM NON-SNATCH SPEED: 20 m.p.h. in top gear.

WEIGHT PER C.C.: 0.73 lb.

First published 26 March 1953

499 c.c. Overhead-valve

A Robust, Economical Roadster with First-class

THE B.S.A. B33, with standard or spring-frame specification, is the lowest-priced overhead-valve five-hundred on the British market. Its comparatively low price is not, however, achieved at the expense of quality or performance. Robustly constructed and good-looking, the B33 combines lively and tireless engine performance with first-class steering and suspension, powerful braking and commendable fuel economy. Reasonably smooth and usable power is produced over the major portion of the engine's r.p.m. range. This flexibility, together with transmission sweetness, renders the machine equally pleasant for town or open-road travel. Manual ignition control is provided, and the engine proved to be sensitive to its use. On full advance, engine performance was very brisk; one-third to a half retard endowed it with a degree of docility appropriate to heavy traffic conditions; full retard, though used only for test purposes, provided the lusty pulling characteristics normally associated with large-capacity, side-valve engines.

In town, engine and transmission were perfectly happy at 30 m.p.h. in top gear. Indeed, the B33 would accelerate smoothly in this gear from the minimum non-snatch speeds of 18 m.p.h. on full retard and 22 m.p.h. on full advance, with no precaution other than reasonably slow initial opening of the throttle. In bottom gear, with the ignition retarded, smooth travel at a pace too low to register on the speedometer was easily achieved.

Away from built-up areas, a top-gear cruising speed of anything up to 75 m.p.h. on the speedometer could comfortably be maintained for as long as the rider wished. A trace of engine vibration was perceptible, but this did not reach an objectionable magnitude until the speedometer needle was approaching the 80 m.p.h. mark in top gear, or at corresponding readings in the indirect ratios. An accurate check of the speedometer showed it to record approximately seven per cent fast up to 40 m.p.h., and ten per cent fast from 50 m.p.h. upward.

At moderate throttle openings, the exhaust note was not offensive, but it was inclined to be loud and "flat" at wide throttle openings. This noise tended to restrict the degree of acceleration which could be used without embarrassment in built-up areas, and proved tiring on long, fast runs. Banging in the silencer occurred occasionally when the engine was on the overrun, and could not be alleviated by adjustment of the pilot air screw. Both the piston and valve gear were audible with the engine cold or hot.

In the matter of cold starting, the engine was sensitive to carburettor flooding. If the float tickler was depressed, two or three kicks were required to bring the engine to life. Better results were obtained by ignoring the tickler and merely leaning the machine slightly to the right for a few seconds after turning on the petrol. This drill usually brought a first-kick response. Full advance could be employed for starting purposes, provided that only a minute throttle opening was used. Starting with the engine warm was simple and certain. As one would expect, idling was slightly erratic with the ignition fully advanced; retardation produced a reliable tickover which was sufficiently slow for individual power strokes to be easily counted.

The gear change could have been sweeter and more positive with advantage. The gear box is of the wide-ratio type, and pedal movement was accompanied by a "scrunch" which could be felt rather than heard; if clean upward changes were to be made, an extremely leisurely movement of the pedal was required. Sometimes, when changing up from second gear at a lowish speed, it was found that a false neutral between third and top ratios had been selected. Neutral was easy to locate from either bottom or second gear. Clutch operation was moderately light; take-up of the drive was smooth and positive.

The B.S.A.'s riding position was excellent for a rider of average build. The relationship of footrests and seat was such as to provide a comfortable knee-angle. Long distances could be covered without fatigue. A pillion passenger could comfortably be accommodated on the dual-seat. All controls could be adjusted for convenient operation. When the gear pedal was suitably positioned for operation without removing the right foot from its rest, however, it was found to foul the shank of the footrest during upward changes. Appropriate filing of the pedal on the test machine overcame this problem.

Robust construction and pleasing appearance characterize the B33

The engine revelled in hard work and remained commendably oil-tight

B.S.A. B33

Steering and Road-holding

Wheel suspension, too, made an important contribution to rider comfort; both front and rear springing operated admirably with either one or two people aboard the machine. Soft around the static-load position, the front fork absorbed small and large road shocks effectively, while the plunger rear springing had a moderately soft and useful range of movement. Together, they resulted in a high standard of road holding. Occasionally, there was slight pitching when travelling fast over bumpy surfaces, but this was never sufficient to be of more than academic interest. Slight fork chopping could be induced only by very heavy use of the powerful front brake.

Under all road conditions the steering of the B33 was first-class and rock steady. A trifle heavy at low speeds, the steering had a strong self-centring characteristic and was noticeably positive. Never was there the slightest suspicion that the steering damper was other than an ornament. Whether the machine was heeled over slightly or generously, the front wheel automatically turned inward by just the right amount to provide safe and confident cornering.

Powerful Brakes

The efficiency of the brakes was such as to encourage the rider to make full use of the machine's road performance. The 8in front brake, previously fitted only to the Gold Star and twin-cylinder models, is now standardized on the B33. Light and smooth in operation, it is extremely powerful. In use, from any speed within the model's capabilities, it could be made to provoke a squeal of protest from the front tyre. For most of the test period, brake application gave rise to a loud squeal from the brake drum. Dismantling of the brake and the cleaning out of an accumulation of friction-material dust largely mitigated, but did not entirely eliminate, this tendency. The rear brake was also smooth and efficient; employment of both brakes together brought the machine to a safe and rapid halt whenever required.

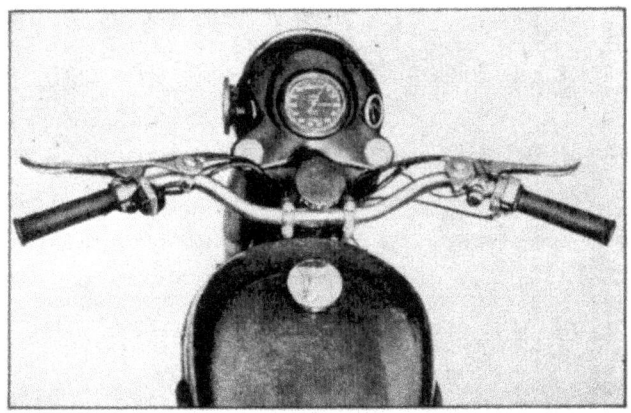

Rider's view of the new headlamp cowl; light switch is on the left, ammeter on the right

The headlamp afforded an adequate beam for night riding. It was by no means easy to check the charging rate accurately owing to the angular disposition of the ammeter in the head-lamp cowl.

Throughout a hard, 1,000-mile test, the engine and gear box remained commendably oil-tight, save for a slight leakage from the gear-pedal shaft. A small quantity of grease leaked from the right-hand rear-springing unit and discoloured the silencer. Some blueing of the exhaust pipe and silencer took place. There was also a tendency for the rear chain to run dry.

The deeply valanced front mudguard proved effective in keeping a good deal of road filth from the machine. The chromium-plated wheel rims proved easy to clean. With its chromium-plated tank panels and excellent maroon enamel finish, the B33 has an attractive appearance. An excellent kit of tools is provided, and proved adequate for all routine maintenance.

To sum up, the B.S.A. B33, in performance and quality, represents excellent value for money.

Information Panel

499 c.c. B.S.A. B33

SPECIFICATION

ENGINE: 499 c.c. (85 × 88mm) single-cylinder o.h.v. with fully-enclosed valve gear. Ball and roller bearing for drive-side mainshaft; ball bearing and plain outrigger bearing for timing side. Gear driven magneto. Dry-sump lubrication by gear pumps; oil tank capacity, 4 pints.

CARBURETTOR: Amal, with twistgrip throttle. Air slide operated by handlebar lever.

TRANSMISSION: B.S.A. four-speed gear box with positive-stop foot control. Bottom, 14.9 to 1. Second, 10.3 to 1. Third, 6.59 to 1. Top, 5 to 1. Multi-plate clutch. Primary chain, ½ × 0.305in, in oil-bath case. Rear chain, ⅝ × ¼in, with guard over top run. R.p.m. at 30 m.p.h. in top gear, 1,950.

IGNITION and LIGHTING: Lucas Magdyno with manual ignition control on handlebar. 7in-diameter headlamp with sealed-beam light unit.

FUEL CAPACITY: 3 gallons.

TYRES: Dunlop Universal, 3.25 × 19in front, 3.50 × 19in rear.

BRAKES: 8in diameter front, 7in diameter rear; hand adjusters.

SUSPENSION: B.S.A. telescopic front fork with hydraulic damping; plunger-type rear springing.

WHEELBASE: 54½in unladen. Ground clearance, 5½in unladen.

SEAT: B.S.A. dual-seat. Unladen height, 30½in.

WEIGHT: 420lb with no fuel, full oil tank, and fully equipped.

PRICE: £140 10s; with purchase tax (in Britain only), £179 10s 7d. Extras: Rear springing, £9 (P.T., £2 10s); dual-seat, £3 (P.T. 16s 8d); pillion footrests, 10s (P.T., 2s 10d).

ROAD TAX: £3 15s a year; £1 0s 8d a quarter.

MAKERS: B.S.A. Cycles, Ltd., Birmingham, 11.

DESCRIPTION: *The Motor Cycle*, 25 September, 1952.

PERFORMANCE DATA

MEAN MAXIMUM SPEED: Bottom :* 31 m.p.h.
Second :* 44 m.p.h.
Third :* 69 m.p.h.
Top: 80 m.p.h.
* Valve float occurring.

MEAN ACCELERATION:

	10-30 m.p.h.	20-40 m.p.h.	30-50 m.p.h.
Bottom	2.8 secs	—	—
Second	3.6 secs	3.5 secs	—
Third	—	5 secs	5.4 secs
Top	—	7.5 secs	7.6 secs

Mean speed at end of quarter-mile from rest: 70 m.p.h.
Mean time to cover standing quarter-mile: 18.2 secs.

PETROL CONSUMPTION: At 30 m.p.h., 112 m.p.g. At 40 m.p.h. 90 m.p.g. At 50 m.p.h., 66 m.p.g. At 60 m.p.h., 53 m.p.g.

BRAKING: From 30 m.p.h. to rest, 28ft 6in (surface, dry tarmac).

TURNING CIRCLE: 15ft.

MINIMUM NON-SNATCH SPEED: 18 m.p.h. in top gear, with ignition fully retarded.

WEIGHT PER C.C.: 0.84lb.

997 c.c. Mark II Ariel

First published 23 April 1953

A Unique High-performance Mount with Gentle Manners

SINCE only two British manufacturers market machines in the 1,000 c.c. class, it might be asserted that the thousand, as a type, has a limited appeal—an appeal restricted to fastidious connoisseurs. However, the latest version of the long-established Ariel Square Four—the 997 c.c. Mark II—by the enhanced versatility of its performance over that of its predecessors, extends the appeal of the 1,000 c.c. machine to the widest possible range of tastes. An outstanding trait of the model is the smoothness and flexibility of its engine torque over an unusually large range of r.p.m. The outcome of more than 20 years' development of the original concept, the 4G Mark II combines, in large measure, the docility for which Ariel Fours have always been renowned with an open-road potential capable of satisfying the most hardened road burner.

The lines of the latest Ariel Four are distinctly sleek and well proportioned. Chromium-plated flashes enhance the appearance of the five-gallon fuel tank

The Ariel's repertoire contains a type of performance to suit a rider's every mood. It may be ridden in top gear at speeds below 20 m.p.h. Alternatively, full use may be made of the engine's high power output in all gears. In either case, acceleration is exceptionally smooth, quiet and unhesitant; if the full performance is used, acceleration has an urgency matched by few road-going vehicles. Intermediately, the Square Four will cruise quietly and unostentatiously at 50, 60 or 70 m.p.h. on a mere "whiff" of throttle.

For long or short journeys, the Ariel was easy and pleasant to ride. Factors contributing to this characteristic were comfortable wheel suspension, excellent riding position and control layout, a large reserve of engine power, good brakes and—not least in importance—a high degree of exhaust and mechanical quietness. At no period in the performance range does the exhaust note rise above a pleasant, subdued hum. Mechanical noise, except when the engine was idling, was reminiscent of that of a well-oiled sewing machine. On tickover, the only audible noises were in the form of a rumble from the crankshaft coupling gears, and a slight rustle from the valve-gear.

In spite of its weight, the 4G Mark II has a high degree of handleability. On slow and medium-pace corners it could be heeled over confidently until the prop stand or silencers grounded — which could occur readily when the suspension was loaded by the added weight of a pillion passenger. This ease of handling, coupled with the machine's zestful but unobtrusive acceleration, made the Ariel a commendably safe and pleasant machine to use under traffic conditions.

The riding position is a fine compromise between an "armchair" layout for maximum comfort at town speeds, and a slight crouch for fatigue resistance at high speeds—with, perhaps, a slight bias towards the former. Relationship of seat and footrests resulted in an agreeably wide knee angle. The shape of the handlebar provided a natural position for the grips. Seat height was such as to enable a rider of average height easily to place his feet on the ground at traffic halts. All controls could be well placed for ease of operation and were silky to use. Those on the handlebar are reduced to a minimum number. The twistgrip has a somewhat longer than usual rotary travel, a feature providing a delicacy of throttle control which enhances the already outstanding sweetness of the engine.

Starting the four-cylinder engine was always simple. No great muscular effort was required to operate the kick-starter, even when the machine had been standing outdoors overnight in the cold weather experienced in March. Under such conditions, three depressions of the starter pedal were normally sufficient to start the engine with the carburettor bi-starter control in operation. This control could be moved to its intermediate stop after a few seconds' running, and moved to its normal-running position when the machine had covered about a quarter of a mile. When warm, the engine could be brought to life by no more than a leisurely movement of the kick-starter. Carburation at very small throttle openings was uneven, particularly when the engine was cold.

With the engine idling, bottom gear could be engaged noiselessly from neutral. Occasionally, partial release of the clutch was required for gear selection. Neutral was at all times easy to locate from either bottom or second gears. Clutch operation was reasonably light and entirely positive. Gear changes, both upward and downward, could be effected with great rapidity. Owing to the engine's unusually quick response to throttle opening and

Close-up view of the massive, yet compact, four-cylinder engine. The distributor is seen in front of the oil tank

Square Four
and Outstanding Acceleration

closing, it was found that a fast gear-changing technique achieved the best results. Partial clutch and throttle operation, with a simultaneous, light depression of the gear pedal, produced excellent upward changes, though sometimes second and top gear engagement could be felt slightly. Second to third was a particularly sweet change. Clean and ultra-rapid downward changes were easily made.

Both front and rear wheel suspensions possessed an adequate range of movement and worked well at all speeds. A reasonably soft response around the static-load position and a progressively increasing resistance to deflection brought both small and large surface irregularities within the compass of the springing. Only at ultra-high speeds, on surfaces which were not smooth, did a certain amount of pitching set in. Steering was first class, being both light and positive; bend-swinging was quite effortless. A slight tendency to weave was apparent only when travelling at very high velocities on bad surfaces. The top hamper of a full, five-gallon fuel tank was virtually unnoticeable, except under extreme conditions.

Both brakes were pleasantly light to operate, smooth and extremely powerful. Though their hard use incurred frequent need for adjustment in the early stages of the test, the adjustment took only a matter of seconds.

In the matter of ultimate road performance, the figures shown in the panel speak for themselves. In fact, these data were obtained after the machine had been ridden exceptionally hard for 1,500 miles with little attention, and when a gusty, 15-20 m.p.h. three-quarter wind prevailed. There can be little doubt that, under more favourable conditions, a mean maximum speed of 100 m.p.h. would have been recorded. The fastest one-way run in top gear was at 107 m.p.h.

Under suitable road and traffic conditions, speeds of 80-85 m.p.h. could be maintained for as long as required. In a deliberate attempt to tire the engine, the machine was ridden for many miles with the speedometer needle hovering between 90 and 95 m.p.h., but the engine betrayed not the least sign of distress. Its reserve of power enabled high cruising speeds to be sustained against headwinds and up long gradients, thus making high average speeds commonplace. A slight vibration period

Noteworthy features are the neatness of the power unit and the 20-amp-hour battery. The ignition coil and voltage regulator are mounted beneath the seat

sets in between 50 and 55 m.p.h., but is not felt above 60 m.p.h.

The minimum non-snatch speed is of more than academic interest in the case of the Ariel. In the normal course of town riding, it was frequently throttled back below 20 m.p.h. in top gear and accelerated away sweetly.

The speedometer fitted to the test machine had a high standard of accuracy up to 60 m.p.h. There was virtually no error up to 50 m.p.h.; from 60 to 90 m.p.h. the instrument registered four to five m.p.h. fast. Failure of the ammeter necessitated a replacement during the test. When riding on flooded roads, there was a tendency for one sparking plug to cut out.

The main head lamp bulb provided an adequate beam for fast night riding. The dynamo balanced the full ignition and lamp load at 30 m.p.h. in top gear.

The discerning Ariel Four owner will appreciate the 20-amp-hour battery and its accessibility for topping-up purposes. Another praiseworthy feature is the fuel-tank capacity, which enables 200-250 miles to be covered at high cruising speeds without refuelling. In spite of the machine's weight, it is a relatively easy matter to place it on its rear stand. The accessible prop stand is excellent for use on cambered roads.

Information Panel

997 c.c. Ariel Square Four Mark II

SPECIFICATION

ENGINE: 997 c.c. (65 × 75 mm) four-cylinder o.h.v. Aluminium-alloy cylinders cast *en bloc* in square formation. Detachable light-alloy cylinder head embodying cruciform induction manifold; totally enclosed and positively lubricated valve gear, with push-rod operation; separate exhaust manifolds. Twin crankshafts coupled by hardened and ground gears. Light-alloy connecting rods with plain, shell-type big-end bearings. Compression ratio, 7.2 to 1. Dry sump lubrication; oil-tank capacity, 6 pints.

CARBURETTOR: Solex, Bi-starter type; twistgrip throttle control.

IGNITION and LIGHTING: Coil ignition. 70-watt, voltage-controlled Lucas dynamo incorporating distributor with automatic timing variation. 7 in-diameter headlamp with sealed-beam light unit. 6-volt, 20-amp-hour Lucas battery.

TRANSMISSION: Burman four-speed gear box with positive-stop foot control. Bottom, 11.07 to 1. Second, 7.1 to 1. Third, 5.46 to 1. Top, 4.18 to 1. Multi-plate clutch with Neoprene inserts, operating in remote case. Primary chain, ⅜ × 0.305 in. in oil-bath case. Secondary chain, ⅝ × ⅜in, lubricated by adjustable bleed from primary chaincase; guards over top and bottom runs. R.p.m. at 30 m.p.h. in top gear, 1,675.

FUEL CAPACITY: 5 gallons.

TYRES: Dunlop. Front, 3.25 × 19in Ribbed. Rear, 4.00 × 18in Universal.

BRAKES: 7 × 1¼in front; 8 × 1¼in rear. Fulcrum adjusters.

SUSPENSION: Ariel telescopic front fork with hydraulic damping. Ariel link-action rear springing.

WHEELBASE: 56½in. Ground clearance, 4½in unladen.

SEAT: Ariel dual-seat. Unladen height, 30in.

WEIGHT: 460 lb fully equipped, with no fuel and full oil tank.

PRICE: £225. With purchase tax (in Gt. Britain only), £271 17s. 6d. Extras: Spring frame, £16 (with P.T., £19 6s 8d.)

ROAD TAX: £3 15s a year; £1 0s 8d a quarter.

MAKERS: Ariel Motors, Ltd., Selly Oak, Birmingham, 29

DESCRIPTION: *The Motor Cycle*, 6 November, 1952.

PERFORMANCE DATA

MEAN MAXIMUM SPEED: Bottom: *40 m.p.h.
Second: *62 m.p.h.
Third: *79 m.p.h.
Top: 97 m.p.h.
* Valve float occuring.

MEAN ACCELERATION:

	10-30 m.p.h.	20-40 m.p.h.	30-50 m.p.h.
Bottom	2 secs	2 secs	—
Second	3.2 secs	2.6 secs	2.5 secs
Third	4.4 secs	3.8 secs	3.4 secs
Top	—	5.4 secs	5 secs

Speed at end of quarter-mile from rest: 85 m.p.h.
Mean time to cover standing quarter-mile: 15.4 secs.

PETROL CONSUMPTION: At 30 m.p.h., 57 m.p.g. At 40 m.p.h., 55 m.p.g. At 50 m.p.h., 54 m.p.g. At 60 m.p.h., 50 m.p.g.

BRAKING: From 30 m.p.h. to rest, 26ft 6in (surface, dry tarmac).

TURNING CIRCLE: 15ft.

MINIMUM NON-SNATCH SPEED: 13 m.p.h. in top gear.

WEIGHT Per C.C.: 0.46 lb.

> First published 30 April 1953

122 c.c. Spring-frame

A Well-finished Lightweight, with Tireless Performance

THE James Cadet J/5 caused a stir at the London Show last November when it was seen to be the lowest-priced, fully sprung 125 c.c. machine on the British market. Retailing today for less than £85, including British purchase tax, it offers not only an all-round performance equal to the best in its class, but also a standard of detail design and finish worthy of a much more costly machine. The acknowledged advantages of its type—economy, light weight, ease of handling both on the road and in the garage—it possesses in full measure. With

In spite of its low price, the James is beautifully finished. The riding position is first class

these attractions of the Cadet J/5 go such refinements as P.V.C.-covered control cables, a sealed-beam headlamp unit and adjustable footrests.

As a utility mount, the James proved equally suitable for use on crowded city roads or for long-distance touring. Its Villiers Mark 13D engine—latest version of the 122 c.c. unit—delivered its power smoothly and lustily over a commendably wide range of r.p.m. Once the engine was warm, acceleration was quite lively for a unit of this capacity. This characteristic, in conjunction with the small overall dimensions, rendered the machine very handy for negotiating city traffic. The engine would two-stroke well from idling speed upward, provided that it was pulling—however lightly. At traffic halts, the engine's excellent idling manners were appreciated. Tick-over was slow and reliable, with only a minimum of the irregular firing which is common to all two-stroke engines under these conditions.

Away from legal speed restrictions, a happy, indefinite, top-gear cruising speed was with the speedometer needle anywhere between 15 and over 40 m.p.h. When pottering at the lower end of this range, both engine and transmission were smooth, though four-stroking, of course, set in under conditions of overrun. At the upper figure, the engine was perfectly content for as long as might be required and exhibited no signs of distress. Indeed, once it was adequately run-in, the engine readily endured prolonged use of full throttle without any indication of fatigue.

On long, main-road journeys, all-in average speeds in excess of 35 m.p.h. were comfortably achieved without recourse to full throttle. Engine balance was excellent and there was no appreciable vibration period to dictate cruising speed. Neither was it possible to provoke transmission snatch except by the use of inordinately low engine r.p.m.

Thanks to the machine's light weight and the engine's excellent pulling power and flywheel inertia, hill climbing was good. Long, main-road gradients of average severity could, if required, be climbed at a speedometer 40 m.p.h. An accurate check of the speedometer showed it to register fast by approximately 1 m.p.h. at 20, 2 m.p.h. at 30 and 3 m.p.h. at 40.

Starting the engine was delightfully easy whether it was hot or cold. Throughout the test, it was quite exceptional for more than one depression of the kick-starter to be required, even when the James had been standing outdoors overnight. Closing the air strangler, flooding the carburettor and opening the throttle about one-third were the requirements for a cold start. The first two operations mentioned were not necessary once the engine was warm. Full kick-starter movement could be used without the rider's foot fouling the footrest.

When getting away with the engine cold, it was necessary to leave the strangler nearly closed for about a quarter-mile, after which it could be opened farther and eventually moved to full open when approximately half-a-mile had been covered. The only audible mechanical noise from the engine was a whine, more pronounced at high speeds but not regarded as offensive. It was considered that the exhaust note could, with advantage, have been quieter at large throttle openings (at over 35 m.p.h. in top gear and at corresponding speeds in the lower ratios).

Gear changing was a pleasure. With the machine at rest and the engine idling, bottom gear could be engaged noiselessly from neutral, though sometimes partial release of the clutch lever was required to assist engagement. The clutch was light to operate and sweet and positive in its take-up of the drive. An accessible, finger-operated fulcrum adjuster is provided. Movement of the gear pedal

At no time during the course of the test did the plunger-type rear suspension bottom

James Cadet
and Excellent Riding Comfort

was short and light, and clean, rapid changes were easily effected. Only the slightest pause in gear pedal movement was required to ensure a quiet change from bottom to second gear. The other upward change and both downward changes, at appropriate speeds, could be made cleanly as quickly as the controls could be operated. No difficulty was experienced in selecting neutral from bottom or second gears.

Though the machine is small, its riding position was found to be comfortable for a rider of medium stature. Saddle height was just right for traffic stops. A useful range of footrest adjustment is provided, and the handlebar can be swivelled in its clamps. Several hours at a time spent in the saddle produced no discomfort. The gear pedal could be positioned ideally relative to the right footrest. The rear-brake pedal could be operated without removing a foot from the rest though, with the rest in the preferred position, the pedal was a shade high and tucked in. Their pivot blocks welded in position, the handlebar levers were excellently placed.

Steering and Stability

Both front and rear wheel suspension layouts are neat in appearance. In use, they have a taut feeling and the machine is innocent of any tendency to pitching. Neither front nor rear springing was bottomed in normal use on rough roads, and a good degree of rider comfort was provided. Bumpy surfaces could be negotiated at speed without wheel hop and with the rider largely insulated from road shocks.

Steering and stability of the James were first class. Straight-ahead steering was positive down to single-figure speeds; on bends, the machine could be heeled well over with confidence and would hold a chosen line steadily. Only by excessively exuberant cornering could the footrests be made to touch the ground. For test purposes, it was found quite easy to control the machine both on straights and bends with the hands removed from the handlebar, even at comparatively low speeds.

Cruising speeds of over 40 m.p.h. are possible with the new 122 c.c. Mark 13D Villiers engine

As mentioned earlier, the Cadet J/5 required a minimum of physical effort for its handling, both in motion and when stationary. It was very easy to lift on to its centre stand, by which means either wheel could be brought well clear of the ground—a riding coat placed over the front wheel provided the necessary bias to raise the rear wheel.

Both brakes were smooth and light in operation, and provided adequate stopping power for the machine's weight and performance. The headlamp furnished a driving beam which, on the majority of roads, enabled daytime speeds to be maintained after dark.

The only blemishes on the machine at the end of the test were slight oil stains at the silencer joints, and some messiness around the carburettor as a result of flooding for starting purposes. Well-proportioned lines and excellent finish give the James an attractive appearance. Delivery tune of the test model was of a very high standard. The instruction book is unusually comprehensive and well set out.

Information Panel

122 c.c. James Cadet J/5

SPECIFICATION

ENGINE: Villiers 122 c.c. Mark 13D (50 × 62 mm) single-cylinder two-stroke. Flat-crown, die-cast, aluminium-alloy piston. Roller bearing big-end; mainshaft supported on three ball bearings. Detachable, light-alloy cylinder head. Compression ratio, 8 to 1. Petroil lubrication.
CARBURETTOR: Villiers Single-lever, with twistgrip throttle control. Air filter, incorporating strangler.
TRANSMISSION: Villiers three-speed, foot-change gear box in unit with engine. Bottom, 19.5 to 1. Second, 10.2 to 1. Top, 7.33 to 1. Primary chain, ⅜ × 0.225in, in oil-bath case. Rear chain, ½ × 0.205in, with guard over top run. R.p.m. at 30 m.p.h. in top gear, 3,050.
IGNITION and LIGHTING: Villiers flywheel magneto incorporating lighting coils. 6in-diameter headlamp with sealed-beam light unit; twin filament 30/24-watt main bulb. Dry batteries in separate container for parking lights.
PETROIL CAPACITY: 2 gallons.
TYRES: Dunlop lightweight, 2.75 × 19in front and rear.
BRAKES: 4in diameter internal expanding, front and rear.
SUSPENSION: James undamped telescopic front fork. James plunger-type rear springing, with impact and recoil springs.
WHEELBASE: 49in. Ground clearance, 4½in unladen.
SADDLE: James. Unladen height, 29½in.
WEIGHT: 168lb fully equipped and with approximately half a gallon of petroil.
PRICE: £70. With purchase tax (in Britain only), £84 11s 8d.
ROAD TAX: 17s 6d a year; 4s 10d a quarter.
MAKERS: The James Cycle Co., Ltd., Greet, Birmingham, 11.
DESCRIPTION: *The Motor Cycle*, 23 October, 1952.

PERFORMANCE DATA

MEAN MAXIMUM SPEED: Bottom: 19 m.p.h.
Second: 36 m.p.h.
Top: 46 m.p.h.

MEAN ACCELERATION:

	10-20 m.p.h.	15-25 m.p.h.	20-30 m.p.h.
Second	3.4 secs	3.4 secs	3.8 secs
Top	—	4.4 secs	5 secs

Mean speed at end of quarter-mile from rest: maximum.
Mean time taken from 0-30 m.p.h.: 7.2 secs.
PETROIL CONSUMPTION: At 20 m.p.h., 140 m.p.g. At 30 m.p.h., 128 m.p.g. At 40 m.p.h., 100 m.p.g.
BRAKING: From 30 m.p.h. to rest, 33ft (surface, dry tarmac).
TURNING CIRCLE: 11ft.
MINIMUM NON-SNATCH SPEED: 13 m.p.h. in top gear.
WEIGHT Per C.C.: 1.36 lb.

First published 7 May 1953

122 c.c. D.M.W.
Versatile Lightweight With

THE D.M.W. Coronation model, it will be recalled, made its debut at the 1952 London Show. Since then this 122 c.c. Villiers-engined lightweight has been further developed and is now in production. Most notable feature on the machine is the leading, bottom-link front fork—a Metal Profiles product. Movement of each leading link is controlled by a spring unit which provides resistance on both depression and rebound. Silentbloc bearings are employed at the pivots. Total range of movement possible at the front wheel spindle is four inches.

An interesting feature of the D.M.W. is the all-welded frame. Note the deeply valanced, fully-sprung front mudguard

Under all normal road conditions experienced during the test, the fork contributed in full measure to a high standard of steering excellence. At low speeds the steering was light and positive; the machine could be ridden unwaveringly to a standstill without conscious effort on the part of the rider. During the negotiation of wet, treacherous road surfaces, the steering, coupled with the riding position (about which more later) engendered complete confidence. Under normal conditions on the open road the steering was rock steady and positive. As might be expected with a solid-frame machine, rear-wheel hop could be induced by cornering fast on bumpy surfaces.

The capacity of the front suspension to absorb heavy shocks imparted by road irregularities encountered at speed was not so good as that afforded by some types of lightweight telescopic fork. However, for the vast majority of road irregularities encountered at the machine's normal cruising speed with 40-45 m.p.h. showing on the speedometer, the standard of comfort provided by the fork was judged to be adequate. Fork action was reasonably light around the static load position.

Mounting of the saddle is by means of single-point attachment to an extended seat pillar which is adjustable for height through 3½ inches of travel. While not providing as great a degree of springing as a three-point saddle mounting, this layout was found to permit a tailor-made riding position to be obtained. Horizontal adjustment through two inches is also possible. After the saddle had been adjusted to suit the height (average) of the rider, the riding position was all that could be desired; it afforded perfect relationship between the seat, footrests and handlebar, which last is of fixed height. However, larger saddle dimensions would have been appreciated.

The location of the controls also contributed to riding comfort; each fell readily to hand or foot. A two-piece handlebar is employed. By loosening two nuts and swivelling each bar in its respective socket, the angle of the handlebar levers—otherwise fixed—can be varied. The footrests are also adjustable.

In town traffic, the D.M.W. excelled for its handleability and its wide range of performance in the well-chosen intermediate gear ratio. Second gear was most useful when overtaking slow-moving traffic on winding, rural rounds. In this gear, and at a speed of around 10 m.p.h., the throttle could be opened quickly and the machine accelerated until 35 or even 40 m.p.h. showed on the speedometer. This instrument, incidentally, registered fast by approximately 1 m.p.h. at 30, 2 m.p.h. at 40, and 4 m.p.h. at 50.

A certain amount of engine vibration was discernible at high r.p.m. in second gear accompanied by a fair amount of whine from the power unit, but it was noted with satisfaction that at these high revs the noise from the exhaust was reasonably subdued. At 30 m.p.h. in top gear the exhaust was, for a two-stroke machine, most unobtrusive.

It has already been mentioned that cruising speed could be anything up to an indicated 40 to 45 m.p.h. At sustained speeds of this order the engine turned over quite happily and remained extremely cool. Average main-road gradients affected the cruising speed but little. It was far more affected by wind conditions. Against a really strong head wind the machine's speed was occasionally reduced to 30 m.p.h. in top gear. On a calm day along a fast road no difficulty was experienced in packing 40 miles into the hour. The power unit remained perfectly oil-tight, but gas leakage occurred at the joint of

An unusually wide range of adjustment is provided for the saddle height. The engine remained oil-tight throughout the duration of the test

Coronation Model

Bottom-link Front Suspension

exhaust pipe and silencer, resulting in discoloration of the pipe.

At the lower end of the scale, the engine and transmission possessed a high degree of smoothness. Carburation was clean throughout the range; two-stroking was perfectly maintained provided the engine was under load and the handlebar-mounted mixture control set two-thirds towards the rich position. A reliable tick-over was readily obtainable as soon as the engine had warmed up; on tick-over, the engine did not, of course, two-stroke, but its idling was slow and even.

Engine starting was in all circumstances extremely easy. When the machine had been standing overnight, the drill was to set the mixture control to rich, flood the carburettor liberally, open the throttle one-third and depress the kick-starter through its full travel. A first-kick start was invariably obtained. To take the kick-starter through its full travel, it was necessary to operate the pedal with the ball of the foot, as distinct from the arch; otherwise, the foot came into contact with the right-hand foot-rest. To start up with the engine already warm, the mixture control lever was left in its normal running position and the throttle was set rather less than one-quarter open; a gentle prod on the kick-starter would then produce immediate results.

Slightly stiff initially, the gear change improved with use. Pedal movement was short and light. Clean changes could be made upward or downward provided the controls were not operated too rapidly when changing up. If the controls were operated very quickly, the upward changes were not quite so clean though, in this case, engagement of the pinions could be felt rather than heard. Neutral could be selected easily from either first or second gear. In order to engage bottom gear with the machine stationary and the engine idling, it was usually necessary to inch the machine forward a little—or an alternative method was partially to engage the clutch. Clutch operation was pleasantly light and the take-up of the drive smooth and positive.

Direct lighting equipment is fitted. The main beam furnished sufficient light to enable the full engine performance to be used after dark. A small bulb horn is clipped to the handlebar, but this instrument was felt to be legal rather than useful.

Several detail features of the D.M.W. are worthy of special

The Metal Profiles bottom-link front fork incorporates two-way springs in the telescopic units

mention. The filler cap is offset on the top of the fuel tank so that a check of the fuel level can readily be made—the bottom of the tank could be seen clearly without any acrobatics on the part of the rider. Further, the cap proved to be liquid-tight, and the 2½-gallon capacity of the tank was appreciated.

The centre-stand is equipped with a peg which simplifies operation of the stand by the rider's foot. The machine is extremely light (158 lb) and the stand was very easy to bring into use. Normally, the front wheel was brought clear of the ground, but the weight of a riding coat thrown across the handlebar was sufficient to alter the balance so that the rear wheel was raised clear. Fully sprung (i.e., not moving with the wheel), the front mudguard is deeply valanced.

Fitted as standard is a rear carrier; it proved useful for carrying small items of luggage, and would be capable of taking a pillion seat if required.

To enable the silencer to be dismantled for decarbonization, the tail pipe is readily removable. A comprehensive set of tools is provided in a large-capacity tool box.

Information Panel

122 c.c. D.M.W.

SPECIFICATION

ENGINE: Villiers 122 c.c. Mark 10D (50 x 62 mm) single-cylinder two-stroke with three-speed gear box in unit. Flat-crown, die-cast aluminium-alloy piston. Roller-bearing big-end; mainshaft supported by three ball bearings. Detachable, light-alloy cylinder head Petroil lubrication.

CARBURETTOR: Villiers Two-lever, with mixture control lever on handlebar; twistgrip throttle control. Air filter fitted as standard.

TRANSMISSION: Villiers three-speed gear box in unit with engine. Gear ratios: Bottom, 18.6 to 1. Second, 9.8 to 1. Top, 7.0 to 1. Primary chain, ⅜ x 0.225in. in oil-bath case. Rear chain, ½ x 0.205in, with valanced guard over top run. R.p.m. at 30 m.p.h. in top gear, 2,850.

IGNITION and LIGHTING: Villiers flywheel magneto incorporating lighting coils. Twin-filament 24/24-watt main bulb Dry battery in headlamp for parking lights.

PETROIL CAPACITY: 2½ gallons.

TYRES: Dunlop 2.75 x 19in front, 3.00 x 19in rear.

BRAKES: 5in diameter front and rear.

SUSPENSION: Metal Profiles bottom-link front fork employing double-action, undamped coil springs. Silentbloc pivot bearings.

WHEELBASE: 48in. Ground clearance, 7in.

SADDLE: Lycett, adjustable. Height, 28½in minimum, 32in maximum.

WEIGHT: 158 lb fully equipped and with ½ gallon of petroil.

PRICE: £77 9s 7d. With purchase tax (in Britain only), £93 12s 6d.

ROAD TAX: 17s 6d a year; 4s 10d a quarter.

MAKERS: D.M.W. Motor Cycles (Wolverhampton), Ltd., Valley Road, Sedgley, Dudley, Worcs.

DESCRIPTION: The Motor Cycle, 20 November 1952.

PERFORMANCE DATA

MEAN MAXIMUM SPEED: Bottom: 19 m.p.h.
Second: 39 m.p.h.
Top: 47 m.p.h.

MEAN ACCELERATION:

	10-20 m.p.h.	15-25 m.p.h.	20-30 m.p.h.
Second	4 secs	4 secs	4.5 secs
Top	—	7.4 secs	6.8 secs

Mean Speed at end of quarter-mile from rest: maximum.
Mean time taken from 0-30 m.p.h. from rest: 8 secs.

PETROIL CONSUMPTION: At 20 m.p.h., 130 m.p.g. At 30 m.p.h., 120 m.p.g. At 40 m.p.h., 90 m.p.g.

BRAKING: From 30 m.p.h. to rest, 29ft 6in (surface, dry tarmac).

TURNING CIRCLE: 12ft 6in.

MINIMUM NON-SNATCH SPEED: 12 m.p.h. in top gear

WEIGHT per C.C.: 1.29 lb.

> First published 4 June 1953

497 c.c. Norton

A Race-bred Machine with Excellent Suspension,

IN its latest form, with a 19in front wheel and the new rear frame incorporating pivoted-fork springing, the Norton Dominator No. 7 (the home-market version) maintains its position among the best contemporary 500 c.c. vertical twins. It possesses a smooth and sparkling engine performance, a superlative gear box and first-class roadholding, springing and steering characteristics. There is a pleasant tautness about its handling which makes the machine a delight to ride.

For a rider of slightly below average stature the relative position of seat and footrests was rather too close, resulting in some leg cramp on long rides. Lowering the footrests one serration below the rear-horizontal position improved the rider's leg angle.

Compact and functional in appearance, the Dominator is a delightful machine to ride

However, when brake and gear pedals were adjusted to suit the lower footrest position, the brake pedal, in operation, fouled the prop stand, while the gear pedal assumed a less effective angle. On the test machine, a considerable, though temporary, improvement was effected in the riding position by raising the dual-seat an inch or so on its slotted mountings—temporary because the forward mounting would not long remain in the raised position on bumpy roads. Handlebar width and grip angle gave a comfortable arm position, while the slender shape of the rear of the tank and the kneegrip position proved excellent. The front brake and clutch controls could be well positioned for ease of operation. The dual-seat was suitably placed to accommodate two fully clad riders.

Starting the Dominator engine was simple and certain. No knack was called for whether the engine was hot or cold. A cold start required closure of the air lever and light flooding of the carburettor; a first-kick response was assured. Once the engine was warm, it would settle down to a slow, reliable tickover when the throttle was closed, even after long periods of full-throttle running. There was never any tendency for the engine to run-on after the ignition cut-out was operated. The degree of mechanical quietness was average, but the exhaust note was inclined to be raucous on medium and wide throttle openings. Discretion in handling the twistgrip was required if embarrassment was to be avoided when accelerating between buildings.

Throughout the engine's speed range, power delivery was commendably smooth. There was virtually no vibration period to dictate cruising speed. In town, the engine was quite happy at 30 m.p.h. in top gear and would accelerate smoothly from this speed. When full use was made of the gear box, acceleration was pulse-stirring. Pinking was never experienced, however quickly the throttle was opened. Intermediate cruising speeds were equally pleasant and unobtrusive while, at the top end of the performance range, the machine was ridden for many consecutive miles at an indicated 80 m.p.h. when road and traffic conditions permitted. In these circumstances, the engine continued for mile after mile to churn out its power with almost turbine-like smoothness and an entire absence of fuss.

Weather conditions were rather unfavourable when the performance figures were obtained, a 20 m.p.h. three-quarter wind prevailing. A one-way, top-gear speed in excess of 91 m.p.h. was recorded with the rider wearing storm coat and waders. Checked electrically, the speedometer proved accurate at 30 m.p.h. and progressively fast by 1 to 4 m.p.h. between 40 and 90 m.p.h. There was a six per cent discrepancy between the main and trip mileage recorders.

The gear box was a joy to use. Engagement of bottom gear from neutral, with the engine idling, was noiseless. The clutch was sweet to operate and very positive in its take-up of the drive. Neutral selection from bottom or second gear was simple. Movement of the gear pedal was light and short. Clean, silent and instantaneous changes, in either direction, could easily be made between any pair of gears. The ratios themselves are well chosen. Second and third gears could be comfortably employed up to 50 and 70 m.p.h. respectively when accelerating.

As befits a machine with a successful racing ancestry, the suspension, steering and roadholding were outstandingly good. They combined to render the Dominator an extremely safe machine to ride. At all speeds within its compass, the machine could be heeled over confidently almost regardless of surface irregularities. On fast or slow bends a chosen line could be held easily, with the assurance that no drifting whatsoever would occur. On slow and medium-pace bends the prop stand grounded rather easily. During part of the test extremely

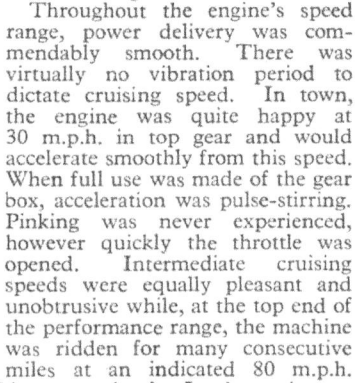

Source of smooth, tireless power. The exhaust ports are widely spaced to assist cooling

Dominator Twin

Hair-line Steering and Smooth Power Output

gusty winds were encountered. Only when the machine was ridden fast over bumpy surfaces under these conditions was there a slight tendency to wandering. At all other times steering was of the hair-line variety and pleasantly light; the damper was never brought into use.

The characteristics of both front and rear springing are exemplary. Together, they provided not only a high degree of physical comfort for the rider but also uncommonly good road-holding under all conditions. Bottoming occurred only on recoil, and that infrequently. At medium and high speeds the wheel suspension assumed in large measure that quality of unobtrusiveness which characterizes well-controlled movement. There was an almost entire absence of pitching. In fact, to be hypercritical, only severe undulations taken at near-maximum velocity could induce the faintest trace of pitching. The impression was formed that slightly heavier recoil damping would render the suspension pluperfect.

No Adjustment Required

The brakes, when used to the full, proved adequate for all occasions. It was felt, however, that they were not quite up to the same high standard as the rest of the machine. A good deal of pressure on the lever was required to obtain the best results from the front brake. Increased leverage in the control mechanism should give improvement. The Bowdenex control cable precluded all trace of sponginess in operation. The rear-brake pedal required a relatively long movement for the optimum retardation. It was difficult to obtain the best results with a bewadered foot. No brake adjustments were called for during the test.

After 1,000 miles of hard riding, engine, gear box and chain case remained reasonably oiltight. Only the slightest discoloration of the exhaust pipes had taken place close to the ports. An unusually wide rear mudguard and a deep-sided rear chainguard

The pivoted-fork, rear-wheel suspension, using proprietary shock-absorber units, operated in exemplary fashion

played a major part in keeping the rear end of the machine reasonably clean in use.

The headlamp beam was adequate for fast cruising after dark, and the dipswitch was accessible. Full lamp load was balanced at 30 m.p.h. in top gear.

The Dominator is provided with three good stands—front, centre and prop; all are easy to use. The prop stand is excellent on a cambered surface but requires both wheel suspensions to be fully extended when employed on a flat surface if the machine is to be supported at a safe angle.

Minor criticisms concern the oil-tank filler cap, which cannot be fully opened owing to the proximity of the dual-seat, and the chaincase oil level plug, which is almost impossible to remove without first detaching the left-hand exhaust system.

Information Panel

497 c.c. Norton Dominator No. 7

SPECIFICATION

ENGINE: 497 c.c. (66 × 72.6 mm) o.h.v. vertical twin. Fully enclosed valve gear operated from a single camshaft. Plain bearing big-ends. Roller main bearing on drive side; ball bearing on timing side. Compression ratio, 6.7 to 1. Dry-sump lubrication; oil-tank capacity, 4 pints.

CARBURETTOR: Amal; twistgrip throttle control; air-slide operated by handlebar lever

IGNITION AND LIGHTING: Lucas magneto with auto-advance. Separate 50-watt Lucas dynamo. 7in-diameter headlamp with sealed-beam light unit.

TRANSMISSION: Norton four-speed gear box with positive-stop foot control. Bottom, 14.9 to 1. Second, 8.85 to 1. Third, 6.05 to 1. Top, 5.0 to 1. Multi-plate clutch with bonded-fabric inserts. Primary chain, $\frac{1}{2}$ × 0.305in, in pressed-steel, oil-bath case. Secondary chain, $\frac{5}{8}$ × $\frac{1}{4}$in. R.p.m at 30 m.p.h. in top gear, 1,980.

FUEL CAPACITY: 3$\frac{3}{4}$ gallons.

TYRES: Avon Front, 3.25 × 19in ribbed Rear, 3.50 × 19in studded.

BRAKES: Both 7in diameter × 1$\frac{1}{8}$in wide; hand adjusters.

SUSPENSION: Norton Roadholder telescopic front fork with hydraulic damping. Pivoted-fork rear springing employing coil springs and hydraulic damping.

WHEELBASE: 57in unladen. Ground clearance, 5in unladen.

SEAT: Norton dual-seat. Unladen height, 30$\frac{1}{2}$in.

WEIGHT: 413 lb with approximately one gallon of fuel, full oil tank and full equipment.

PRICE: £187 With purchase tax (in G. Britain only), £225 19s 2d.

ROAD TAX: £3 15s a year; £1 0s 8d a quarter.

MAKERS: Norton Motors, Ltd., Bracebridge Street, Birmingham, 6.

DESCRIPTION: *The Motor Cycle*, 2 October 1952.

PERFORMANCE DATA

MEAN MAXIMUM SPEED: Bottom:* 34 m.p.h
Second:* 56 m.p.h
Third:* 82 m.p.h
Top: 84 m.p.h
* Valve float occuring.

MEAN ACCELERATION:

	10-30 m.p.h	20-40 m.p.h	30-50 m.p.h
Bottom	2.5 secs	—	—
Second	3.8 secs	3.5 sec	3.6 secs
Third	—	6.0 secs	5.6 secs
Top	—	7.6 secs	7.9 secs

Mean speed at end of quarter-mile from rest: 75 m.p.h.
Mean time to cover standing quarter-mile: 17.2 secs.

PETROL CONSUMPTION: At 30 m.p.h., 72 m.p.g. At 40 m.p.h., 60 m.p.g. At 50 m.p.h., 56 m.p.g. At 60 m.p.h., 54 m.p.g.

BRAKING: From 30 m.p.h. to rest. 33ft 6in (surface dry tarmac).

TURNING CIRCLE: 17ft.

MINIMUM NON-SNATCH SPEED: 14 m.p.h. in top gear.

WEIGHT PER C.C.: 0.83 lb

First published 25 June 1953

249 c.c. Side-valve

Comfortable, Easy-to-ride Machine with

THREE versions of the 249 c.c. side-valve B.S.A. C10 are listed: they comprise the standard model with three-speed gear box and solid rear frame, a de-luxe three-speed model with rear springing, and a de-luxe four-speed model with rear springing. The machine tested was equipped with rear springing and a three-speed gear box. During the 700 miles of the test, the C10 proved to be a most likeable mount. It earned full marks for ease of handling and for the standard of riding comfort it afforded.

Efficient springing, a good riding position and a dual-seat combined to make the C10 extremely comfortable to ride

An admirable contribution to riding comfort was made by the plunger-type rear springing. On bumpy surfaces, road shocks were absorbed in a most satisfactory manner. The springing operated through its full range of movement (2in) but no "clashing" occurred either on full depression or recoil. In the early stages of the test, the springing was not so light as desirable around the static load position; after 500 miles, however, its action in this respect improved considerably.

The B.S.A. front fork, as fitted to this model, would be extremely difficult to better. It was very sensitive at the static load position, and its long, easy action dealt with all road shocks with commendable efficiency. Action was also progressive and bottoming on depression never occurred. What was felt to be a minor criticism was that when corrugated road surfaces were taken fast, light bottoming on the recoil strokes could be felt and heard.

Steering was first-class in almost every respect. At all speeds it was steady and dead positive. Under town conditions, the B.S.A. could be manœuvred through congested traffic, or taken round acute, slow corners with an absolute minimum of effort. In wet weather and on road surfaces far from ideal for a two-wheeler, the machine's behaviour was such as to instil into the rider the utmost confidence. On the open road, the model could be cornered stylishly at any speed of which it was capable and which the road permitted. Usually, both wheels hugged the road on any selected line through a bend. Only when really bumpy corners were taken fast was there a slight tendency for the rear wheel to drift outward. Under all normal conditions, therefore, the handling was exemplary.

Without any adjustments being carried out, the riding position was found to be admirable. Relationship between seat, footrests, and handlebar was well nigh perfect; it afforded the rider a very comfortable leg angle and resulted in his weight being distributed just at the correct place on the well-shaped B.S.A. dual-seat. In delivery trim, hand and foot controls were well positioned for ease of operation. Handlebar levers are fitted on fixed pivot blocks; the handlebar can be adjusted for the angle of the grips. Footrests and gear pedal are fully adjustable. The brake pedal is provided with a non-adjustable stop. Mounted on the front brake lever pivot block, the horn button could not (owing to its location) be operated conveniently while the front brake was being applied.

Flexibility of the engine was all that might be expected from a side-valve unit. True to type, the engine could be made to slog lustily at very low revs without the slightest trace of pinking. Along a level road, the C10 would tick-tock along quietly at 20 m.p.h. in top gear without any protest from the engine or transmission. At this speed, the exhaust note was most unobtrusive, and even when high engine r.p.m. were used in the lower gears, the note was deep and well subdued. The engine was fairly quiet mechanically, but a rather loud whine emanated from the gear box with the transmission on the overrun—particularly in second gear.

Once the engine revolutions had mounted, the machine would respond in lively fashion to a sudden increase in throttle opening. Second gear could be engaged before the speedometer needle had reached 10 m.p.h. and held, if necessary, until 40 m.p.h. was indicated. Above 35 m.p.h. in second there was a certain amount of high-frequency vibration which could be felt at the handlebar and footrests. This recurred at high r.p.m. in top gear, but was negligible at normal cruising speeds. A comfortable cruising speed was anything up to an indicated 45 to 50 m.p.h. An accurate check of the speedometer revealed that the instrument registered fast by approximately 2 m.p.h. at 30, and 3 m.p.h. at both 40 and 50 m.p.h.

A 70-mile journey in hilly country was frequently covered in a few minutes under two hours without either rider or machine being unduly exerted. During such usage the engine remained oil-tight,

Easy to start, unobtrusive and flexible in use—the side-valve engine of the C10

B.S.A. C10

a Flexible Engine

Control lever pivot blocks are welded in position

though the exhaust pipe became discoloured in the vicinity of the port.

In all circumstances engine starting was delightfully easy. For an early morning start from cold, the drill was to flood the carburettor liberally, set the throttle about one-quarter open, and depress the kick-starter through its full arc of travel. A first-kick start was then invariably obtained—assuming one had remembered to switch on the ignition! When the engine had been running for a minute or two it would settle down to a reliable and perfectly even tickover—a tickover so slow that the individual power strokes could easily be counted. To start up with the engine already warm, it was necessary to give only a gentle prod on the kick-starter; this could be accomplished with the rider normally seated. Carburation was clean throughout the throttle range.

In order to engage bottom gear with the machine stationary and the engine idling, it was sometimes necessary to inch the machine forward a little or partially to engage the clutch. Moderately light in operation, the clutch took up the drive smoothly, but progressive engagement was difficult to achieve because the effective range of the handlebar lever was only in the final stages of its arc of movement. Clean upward gear changes could be made provided the gear pedal was moved with some deliberation. Movement of the gear pedal was light, and the control could be operated merely by pivoting the right foot on the footrest. As might be expected with three fairly wide gear ratios, clean downward gear changes were rather more difficult to accomplish and called for high engine r.p.m. while the clutch was withdrawn prior to selecting the lower gear.

It was considered that bottom gear could, with advantage, have been slightly lower. Restarting on steep gradients required the clutch to be slipped fairly generously—though it should be mentioned that the clutch never showed the slightest sign of distress even after deliberately severe usage. Neutral could be selected easily from either first or second gear.

At night, the headlamp main beam furnished ample driving light at normal cruising speeds; the ammeter indicated that the full load on the battery was balanced at 25 m.p.h. in top gear. An ignition warning light is incorporated in the ammeter. The headlamp switch has an unusually large shank; the ease with which the switch could be operated was appreciated.

Mounted at an inclined angle on the steering head, the speedometer was very easy to read by day or night. A Lucas Type 275 Diacon stop/tail lamp is fitted; this blazed out like a beacon in the night—especially when the stop light was in operation.

Applied in unison, the brakes provided adequate stopping power, though the front brake was judged to be below par.

A centre stand is provided. This was reasonably easy to operate, and either front or rear wheel could be raised clear of the ground. Oil from the crankcase breather was blown back and soiled the left-hand leg of the stand. As mentioned earlier, roadholding was excellent and this may have some bearing on the fact that the stand was occasionally grounded when cornering with the machine well heeled over.

The ground clearance of 4⅜in quoted in the Information Panel was measured from the underside of the centre stand legs; clearance at the lowest part of the crankcase is 6in.

A comprehensive, 18-piece tool-kit is provided. The C10 is attractively finished in dark maroon, with chromium-plated tank panels, wheel rims and fittings.

249 c.c., side-valve B.S.A. C10

Information Panel

SPECIFICATION

ENGINE: 249 c.c. (63 × 80 mm) single-cylinder side-valve. Detachable light-alloy cylinder head with cast-iron barrel. Light-alloy piston. Roller-bearing big-end; ball bearing on drive side of crankshaft, plain bearing on timing side. Dry-sump lubrication; oil-tank capacity, 4 pints. Gear-type oil pump. Compression ratio, 5 to 1.
CARBURETTOR: Amal single-lever (no air slide); twistgrip throttle control.
IGNITION and LIGHTING: By battery and coil, with auto-advance mechanism integral with contact-breaker. Lucas 3in dynamo; 7in headlamp with 30/30-watt main bulb controlled by handlebar switch.
TRANSMISSION: B.S.A. three-speed gear box. Top, 6.6 to 1. Second, 9.8 to 1. Bottom, 14.5 to 1. Clutch has two friction plates, with cork inserts. Primary chain, ⅜ × 0.305in in pressed-steel oil-bath chaincase. Rear, ½ × 0.305in, with guard over top run. R.p.m. at 30 m.p.h. in top gear, 2,700 approximately.
FUEL CAPACITY: 2½ gallons.
TYRES: Dunlop 3.00 × 19in front and rear.
BRAKES: 5½in diameter front and rear.
SUSPENSION: B.S.A. hydraulically damped telescopic front fork. Plunger-type rear springing employing coil springs.
WHEELBASE: 52in. Ground clearance, 4⅞in unladen.
SEAT: B.S.A. dual-seat. Unladen height, 30in.
WEIGHT: 318 lb with fuel tank dry, but otherwise fully equipped.
PRICE: £107. With purchase tax (in G. Britain only) £129 5s 10d.
ROAD TAX: £1 17s 6d a year; 10s 4d a quarter.
MAKERS: B.S.A. Cycles, Ltd., Birmingham, 11.
DESCRIPTION: *The Motor Cycle*, 25 September 1952.

PERFORMANCE DATA

MEAN MAXIMUM SPEED: Bottom: 28 m.p.h.*
Second: 42 m.p.h.*
Top: 56 m.p.h.
* Valve float starting.

MEAN ACCELERATION:

	10-30 m.p.h	20-40 m.p.h	30-50 m.p.h
Second	6 secs	6.2 secs	—
Top	—	11 secs	13.6 secs

Speed at end of quarter-mile from rest: 53 m.p.h.
Mean time to cover standing quarter-mile: 24.4 secs.
PETROL CONSUMPTION: At 30 m.p.h. 120 m.p.g. At 40 m.p.h. 92 m.p.g. At 50 m.p.h., 76 m.p.g.
BRAKING: From 30 m.p.h. to rest, 34 feet (surface, dry tarmac)
TURNING CIRCLE: 12 feet
MINIMUM NON-SNATCH SPEED: 15 m.p.h. in top gear.
WEIGHT per C.C.: 1.27 lb.

> First published 30 July 1953

Royal Enfield

A Modern Single with Good Low-speed

THE 499 c.c. Royal Enfield Bullet was re-introduced at last year's London Show. In its latest form the machine conforms to modern Royal Enfield practice and features hydraulically damped front- and rear-wheel suspension. Possessing all the charms inherent in a modern, 500 c.c. overhead-valve, single-cylinder engine, the Bullet offers reasonably good fuel economy, simplicity, and the effortless, loping gait on part-throttle openings resulting from the use of large, effective flywheels.

All enamelled parts are in polychromatic copper beech: crankcase castings are externally polished. Note the box-shape air cleaner

Two conditions were essential to a first-kick start when the Bullet engine was cold. First, the carburettor tickler had to be depressed only momentarily; secondly, the barest throttle opening has to be precisely set. Granted these two conditions, the ignition lever could be left at full advance without risk of the engine kicking back; slight ignition retard could be employed as a safety precaution, without detriment to the certainty of starting. With the engine hot, the carburettor tickler could be ignored, but the throttle opening was critical if first-kick results were to be obtained. Assuming the foregoing conditions were not fulfilled, and the engine failed to respond after, say, three kicks, it would fire readily if the throttle was opened fully while kickstarting.

When it was running, the engine amply repaid skilled handling of the ignition control, and the most regular idling resulted from a half-retard setting. Although the engine would pull quite happily at 30 m.p.h. in top gear, it was found advisable under conditions of heavy city traffic to set the ignition lever fractionally retarded. The engine then provided lusty and pink-free pulling characteristics at low r.p.m. Out of built-up areas, the same beefy acceleration from the lower engine-speed ranges was notable and upward gear changes could be made at comparatively low r.p.m. When extra-rapid acceleration was required, second and third gears could be employed up to speedometer readings of 45 m.p.h. and 60 m.p.h. respectively.

On a small throttle opening, the Bullet would cruise smoothly at 40 or 50 m.p.h. with the engine spinning at no more than a fast tickover. Farther up the scale, an indicated 70 m.p.h. proved to be the fastest comfortable speed for continuous cruising under average conditions. This speed could normally be maintained on approximately half throttle; higher speeds, or hard accelerating resulted in the exhaust becoming obtrusive. On small throttle openings the exhaust was deep-toned and not offensive, either to the rider or to pedestrians. Mechanical noise was average for an engine of this type and both piston and valve gear were slightly audible. A temporary increase in valve-gear noise was traced to an excessive inlet valve clearance, resulting from a loose pushrod cup.

As a result of the engine's excellent torque and flywheel characteristics, main-road cruising speeds were effortlessly maintained on average gradients without the need for appreciable increase in throttle opening. With the exception of a slight period from 60 to 65 m.p.h., there was no perceptible engine vibration. The speedometer read approximately 6 per cent fast throughout the Bullet's performance range.

At the conclusion of 1,500 miles of hard riding, the exhaust pipe had blued considerably near the port, and slight oily messiness was apparent around the oil-filler cap. The polished crankcase and chaincase proved entirely oil tight, however, and they were easy to clean. Checking or adjustment of the primary chain tension called for removal of the outer half of the chaincase which is retained by a single nut.

The range of movement of the gear pedal is unusually short. Owing to the high position of the pedal pivot, it was found impracticable to change gear by pivoting the right foot on its footrest. Rapid, noiseless gear changes could be made in either direction and engagement of bottom gear from neutral was only slightly audible. No undue difficulty was experienced in selecting neutral from bottom or second gears when coming to a standstill and an overriding neutral finder to the rear of the gear pedal can be operated from all gears except bottom. A shade heavy in operation, the clutch took up the drive in a sweet and positive manner. A tendency to slipping could be induced by prolonged hard driving.

The steering of the Bullet was first-class, being precise and rock steady at all times. At high or low

The rear-suspension layout is compact, the mudguard mounting robust. Rear-chain adjustment is effected by serrated cams

499 c.c. Bullet

Torque and Excellent Handling Qualities

speeds the machine could be banked over without the least tendency for the front wheel to waver; in strong, gusty winds, and on wet city cobbles, stability was of a high order.

The relative positioning of seat and handlebar resulted in a comfortable angle for the rider's arms. Both from considerations of riding comfort and convenience of gear-pedal operation, it was desired to move the right-hand footrest upward and backward, but adjustment was impossible because of the proximity of the gear box to the footrest hanger. Partly because of the relatively low footrest position, there was a tendency on long runs for the top edges of the dual-seat to be felt at the thighs by a rider of slightly below average leg length.

The rear-brake pedal and all hand controls were well placed, though the hand reach to the front brake lever was considered too great for a hand of average proportions. Stickiness in twistgrip action in the initial stages of the test was cured by re-running the cable in easier sweeps.

Floating Brake Cam

Both front and rear springing were somewhat hard by modern standards, and the degree of comfort was improved when a pillion passenger was carried. Bottoming on recoil was sometimes experienced.

At the beginning of the test, the front brake was rather poor. Inspection showed that wear on the leading shoe (the machine had previously covered a fair mileage) had resulted in the floating cam reaching the limit of its travel. Reversal of the brake shoes was all that was required to bring the cam back within the floating range. Thereafter, the brake was light in operation and adequate in power, though it required adjustment

The easy-to-clean, brilliantly polished chaincase cover is retained by a single nut

after extended heavy usage during the remainder of the test.

After dark, the headlamp beam gave a spread of light which rendered main-road cruising speeds up to 60 m.p.h. quite permissible. Although the crankcase breather is led to the rear chain, the chain ran dry throughout the test and had to be lubricated by means of an oil can. A centre stand and a prop stand are provided; both are easy to operate and give safe support to the machine. Neither wheel could be raised clear of the ground by means of the centre stand.

The Bullet's polychromatic copper-beech finish is smart and distinctive in appearance. The wheel rims are bright zinc plated—a finish which is indistinguishable in appearance from the chromium plating on the exhaust pipe and handlebar.

Information Panel

499 c.c. Royal Enfield Bullet

SPECIFICATION

ENGINE: 499 c.c. (84 × 90 mm) single-cylinder o.h.v. with fully enclosed valve gear; Duralumin pushrods. Aluminium-alloy cylinder head. RR56 alloy connecting rod; plain-bearing big end; double-row roller bearing on timing-side mainshaft; ball and roller bearings on drive side. Compression ratio, 6.2 to 1. Dry-sump lubrication; oil tank integral with crankcase; capacity, 4 pints.

CARBURETTOR: Amal; twistgrip throttle control; air-slide operated by handlebar lever. Air filter.

IGNITION and LIGHTING: Lucas Magdyno with manual ignition control; 7in-diameter headlamp with sealed-beam light unit.

TRANSMISSION: Royal Enfield four-speed gear box with positive-stop foot control and neutral finder. Bottom, 13.65 to 1. Second, 8.82 to 1. Third, 6.37 to 1. Top, 4.9 to 1. Multi-plate clutch with cork inserts operating in oil. Primary chain, ⅜in duplex, in cast-aluminium, oil-bath case. Secondary chain, ⅝ × ⅜in. R.p.m. at 30 m.p.h. in top gear 1,950.

FUEL CAPACITY: 3¼ gallons

TYRES: Dunlop. Front, 3.25 × 19in Ribbed. Rear, 3.50 × 19in Universal.

BRAKES: 6in diameter front and rear; hand adjusters.

SUSPENSION: Royal Enfield telescopic front fork with two-rate coil springs, hydraulically damped. Pivoted-fork rear springing with hydraulic damping.

WHEELBASE: 54in unladen. Ground clearance, 6in unladen.

SEAT: Royal Enfield dual-seat. Unladen height, 31in.

WEIGHT: 420lb with approximately one gallon of fuel, full oil tank and equipment.

PRICE: £167 10s. With purchase tax (in Gt. Britain only), £202 /s 11d. Dual-seat, extra, £4 (with P.T., £5 2s 3d).

ROAD TAX: £3 15s a year; £1 0s 8d a quarter.

MAKERS: The Enfield Cycle Co. Ltd., Redditch, Worcs.

DESCRIPTION: The Motor Cycle, 2 October 1952

PERFORMANCE DATA

MEAN MAXIMUM SPEED: Bottom: 35 m.p.h.
Second: 53 m.p.h.
Third: 70 m.p.h.
Top: 78 m.p.h

MEAN ACCELERATION:

	10-30 m.p.h	20-40 m.p.h	30-50 m.p.h
Bottom	2.8 secs	—	—
Second	4 secs	3.8 secs	5 secs
Third	—	5 secs	5.6 secs
Top	—	7 secs	7.8 secs

Mean speed at end of quarter-mile from rest: 68 m.p.h.
Mean time to cover standing quarter-mile: 19.2 secs

PETROL CONSUMPTION: At 30 m.p.h., 100 m.p.g. At 40 m.p.h. 88 m.p.g. At 50 m.p.h., 74 m.p.g. At 60 m.p.h., 60 m.p.g.

BRAKING: From 30 m.p.h. to rest, 29ft 6in (surface, dry tarmac).

TURNING CIRCLE: 15ft.

MINIMUM NON-SNATCH SPEED: 15 m.p.h. in top gear.

WEIGHT PER C.C.: 0.84lb.

First published 8 October 1953

197 c.c. Greeves De

Riding Comfort and Good All-round Performance the

THE Greeves range of machines, latest addition to the expanding field of lightweights, possesses several features of technical interest and novelty. Common to all models in the range is the composite frame incorporating a light-alloy beam which is cast around the steering head and forms the front down member and, cast in the same material, a duplex cradle for the power unit. Front- and rear-wheel suspensions are controlled by rubber torsion units and friction dampers. In the case of the De Luxe Roadster model 20D tested, the power unit

The Greeves is finished in attractive blue enamel. The valanced mudguards proved to be commendably effective

was the latest four-speed Villiers 197 c.c. Mark 8E/4. The test machine was also equipped with plain-bearing hubs, available as an extra.

The behaviour of the Greeves on the road amply justifies the makers' faith in rubber-controlled wheel suspension; a high degree of road-holding excellence and rider comfort has been achieved. The most comfortable ride on bumpy road surfaces was obtained with the friction dampers adjusted so that they were just biting. With that setting, the wheel suspension was remarkably responsive to minor surface irregularities whether they were traversed at high or low speeds. Slight pitching at the rear of the machine was induced by more severe bumps, but could readily be mitigated by tightening the rear friction dampers a shade more. These dampers are easily accessible from the riding seat.

Heavy braking on the front wheel alone produced a tendency for the front fork to judder, particularly on bumpy surfaces. Again, this tendency could be reduced by employing heavier front-fork damping. It was not desirable, however, to employ more damping than was strictly necessary at the front end, since the front-wheel suspension units were slightly harder in action than those at the rear.

The steering and general handling of the Greeves were first class. On bends and corners the machine could be heeled over to any desired degree without the footrests or any other components fouling the ground. Rapid changes of steering lock could be effected with commendably little effort. Straight-ahead steering was light yet positive. The relationship of handlebar, seat and footrests provided a riding position which was quite comfortable for a person of medium stature. No cramp or fatigue was felt after several consecutive hours' riding. The downward slope of the dual-seat, however, tended to throw the rider on to the forward extremity of the seat, where the reduced width and depth of the upholstery detracted slightly from rider comfort.

All controls, both hand- and foot-operated, could be readily adjusted for convenient manipulation. The handlebar shape gave a comfortable wrist angle, but it was considered that the overall width of the bar (28in) could be reduced with advantage.

Villiers power units have long earned a reputation for stalwart and unflagging performance; that fitted to the Greeves De Luxe Roadster was no exception, and it provided smooth, tractable power over a wide engine-speed range. Engine starting was invariably a first-kick affair provided that, when the engine was cold, the carburettor was well flooded and the strangler closed. With the engine warm, these measures were not required. Idling was erratic—as is common with orthdox two-strokes—but reliable.

At all times when the engine was firing evenly, the silencer reduced the exhaust note to an inoffensive drone; irregular firing, such as on tick-over or when the engine was running light, produced a rather "tinny" note. More obtrusive to the rider than the exhaust note was induction roar, which was apparent at throttle openings of one half or more. The engine was notable for its mechanical quietness and the absence of the elusive ringing noise which characterizes many small two-strokes.

The Greeves was a delightful machine to ride in town. At 30 m.p.h. in top gear, the engine pulled very sweetly and the only audible noise was a subdued drone from the exhaust. Smooth, gentlemanly acceleration from that speed was available in either third or top gears.

On the open road, the Greeves would cruise at an indicated 45-55 m.p.h. according to prevailing conditions. Reasonably stiff main-road gradients could be surmounted at the lower figure; an adverse combination of wind and gradient was required to bring the speed of the machine

The 197 c.c. power unit incorporates a four-speed gear box and the latest Villiers carburettor with adjustable pilot air screw

Luxe Roadster

Keynote of a New Lightweight

down to 40 m.p.h. Prolonged hard riding failed to tire the engine. At high engine speeds a faint, high-frequency vibration was perceptible through the handlebar and seat. The speedometer registered fast by approximately 1½ m.p.h. at 30 m.p.h., 2½ m.p.h. at 40 m.p.h. and 4 m.p.h. at 50 m.p.h.

The provision of four well-chosen gear ratios enabled the engine performance to be used to great advantage. Clean gear changes could be made in either direction without any hesitation in pedal movement. The travel of the gear pedal is uncommonly short; consequently neutral selection required an undesirably delicate movement of the right foot. Bottom-gear engagement, with the machine stationary and the engine idling, was noiseless; partial release of the clutch was sometimes necessary to effect the engagement. The clutch was light to operate and sweet in action. It freed perfectly, took up the drive positively and seemed impervious to abuse.

The friction of the four-speed gear box, and the use of gear oil, detracted slightly from the remarkable liveliness for which the 197 c.c. Villiers engine, in its three-speed form, is renowned. On long, main-road journeys, a perceptible improvement became apparent when the unit was thoroughly hot and the gear oil less viscous in consequence.

The rear chain tended to run dry. When adjusting it, care was required to make allowance for an appreciable increase in chain tension when the machine—a pre-production model—was laden; there was also a tendency for the chain to tighten still more after the machine had been run for a few miles. On the production machines, modified rear-fork geometry has eliminated the difficulty.

Both brakes were adequately powerful, light and positive in operation and required no adjustment for wear throughout the 1,000-mile test. In the early stages of the test the rear brake lost efficiency. Inspection showed that this was the result of leakage of a small amount of oil from the hub to the brake drum. Substitution of new brake shoes for those which had become impregnated with oil effected a complete cure. Torque reaction of the front brake is transmitted through the fork links, and use of the brake resulted in lifting of the front of the machine.

This close-up shows one of the links which connect the pivoted rear fork with the rubber suspension units

The valanced mudguards proved commendably effective when the machine was ridden under dirty weather conditions; there was a high degree of protection from mud, both for the engine and for the rider's shoes.

After dark, with the battery circuit in use, the main headlamp bulb provided a beam which was adequate for the maintenance of daytime cruising speeds. The generator did not, however, balance the load under those conditions. The drain on the battery could be obviated by turning the head-lamp switch to the direct lighting position, though it involved some reduction in the brilliance of the light beam.

A rattle from the rear number plate which occurred at high engine speeds at the beginning of the test was eliminated by substituting a rubber sleeve for the steel distance piece on the number-plate lower attachment bolt.

To sum up, the excellent riding comfort and sound all-round performance provided by the Greeves De Luxe Roadster make it an attractive proposition for the lightweight buyer.

Information Panel

197 c.c. Greeves 20D

SPECIFICATION

ENGINE: Villiers 197 c.c. Mark 8E/4 (59 × 77 mm) single-cylinder two-stroke. Roller-bearing big end; ball bearings supporting mainshafts. Flat-crown, die-cast, aluminium-alloy piston. Detachable, light-alloy cylinder head with hemispherical combustion chamber. Compression ratio, 7.25 to 1. Petroil lubrication.
CARBURETTOR: Villiers type S24 single-lever, with twist grip throttle control. Detachable air filter incorporating strangler.
TRANSMISSION: Villiers four-speed gear box in unit with engine. Gear ratios: Bottom, 18.15 to 1. Second, 11.27 to 1. Third, 8.45 to 1. Top, 6.26 to 1. Primary chain, ⅜ × 0.225in, in oilbath case. Rear chain, ½ × 0.205in, with guard over top run. Engine r.p.m. at 30 m.p.h. in top gear, 2,500.
IGNITION and LIGHTING: Villiers flywheel magneto with lighting coils. Westinghouse rectifier and Lucas 6-volt, 5-ampere-hour accumulator. 6in-diameter headlamp with sealed-beam light unit; A.C./D.C. headlamp switch.
TANK CAPACITY: 2½ gallons.
TYRES: Avon. Front, 3.00 × 19in ribbed; rear, 3.25 × 19in studded.
BRAKES: 6in diameter front and rear; hand adjuster to rear.
SUSPENSION: Greeves pivoted-fork springing front and rear, employing rubber in torsion and friction damping.
WHEELBASE: 52in unladen. Ground clearance, 6in unladen.
SEAT: Greeves dual-seat. Unladen height, 32in.
WEIGHT: 245 lb fully equipped and with approximately half a gallon of fuel.
PRICE: £125. With purchase tax (in Gt. Britain only), £150. Plain bearing hubs, extra £5 (P.T. £1).
ROAD TAX: £1 17s 6d a year; 10s 4d a quarter.
DESCRIPTION: *The Motor Cycle*, 17 September 1953.
MAKERS: Invacar, Ltd., Church Road, Thundersley, Essex.

PERFORMANCE DATA

MEAN MAXIMUM SPEED: Bottom: 23 m.p.h.
Second: 37 m.p.h.
Third: 48 m.p.h.
Top: 57 m.p.h.

MEAN ACCELERATION:

	10-20 m.p.h.	15-25 m.p.h.	20-30 m.p.h.
Bottom	2.4 secs	—	—
Second	3.2 secs	3.6 secs	4 secs
Third	4.4 secs	4.8 secs	5.6 secs
Top	—	—	8 secs

Mean speed at end of quarter-mile from rest: 48 m.p.h.
Mean time taken from 0-30 m.p.h.: 7 secs.
PETROIL CONSUMPTION: At 30 m.p.h., 112 m.p.g. At 40 m.p.h., 90 m.p.g. At 50 m.p.h., 68 m.p.g.
BRAKING: From 30 m.p.h. to rest, 32ft (surface, dry, smooth tarmac).
TURNING CIRCLE: 12ft.
MINIMUM NON-SNATCH SPEED: 14 m.p.h. in top gear.
WEIGHT PER C.C.: 1.24lb.

The 148 c.c. Excelsior

First published 15 October 1953

An Attractively Finished Two-stroke Lightweight with a

INTRODUCED just before the 1952 London Show, the Excelsior Courier, along with other makes, focused attention on a capacity class that was extremely popular before the last war. The 150 c.c. engine was new to the post-war home market. Experience gained in the course of road-testing the 148 c.c. Courier served to pin-point the excellent performance that can be expected from a one-fifty two-stroke

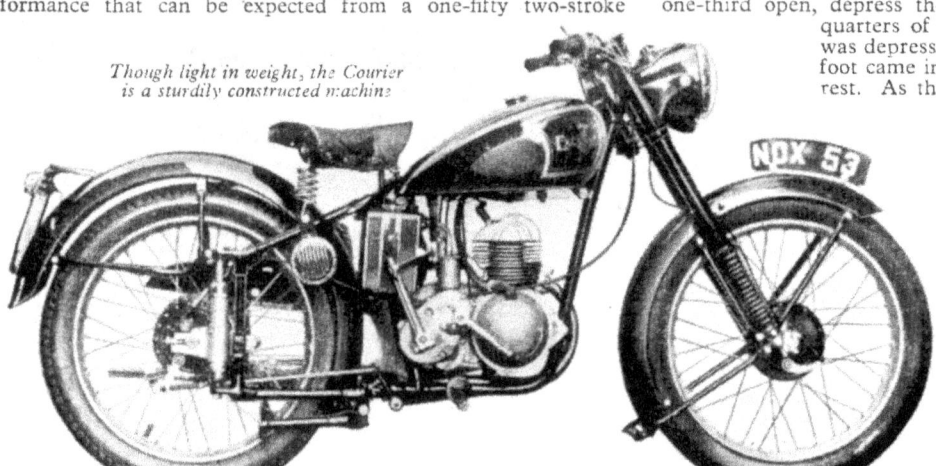

Though light in weight, the Courier is a sturdily constructed machine

engine. On a mildly undulating road, a cruising speed of 40-45 m.p.h. could be held indefinitely without the slightest sign of fuss from the engine. Never was there any indication of overheating. In most circumstances there was sufficient power in hand to enable the cruising speed to be maintained in the face of moderate headwinds. On long, main-road climbs, provided that the machine was not baulked by other traffic, engine r.p.m. dropped but slowly; indeed, some of the long hills were breasted at 40 m.p.h. in top gear. The Courier was found to possess a good measure of slogging power at low revs. A wide range of performance in second gear was available—from 10 to 40 m.p.h. Coupled with the attractive all-round performance, was very economical consumption of fuel.

In the matter of easy engine starting the Courier excelled. Almost without exception, the engine started at the first kick. With the engine cold, the procedure adopted was to flood the carburettor at least until fuel could be discerned at the base of the mixing chamber, close the air-lever and, with the throttle one-third open, depress the kick-starter through about three-quarters of its arc of travel. (When the crank was depressed through its full travel, the rider's foot came into contact with the right-hand footrest. As the engine started so easily, however, little inconvenience was caused in practice.) Even after the machine had been unavoidably left exposed to a night's heavy rain, the procedure outlined produced an immediate start. On a cool autumn morning it was necessary to ride about half a mile before the air-lever could be fully opened.

When warm, the engine would idle in neutral reliably and reasonably slowly, though not, of course, two-stroking evenly. Starting up with the engine warm merely required the throttle to be set rather less than one-quarter open, when a gentle dig on the kick-starter invariably produced the desired effect.

General mechanical noise audible from the engine was not exceptional though, on the overrun in top gear, piston rattle was at times rather pronounced. Power delivery was very smooth and pleasant.

Good Two-stroking

Two-stroking was perfectly maintained whenever the engine was running under load—even under light load. At 30 m.p.h. in top gear the degree of exhaust silencing was adequate. When wide throttle openings were employed, such as for maximum acceleration or at speed on the open road, the exhaust noise was considered to be obtrusive. Gas leakage occurred at the joint between the exhaust pipe and silencer.

Rather stiff in operation, the gear pedal also required appreciable movement to effect a change. When making downward changes, it was necessary to lift the right foot off the footrest in order to depress the pedal. Advantage could not be taken of the pedal adjustment provided because further lowering of the pedal brought it too close to the footrest. This condition arises from the fact that the pedal is pivoted high up on the gear box, so that the pedal arm slopes downward at an angle of roughly 45 degrees to the horizontal. For upward gear changes, on the other hand, it was necessary only to pivot the foot on the footrest.

Clean gear changes, either up or down, could be made provided that the controls were operated with some deliberation and, when changing down, that the engine was revved hard with the clutch withdrawn. Clutch operation was light and the take-up of the drive smooth and positive. Neutral could be selected easily from first or second gear.

Handling of the one-fifty Courier was exemplary under all conditions. Steering was light and positive at low speeds and rock steady at high

The engine has a wide power range and is particularly economical of fuel

Courier

Lively Performance

speeds. On the open road, any selected line through fast bends could be held unwaveringly. A very fair measure of riding comfort was afforded by the telescopic front fork and the plunger-type rear springing. Under normal road conditions, bottoming of either suspension was never discernible.

The relationship between handlebar, seat and footrests afforded a first-class riding position for a rider of average stature. The two-piece handlebar is adjustable for angle of grip. A slightly larger saddle would have been appreciated (a dual-seat is available at extra charge). The saddle is adjustable for height and longitudinally through approximately one inch. A 65 m.p.h. speedometer is mounted on the steering crown. The instrument, which was easily readable, was accurate at 30 m.p.h. but registered fast by approximately 2½ m.p.h. at a true speed of 40 m.p.h.

Both brakes were light and smooth in operation; they afforded really good stopping power from any speed of which the machine was capable. An adjustable stop is provided for the brake pedal. However, with the adjustment at its maximum setting, the pedal was still just a shade too high in relation to the desired footrest position.

Rectifier and battery lighting equipment is standardized. Sufficient light was furnished by the main beam to enable the full engine performance to be used after dark. Of the underslung type, the pilot light, though satisfactory for parking purposes, was considered to be too inconspicuous to other road users to warrant riding the machine in towns at night other than on the dipped beam. Equipped with a plastic-type lens, the rear lamp produced a penetrating light. An appreciated feature was the long shank provided on the headlamp switch, which greatly facilitated manipulation of the switch. The full lamp load was balanced on the ammeter at a speed of 30 m.p.h. in top gear.

Included in the equipment is an electric horn. The position on the handlebar of the horn button was such that its operation necessitated removal of the rider's hand from the twistgrip. The dip-switch and other handlebar controls were well placed for ease of operation.

Robust rear springing is a feature of the Courier

Placing the Courier on its centre stand involved very little effort. The stand embodies an extension peg which facilitates its being located, and curved feet which allow the machine to be rolled on and off the stand; in addition, a lifting handle is conveniently placed on the left side of the machine. The only drawback was that care was necessary to avoid contact with the underside of the silencer; otherwise, the rider's shoe became soiled by the accumulation of oil from the exhaust gases.

A minor criticism was that the fuel tap was so stiff that it could not be operated from the saddle, though the tap appeared to be easing slightly with use. Because the filler cap is offset from the centre line of the fuel tank, inspection of the fuel level was easy with the cap and separate oil measure removed. Even with the tank full, there was no leakage of petroil past the filler cap.

In its finish of glossy black enamel, with gold-lined tank and chromium-plated wheel rims, the Courier looked most attractive. A comprehensive set of tools is provided.

Information Panel

148 c.c. Excelsior Courier

SPECIFICATION

ENGINE: Excelsior 148 c.c. (55 × 62 mm) single-cylinder two-stroke with three-speed gear box in unit. Aluminium-alloy piston with slightly domed crown. Double-row roller-bearing big end; mainshafts supported by three ball journal bearings. Detachable light-alloy cylinder head. Petroil lubrication.

CARBURETTOR: Amal two-lever with air control lever on handlebar; twistgrip throttle control. Air filter fitted as standard.

TRANSMISSION: Three-speed gear box in unit with engine; positive-stop foot control. Gear ratios: Bottom, 17.24 to 1. Second, 9.64 to 1. Top, 6.52 to 1. Primary chain, ⅜ × 0.225in, in oil-bath case. Rear chain, ½ × 0.205in, with deeply valanced guard over top run. Two-plate, cork-lined clutch, running in oil, with built-in shock absorber. Engine r.p.m. at 30 m.p.h. in top gear, 2,700.

IGNITION and LIGHTING: Wico-Pacy flywheel magneto incorporating lighting coils. Rectifier and 6-volt, 12-ampere-hour accumulator. Twin-filament 24/24-watt main bulb.

FUEL CAPACITY: 2¼ gallons.

TYRES: Dunlop, 3.00 × 19in front and rear.

BRAKES: 5in diameter front and rear.

SUSPENSION: Excelsior telescopic front fork. Plunger-type rear springing.

WHEELBASE: 49½in. Ground clearance, 5½in. unladen.

SEAT: Wrights saddle. Unladen height, 3Cin.

WEIGHT: 217 lb fully equipped and with one gallon of fuel.

PRICE: £94. With purchase tax (in Gt. Britain only), £112 16s.

ROAD TAX: 17s 6d a year; 4s 10d a quarter.

MAKERS: Excelsior Motor Co., Ltd., Kings Road, Tyseley, Birmingham.

PERFORMANCE DATA

MEAN MAXIMUM SPEED: Bottom: 24 m.p.h.
Second: —
Top: 48 m.p.h.

MEAN ACCELERATION:

	10-20 m.p.h.	15-25 m.p.h.	20-30 m.p.h.
Bottom	3 secs	—	—
Second	4 secs	4.2 secs	4.4 secs
Top	—	6.2 secs	6 secs

Mean speed at end of quarter-mile from rest: maximum.
Mean time taken from 0-30 m.p.h.: 9 secs.

PETROIL CONSUMPTION: At 20 m.p.h., 150 m.p.g. At 30 m.p.h. 131 m.p.g. At 40 m.p.h, 98 m.p.g.

BRAKING: From 30 m.p.h. to rest, 29ft 6in (surface, dry tarmac).

TURNING CIRCLE: 11ft 9in.

MINIMUM NON-SNATCH SPEED: 14 m.p.h. in top gear.

WEIGHT per C.C.: 1.46 lb.

First published 17 January 1952

The 125 c.c. Douglas

A Practical, Likeable Runabout : Excellent Weather Protection :

WHEN the Douglas Vespa was introduced in 1949 it was one of the major attractions at the London Show, and even though the model has been in production for some time, machines on the road still attract a great deal of attention. The machine embodies many advanced technical features and its styling is uncommonly appealing to the eye.

Excellent weather protection coupled with a nippy performance make the Vespa a most attractive scooter

The combined large weather shield and footplate provide almost perfect protection. Water and road filth are prevented from soiling the rider's clothing at all times, but there is a tendency for wind to whip round the edges of the shield and create an up-draught at the rider's legs. It was felt that some form of valance would have been a useful addition.

Starting was simple and certain in all circumstances. In average winter weather, one gentle prod on the forward-acting kick-starter would bring the engine to life, providing the carburettor had been liberally flooded beforehand. An alternative was to close the air slide by means of the spring-loaded lever under the saddle instead of flooding the carburettor, but usually in these circumstances three or four prods on the kick-starter crank were necessary. If the weather was unusually cold, it was necessary to retain a hold on the air lever for about 15 seconds after the engine had started, but subsequently the lever could be released without fear that the engine would stall. Once the Vespa was under way the engine warmed up in a very short time, and usually after about a quarter-of-a-mile had been covered it would tick over quietly and reliably when the twistgrip was rolled right back. Two-stroking was exceptionally good, even on very small throttle openings, and the only occasions when four-stroking occurred was when the engine was on the overrun.

Some riders might prefer to start the engine with the machine on its centre stand. However, this is no hardship because the stand is uncommonly easy to bring into use.

To British eyes, the clutch lever and gear-change twist grip mounted together on the left-hand side of the handlebar is unusual. The clutch lever rotates with the grip, and the whole arrangement is most convenient. In the early stages, the mechanism was rather stiff, but after about 100 miles had been covered it began to free up, and towards the end of the test it was pleasantly light in operation. First gear was, occasionally, a little difficult to engage.

The makers suggest that, once on the move, there is no need to use the clutch for gear changing, and it was found that this method was perfectly satisfactory provided the rider did not object to slight clashing as the gears were engaged. If the clutch was employed, silent changes could be made given a slowish movement of the grip and correctly judged engine speed in relation to road speed. The gear change has no positive-stop mechanism, but there was no trouble with "missing" gears. Finger-light in operation, the clutch took up the drive sweetly and without snatch. Because the engine pulled extremely well at low revolutions, the clutch could always be fully engaged within the first few feet of starting from rest.

The twistgrip throttle was commendably light in operation and was most pleasant to use. Throughout the range, the pick-up was clean and responsive, and by using a fast gear change, acceleration was good enough to keep up with the average saloon car of, say, 12 h.p. At 35 m.p.h. the Vespa was running well within its limits, though, in fact, the engine did not seem to be stressed at full throttle. The engine is tractable and provides a smooth top-gear range of 15 to over 35 m.p.h. in pleasant, effortless

Mounted on the right-hand side, the fan-cooled 125 c.c. engine is partly enclosed by a neat "blister"

Vespa

Attractive Appearance

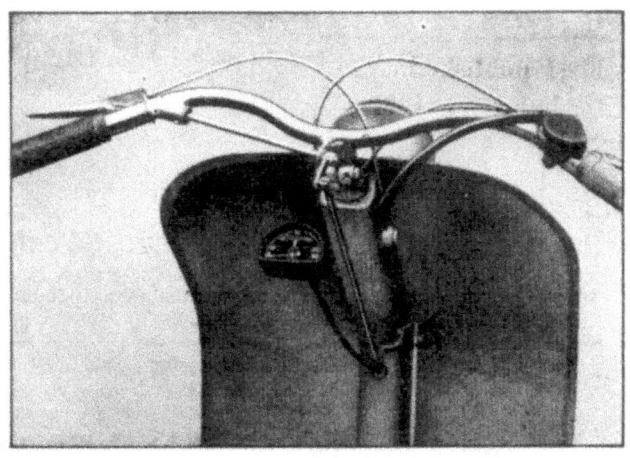

An ingenious and useful feature of the Vespa is the Yale-type lock on the steering column

style. Except at about 25 m.p.h., when a slight tremor ran through the footplate, vibration was virtually non-existent. The exhaust is well silenced, and from the saddle could be heard only as a low-pitched burble; even if hard acceleration was used, no undue noise was created.

Riding position is eminently satisfactory. The fairly wide flat handlebar makes for a comfortable wrist position, and the large Milverton saddle is positioned so that the rider sits nearly upright. Riders of a wide variety of stature can be comfortably accommodated although no adjustment is provided for either the bar or the saddle.

Handling of the Vespa was above reproach. Even on the worst surfaces, the machine felt completely stable. Bends could be negotiated with complete confidence and the machine held its line with no trace of chopping or sliding. The rear suspension provides about 2½in of movement which is adequately controlled by a hydraulic damper; on no occasion during the test did the pivoted arm reach the limit of its travel. Front suspension has about 2in movement and this bottomed once only during the test period—when the machine was travelling fairly fast over a series of pot-holes. Over "wavy" surfaces the Vespa had a tendency to pitch, but it never developed enough to cause concern.

Fixed to the handlebar near the throttle is an ingenious lighting switch which can be operated by the thumb without moving the hand from the throttle. It was thought that a "click-action" switch would be better than the existing type as on one or two occasions the switch was pushed too far in one direction and the lights extinguished. For night work, the direct lighting set provides enough illumination to enable day-time speeds to be maintained safely. The headlamp is fixed to the weather shield and does not move with the steering column. At speeds of over 15 m.p.h. this was not a disadvantage but at lower speeds, and particularly when manoeuvring in a confined space, it was necessary to get accustomed to the fact that the lamp beam does not follow the front wheel direction on corners. For parking purposes, an 8-ampere-hour battery is fitted. A very useful device on the Vespa is the steering lock. When the bar is turned to the left as far as possible, the steering column is automatically locked and the "joy-rider" thief is foiled. It is not, of course, practicable to turn the handlebar sufficiently when riding to bring the lock into operation.

As already implied, the Vespa is an exceptionally clean machine to ride. After the test had been completed, few traces of road filth (except on the underside of the footplate), or petroil could be located on any part of the machine, although a lengthy mileage, much of it during wet weather, had been covered. Ordinary clothes are quite suitable for everyday riding. The Vespa is a most attractive runabout and light tourer, and deserves the popularity it is earning in this country.

Information Panel

125 c.c. Douglas Vespa

SPECIFICATION

ENGINE: 125 c.c. (56.5 × 49.8 mm) two-stroke. Hardened steel connecting rod with roller bearing big end. Petroil lubrication.

CARBURETTOR: Amal single lever. Twistgrip throttle control. Air lever mounted below saddle.

IGNITION AND LIGHTING: Flywheel magneto incorporating lighting coils. Parking light from 6 v. 8 a.h. battery ; main headlight direct from generator. 24/24 w double-filament headlamp bulb controlled by handlebar switch. A.C. electric horn.

TRANSMISSION: Three-speed gearbox controlled by twistgrip. Gear ratios: Bottom, 12 to 1. Second, 7.5 to 1. Top, 4.78 to 1. Two-plate clutch with cork inserts running in oil. Primary and final drives by gears.

FUEL CAPACITY: 1.3 gallons.

TYRES: 3.50 × 8in Michelin front and rear. Quickly detachable and interchangeable wheels.

BRAKES: 5in diameter × ⅞in wide front and rear.

SUSPENSION: Vespa trailing-link front fork controlled by a coil spring ; hydraulically damped, pivoted-arm rear suspension.

WHEELBASE: 50in. Ground clearance, 8in unladen.

SADDLE: Milverton. Unladen height, 29in.

WEIGHT: 170lb, fully equipped with approximately ½ gallon of fuel.

ROAD TAX: 17s 6d a year : 4s 10d a quarter.

MAKERS: Douglas (Sales and Service), Ltd., Kingswood, Bristol.

PERFORMANCE DATA

MEAN MAXIMUM SPEED: Bottom : 20 m.p.h. Second : 29 m.p.h. Top : 43 m.p.h.

MEAN ACCELERATION:

	10-20 m.p.h.	15-25 m.p.h.	20-30 m.p.h.
Bottom	4 secs	—	—
Second	3.2 secs	4.4 secs	—
Top	7.6 secs	7.2 secs	6.2 secs

Mean speed at end of quarter mile from rest : Maximum.
Mean time taken to cover standing quarter mile : 13.5 secs.

PETROIL CONSUMPTION: At 20 m.p.h., 120 m.p.g. At 30 m.p.h., 93 m.p.g.

BRAKING: From 30 m.p.h. to rest, 32 feet (surface : dry tar macadam).

TURNING CIRCLE: 8ft.

MINIMUM NON-SNATCH SPEED: 12 m.h.p. in top gear.

WEIGHT PER C.C.: 1.3 lb.

The 123 c.c. Lambretta

First published 26 February 1953

A Willing, Lightweight Runabout, Simple to Start and

SINCE the war, the popularity of the motor scooter has been one of the outstanding features of the development of road transport on the Continent. Clean, easy and convenient to ride, these machines have found a considerable demand as a utilitarian means of transport among men and women of all ages and from all walks of life. One of the leading Italian makes is the Lambretta, which sells in very large numbers in its country of origin and elsewhere. Four types are imported into Great Britain; that tested was the model D, which may be described as the austerity model of the two which have the new suspension.

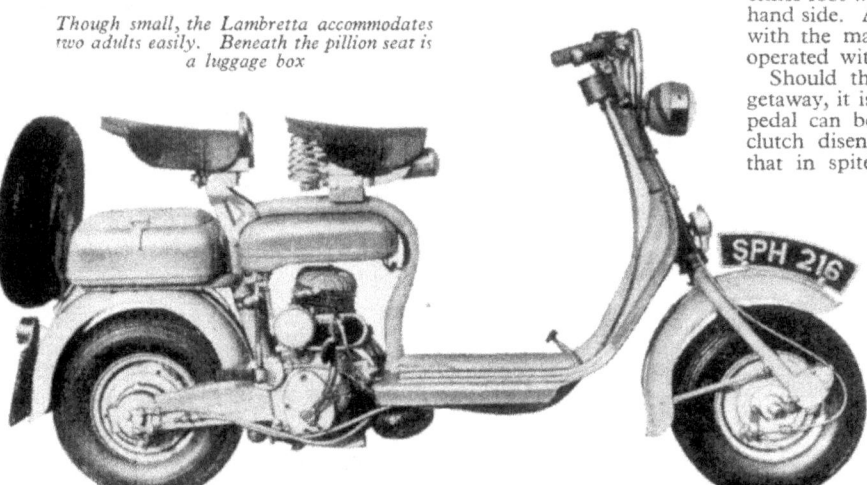

Though small, the Lambretta accommodates two adults easily. Beneath the pillion seat is a luggage box

While retaining such outstanding design features as fully enclosed shaft transmission, torsion-bar rear springing and trailing-link front fork, the model D does not feature a number of the refinements and the comprehensive enclosure which characterize its de luxe brother, the model LD. Docile and economical in performance, reasonably comfortable, and easy to start, control and park, the model D fulfils most of the requirements of a modern utility vehicle. Its open frame and light weight make it equally suitable for riding by either sex, while it provides ample accommodation for two people. Its appearance, too, is attractive: the finish is in light green.

Engine starting was simple at all times, there being little sensitivity to control setting. With the engine cold, it was necessary only to turn on the fuel tap, close the manual carburettor choke and depress the float tickler for a few seconds. First or second depression of the starter pedal invariably brought the engine to life, almost regardless of throttle position. The starter pedal pivots forward and downward, and is easily operated by either foot while supporting the machine from the right-hand side. Alternatively, engine starting can be effected with the machine on its stand, or the pedal can be operated with the rider in the saddle.

Should the rider inadvertently stall the engine on getaway, it is not necessary to select neutral; the starter pedal can be operated with machine in gear and the clutch disengaged. Pedal-to-engine gearing is such that in spite of healthy compression, the engine can effectively be spun without undue effort. It was found convenient to allow the engine to warm up for a few moments so that the choke could be opened fully before moving off; otherwise it was necessary to stop after a few hundred yards to raise the choke lever. Once warm, the engine ticked over reliably when the throttle was closed, though, as is to be expected, it four-stroked under these conditions. Engine stopping is effected by an ignition cut-out operated by an ingenious, handlebar-mounted, combination switch which also controls the lights and horn.

Gear selection is effected by rotating the combined twistgrip and clutch lever on the left side of the handlebar. Engagement of bottom gear with the machine stationary and the engine idling was accompanied by a slight jerk.

Simple Gear Change

The clutch took up the drive rather quickly, as effective movement of the lever was confined to a small range. It was not difficult to master this characteristic and achieve smooth getaways. Gear changing, both upward and downward, was simple. Location of second gear was not so positive as is desirable, but with practice it became an easy matter to judge the correct position of the twistgrip. Second and top gear ratios are rather widely spaced; consequently, for the ultimate in acceleration, it was found advantageous to take the machine up to 30 m.p.h. before selecting top gear. However, when riding normally, a change into top at about 25 m.p.h. was usual.

Both engine and transmission were smooth except for slight snatching at low speeds on the overrun. In motion, exhaust and mechanical noises were well subdued. When idling, the exhaust note was more staccato though by no means offensive, and some mechanical noise was audible.

In top gear the Lambretta cruised easily and indefinitely between 30 and 40 m.p.h., according to wind and gradient, and with the rider clad in the bulky clothing appropriate to mid-winter riding. Alternatively, the engine was quite happy with the machine burbling along at 20-25 m.p.h. Though main-road gradients reduced the speed sharply owing to the rather high top-gear ratio, the Lambretta continued to pull lustily down to less than 20 m.p.h. if required.

In town, the acceleration from traffic halts was more than a match for the average stream of

This view of the power unit shows the air and fuel filters built into the carburetter. Also prominent are the starter pedal and folding pillion footrest

Scooter

Ride, Easy to Clean

The shaft-drive housing forms the pivoted arm of the rear suspension. Note the ribbed rear brake drum

vehicles. Consequent upon its over-gearing, the Lambretta ran happily up to 50 m.p.h. in top gear when conditions of wind and gradient were favourable. The engine well repaid use of the new premier-grade petrols, which considerably lessened a tendency to pink when pulling hard in top gear. Two-stroking at idling speed was also markedly improved on the better fuels. The little engine was quite capable of dealing with the extra weight of an adult pillion passenger. The Smith's magnetic speedometer registered approximately ten per cent fast; it was necessary to replace the head during the course of the test.

Handling the Lambretta was child's play and should present no difficulties to the newcomer to single-track vehicles. Straight-ahead steering was positive at all times, while the machine's light weight and very low centre of gravity make it responsive to the least effort in turning and cornering. This lightness of control, allied to the small overall dimensions, renders traffic negotiation simple. Steering lock is generous; it proved an asset when riding in confined spaces and when manœuvring the machine manually. The centre stand relieves parking of all possible worries. Very little effort is required to bring the stand into operation provided the machine is pulled back by the handlebar rather than lifted by the pillion-seat rail. The stand supports the machine safely on the steepest cambers.

Stability on slippery roads was good. Rear wheel slides were provoked by banking well over on an icy corner, but were immediately corrected without conscious effort. Similarly, although it was not difficult to spin the rear wheel when accelerating on wet wood blocks, the machine always remained quite controllable.

The natural, "easy chair" riding position is suitable for a wide variety of statures. Allied to a sprung saddle and front and rear wheel springing, it furnishes a fair degree of riding comfort. The suspension takes the sting out of road irregularities, but absence of damping of the rear torsion bar resulted in pitching on undulating surfaces. Accommodation for the passenger is generous and comfortable; the added weight was found to improve the behaviour of the rear springing.

Both brakes, particularly the rear one, were reasonably powerful and light to operate. Care was required to avoid locking the wheel when using the rear brake on slippery surfaces; in heavy rain, the front brake lost some degree of efficiency.

Some criticism might be levelled against the weather protection. While the legshield-cum-footboard is adequate to protect the rider's feet from road filth, the shield is too narrow and too short to afford sufficient defence against wind and rain. When riding in wet weather, full-length leg and body waterproofs were required. Another criticism concerns the reserve petrol tap which, on average London roads, provided sufficient fuel for no more than one mile. No parking light is fitted.

The connoisseur will find that the Lambretta possesses several attractive features; not the least are the ease with which it can be cleaned, and the complete oil-tightness of all its mechanism. Both wheels are quickly detachable from their hubs, car fashion, by the removal of three nuts. Removal of three more nuts which secure the split rim enables the tyre to be removed. A detachable, fine-gauze fuel filter is built into the carburettor. An appreciated fitting was the 5in-deep rear luggage box.

Information Panel

123 c.c. Lambretta Model D

SPECIFICATION

ENGINE: 123 c.c. (52 × 58 mm.) single-cylinder two-stroke. Needle roller-bearing big-end. Mainshaft supported on four ball-bearings. Aluminium-alloy piston. Detachable, light-alloy cylinder head. Petroil lubrication.

CARBURETTOR: Dellorto, with twistgrip throttle control and air-slide directly operated. Petrol and air filters incorporated.

IGNITION and LIGHTING: Marelli flywheel magneto with lighting coils. Twin-filament, 24/24-watt headlamp bulb.

TRANSMISSION: Three-speed gear box in unit with engine. Twist-grip control. Bottom, 12.9 to 1. Second, 7.5 to 1. Top, 4.75 to 1. Primary drive by bevel gears. Final drive by shaft and bevels. Multi-plate clutch with Ferodo friction material running in oil.

FUEL CAPACITY: 1.3 gallons.

TYRES: Pirelli, 4.00 × 8in studded front and rear. Spare wheel mounted behind pillion seat. All wheels quickly detachable and interchangeable. Split rims for tyre removal.

BRAKES: Rear, approximately 5½ × 0.8in; front, approximately 4 × 0.9in.

SUSPENSION: Trailing-link front fork controlled by progressive-rate coil springs; pivoted-arm rear springing controlled by torsion-bar and rubber limit stops.

WHEELBASE: 51½in unladen. Ground clearance, 4½in unladen

SADDLES: Aquila. Unladen height, 31in.

WEIGHT: 206 lb fully equipped, including spare wheel and pillion seat, and with one gallon of fuel.

PRICE: £110 7s 7d. With Purchase Tax (in Britain only), £139 17s 6d. Extras: pillion seat, £4 10s; spare wheel, £8 8s.

ROAD TAX: 17s 6d a year; 4s 10d a quarter.

MAKERS: Innocenti Soc. Generale per l'Industria Metallurgica e Meccanica, Milano, Italy.

BRITISH CONCESSIONAIRES: Lambretta Concessionaires, Ltd., 213-219, The Broadway, Wimbledon, London, S.W.19.

PERFORMANCE DATA

MEAN MAXIMUM SPEED: Bottom: 20 m.p.h.
Second: 35 m.p.h.
Top: 40 m.p.h.

MEAN ACCELERATION:

	10-20 m.p.h.	15-25 m.p.h.	20-30 m.p.h.
Bottom	2.6 secs	—	—
Second	4.6 secs	4.2 secs	4.8 secs
Top	—	—	11 secs

Mean speed at end of quarter-mile from rest: maximum.
Mean time taken from rest to 30 m.p.h.: 9 secs

PETROIL CONSUMPTION: At 20 m.p.h., 140 m.p.g. At 30 m.p.h., 110 m.p.g.

BRAKING: From 30 m.p.h. to rest, 44ft (surface, damp tarmac).

TURNING CIRCLE: 11ft.

MINIMUM NON-SNATCH SPEED: 16 m.p.h. in top gear.

WEIGHT PER C.C.: 1.6 lb.

The Bond Minicar is no longer unusual on British roads. Here it is seen in a London park traffic stream

First published 2 April 1953

Mark C Bond Minicar

An Economical 197 c.c. Three-wheeler with Lively Performance and Car Convenience

WITH the arrival of peace in 1945, the traditional three-wheeler of pre-war days appeared to have died. The sporting or semi-sporting vehicles of the type, which had enjoyed only limited popularity in the between-the-wars period, were dropped from their manufacturers' programmes. In 1948 the Bond Minicar—the first post-war three-wheeler—was introduced. Its attractive features included economy in running, convenience in use, exceptional manœuvrability and small overall dimensions. High performance was placed well down the list of essential requirements. By now the Minicar has ceased to be unusual on British roads. Nevertheless, wherever the model submitted for test was parked, it rarely failed to attract interested—if somewhat amused—comment from lay public as well as from motorists and motor cyclists.

Economical running has certainly been achieved. In the four weeks during which the Bond was under test it was used as a home-to-office hack, for going to the cinema, shopping on Saturdays in busy Kingston, for running "up to the ironmongers at the end of the road." The home-to-office run embraced 16 miles each way. The journey lay through bottle-neck streets and involved driving in some of the worst of London's traffic. Since the driver was generally in a hurry, the acceleration performance was always used to the full.

These facts notwithstanding, overall fuel consumption worked out at nearly 70 m.p.g. The fuel consumption figure for steady 30 m.p.h. cruising on the open road was 86 m.p.g. and that for 40 m.p.h. cruising, 72 m.p.g. There was no appreciable difference in fuel consumption whether one person was in the car or two—or, indeed, whether three were squeezed into the single, bench-type seat. This last achievement involved not too much discomfort for the driver and no difficulty in steering or changing gear.

Control layout of the Bond follows orthodox car practice. That is to say, clutch, brake and throttle pedals are situated in line, in that order, from left to right. To the left of the clutch is a fourth pedal which operates the decompressor chamber in the cylinder head. The gear lever protrudes through the facia and is bent at 90 degrees for left-hand operation. The steering wheel is almost vertical. In the instrument panel are situated the ignition switch, choke control, speedometer, dash-light switch, headlamp dipswitch and, in the test model, two extras: an ammeter and a trafficator switch. Protruding from the floor for left-hand operation is a starting handle and, to the right of the steering wheel, there is a pistol-grip, parking-brake lever. The floor is carpeted.

Easy starting from cold demanded generous flooding of the carburettor. It was dependent also upon accurate adjustment of the mixture control needle which, on the Bond, is cable operated from the choke knob in the dash. In delivery tune, the mixture setting was decidedly weak, with the result that starting was difficult, and reliable idling impossible to achieve. Moreover, since the choke knob is spring-loaded, it automatically returns to its normal-use position, and the needle setting cannot be varied by the driver while he is in the car. Once the trouble was diagnosed, however, it was the work of a few minutes only to reset the needle to provide the proper mixture strength. This done, cold starting was generally accomplished after, say, half-a-dozen easy pulls on the starting lever. The degree of muscular effort required was not great, since engine compression was negligible when the decompressor chamber was in use.

Once the engine was warm, it would idle slowly and reliably, although, of course, it was firing irregularly. In view of the fact that no hand throttle is fitted, the carburettor setting has to be such that the engine will not stall when the right foot is away from the throttle. Hence there is always some degree of transmission snatch when the engine is on the overrun. The practice adopted to overcome this was to free the clutch comparatively early when slowing down or coming to a stop.

Acceleration from rest was decidedly brisk and more than sufficient to cope with modern traffic speeds. The Bond would stay with many 10 h.p. saloons with ease and, indeed, be faster off the mark if spirited driving tactics were employed. Second gear could be engaged almost as soon as the car was on the move. Top gear could be snicked home at 20 m.p.h. if only moderate acceleration was required; when peak performance was being sought, upward gear changes were generally made at 10 and 30 m.p.h.

Gear-changing required no special skill or knack. From neutral, the lever is moved up into bottom gear and down to second and top gears. The gear change was much heavier than some might desire, and bottom gear was not always easy to engage from neutral.

Clutch operation when the test vehicle was stationary was unduly fierce. Smooth starting away demanded gentle clutch engagement and a small throttle opening. Once the vehicle was on the move, even slightly, this characteristic disappeared and care in clutch operation during gear-changing was unnecessary.

Happiest maximum cruising speed on the open road with two people on board was 40 m.p.h. At this speed the engine gave little indication of fuss, and main road hills in southern England could be surmounted with ease. Box Hill, which is almost 1½ miles long, and has an average gradient of 1 in 25 and a maximum gradient of 1 in 8, could be effortlessly climbed in second and top gears, and restarting on the steepest gradient was easily accomplished. Two successive climbs of Box Hill, after some 30 miles of near-full-bore driving, were undertaken without the slightest sign of protest from the engine. Highest maximum speed achieved was 49 m.p.h. On several occasions as much as five or six miles were covered on full throttle, again without indication of distress from the engine. At full-throttle speeds,

With the hood raised there was marked freedom from draughts

ENGINE: Villiers 197 c.c. (59 x 72 mm) two-stroke, with gear box in unit. Flat-crown, die-cast, aluminium-alloy piston. Detachable light-alloy cylinder head with hemispherical combustion chamber.

CARBURETTOR: Villiers Middleweight with pedal throttle control and hand-operated mixture control for cold starting.

TRANSMISSION: Villiers three-speed gear box, with dashboard-mounted hand control. Gear ratios: Top, 4.9 to 1. Second, 6.9 to 1. Bottom, 13.1 to 1.

IGNITION AND LIGHTING: Flywheel magneto with lighting coils; Westinghouse rectifier and 6-volt, 13-ampere-hour accumulator. Separate head and side lamps.

FUEL CAPACITY: 2½ gallons.

WEIGHT: 460 lb with no fuel and fully equipped.

ROAD TAX: £5 a year: £1 7s 6d a quarter.

PETROIL CONSUMPTION: At 30 m.p.h., 86 m.p.g. At 40 m.p.h., 72 m.p.g.

PRICE: £224; with purchase tax (in Britain only), £349 18s 10d.

MANUFACTURERS: Sharp's Commercials, Ltd., Ribbleton Lane, Preston, Lancs.

---

however, mechanical and exhaust noises reached an uncomfortable pitch and there was, in addition, some drumming from the light-alloy body. These noises were increased when the car was driven with the hood raised.

Suspension on the Bond is by hydraulically controlled pivoted-arm for the front wheel and by bonded-rubber controlled pivoted-arms for the rear wheels. Wheel movement was approximately 3in at the rear and, partly as a result of this, the standard of road-holding of the little car is of a very high order. Corners may be taken in safety in a manner that would cause many a normal car to roll disconcertingly. Though the Bond is so light that one of the rear wheels could easily be lifted clear of the road, neither of them gave any indication that they would ever lift during cornering. The tendency to skidding appeared to be lower than with many orthodox cars. The combination of small-diameter wheels and three tracks results in the vehicle suffering the effects of road irregularities to a greater extent than two- or four-wheelers; the standard of insulation from road shocks was thus only moderate.

On the latest Minicars, brakes are fitted to all three wheels. The brakes in themselves were powerful and adequate for all normal touring purposes. When they were applied in crash-stop fashion, however, the wheels tended to lock and the car, because of its light weight, skidded for the whole of the stopping distance.

In towns and cities, such as for shopping excursions or theatre visits, the small dimensions and 90-degree steering lock provided the Bond with a degree of manœuvrability in excess of that possessed by almost any other wheeled vehicle, the common bicycle excepted. Parked close between other vehicles, it could be brought out in one movement, merely by locking the wheel hard over. No reverse gear is fitted and none is required. If the vehicle has to be reversed, it can be moved by a single person with no more effort than that required to move a 350 c.c. solo motor cycle (less, indeed, for the Bond has natural stability). First impressions were that the steering was over-heavy, but in the later stages of the test, when the driver had become more accustomed to the Minicar, this heaviness was not considered objectionable.

Ample Luggage Room

Windscreen and sidescreen protection was all that was required on dry days, even during cold weather. Some draught was felt on the back of the driver's and passenger's heads but it was not sufficient, for example, to make the wearing of a hat necessary. The hood could be raised in less than a minute. When the hood was in use, the interior of the car was as snug as that of a normal sports car. Luggage space behind the seats was covered by the hood when it was raised. The room provided was more than ample for luggage for two people for a week's holiday.

An outstanding feature of the Minicar was the intensity of the driving beam from the twin Lucas headlamps mounted in the front of the "wings." Of the modern double-dipping type, they provided more than enough light for a vehicle of the Bond's speed performance. The generator did not balance the discharge rate but no trouble was experienced during the month the car was in use—a month in which it was frequently parked for long periods with the side lights on and two, two-hour night runs in open country were undertaken. Finish of the car submitted for test was a pleasant shade of grey.

The road test model was finished in an attractive grey. The wing-mounted trafficators are available at extra charge

The offset engine, short gear lever and instrument panel are clearly shown in this view

First published 6 August 1953

Reliant Regal Three-Wheeler

A Lively and Economical 750 c.c. Family Vehicle with Excellent Steering and Brakes

THE recent reduction in purchase tax has given the three-wheeler the opportunity of competing on level terms with the sidecar outfit. Whether or not the British public will take to the new school of three-wheelers (which are essentially utilitarian compared with the sporting types popular in the 1930s) remains to be seen; the restricted choice of machines suitable for sidecar work and the need for better sidecars certainly give the three-wheeler a good opportunity.

An attractive example of its kind is the Reliant Regal occasional four-seater, which is in its second season on the market. Several modifications have been made since this machine was introduced, and the Regal is now less a coupé than an open tourer with all-weather equipment. The machine tested was one of the latest series, smartly finished in metallic-lustre blue, with dark red upholstery, and it made a very favourable impression. It was accorded many complimentary remarks when parked or in traffic blocks, and a good deal of time was spent answering questions as to its price and performance.

Though of small overall dimensions, the Regal is a thoroughly practical vehicle. The seating height is about the same as that of the average small sports car, so that the size of other vehicles does not seem overwhelming. An unusual feature is the position of the four-cylinder engine, which is located in the driving compartment forward of the seats and between driver and passenger.

RELIANT REGAL

ENGINE: Reliant four-cylinder, side-valve, water-cooled, 747.5 c.c. (56 × 76 mm), giving 16 b.h.p. at 4,000 r.p.m.; compression ratio 5.7 to 1; detachable cast-iron cylinder head; cast-iron cylinder block mounted on aluminium crankcase; three-point rubber engine mounting; dynamo belt-driven from crankshaft.

CARBURETTOR: Solex downdraught with choke control inter-connected with throttle; A.C. mechanical petrol pump.

TRANSMISSION: Borg and Beck single-plate clutch; four-speed and reverse gear box; gear ratios—top 5.43 to 1, third 8.63 to 1, second 14.6 to 1, bottom 23.18 to 1, reverse 23.18 to 1; Hardy Spicer needle-roller propeller shaft; semi-floating rear axle with differential.

BRAKES: Girling hydraulic, pedal-operated on all wheels; hand brake on rear wheels only.

SUSPENSION: Pivoted-arm front suspension by torsion bar; semi-elliptic rear springs; double-acting hydraulic dampers on all wheels.

WHEELS: Interchangeable, pressed steel, fitted with 4.50 × 14in tyres (export, 5.00 × 14in); spare wheel housed under bonnet.

ELECTRICAL EQUIPMENT: Ignition by 6-volt battery, coil and distributor with centrifugal automatic-advance control; built-in headlamps with twin-filament bulbs; separate side lamps; twin stop-and-tail lamps with separate number-plate illumination; electric starter; electric horn; self-cancelling direction indicators.

FUEL TANK: Rear-mounted, 6 gallons capacity.

DIMENSIONS: Wheelbase, 74in; track, 45in; overall length, 123in; overall width, 54in; overall height (hood raised), 53in; ground clearance, 6in; weight, 890 lb.

PRICE: £362 9s 2d, including purchase tax (in Great Britain only). Annual tax, £5.

MANUFACTURERS: The Reliant Engineering Co. (Tamworth), Ltd., Watling Street, Two Gates, Tamworth, Staffs.

The unit is concealed by a detachable, sheet-aluminium cowling, fabric-covered to reduce heat radiation and noise.

Orthodox car practice is followed in the control layout. The instrument panel is equipped with speedometer and fuel gauge, warning lights for ignition and oil pressure, starter button, choke control, combined lighting and ignition switch, and further switches for the dash light and windscreen wiper. A switch on the steering-wheel hub operates the self-cancelling direction indicators, and the double-dipping headlamps are controlled by a push-push button on the floor near the clutch pedal. The short gear lever is convenient to the left hand and the hand brake lies close to the driver's seat on the left side.

The electric starter never failed to bring the engine to life at the first or second push on the button; inter-connection of throttle and choke ensures the correct throttle opening for starting. When the Reliant was received, the tickover was set too fast, but was quickly adjusted by means of the throttle-stop screw, and thereafter proved slow and reliable when the engine was warm.

Once under way, the machine gave an impression of liveliness which remained throughout the test. Its low weight, barely 8 cwt, and reasonable power output gave it accelerative powers rather above those of the average small family saloon car.

Very high marks must be awarded to the steering, which was light and positive at all speeds and almost entirely free from reaction on bumpy surfaces. Only 1¼ turns of the wheel are required from lock to lock—an excellent lock it is, too—and the Regal can turn in an average suburban road without reversing.

Cornering and stability were also of a high order and, even when the rear tyres were squealed on fast bends, body roll was slight. Comfort, however, was not up to the expected standard: the rear suspension was thought to be much too firm (unless four adults were squeezed in), and this factor, in conjunction with rather hard and not-too-well-shaped seats, resulted in a considerable amount of jolting on other than smooth main roads. Softer rear springs and rather more lavish upholstery would effect a big improvement. The stiff rear suspension no doubt contributes to the absence of roll on corners; front suspension, on the other hand, had an adequately soft, well-controlled action and provided no grounds for criticism.

The crash-type (i.e., non-synchromesh) gear box was audible on the indirect gears. Movement of the lever was considered to be a little on the heavy side and some care was necessary, using double-declutching methods, to ensure quiet changes. Though the clutch-pedal travel between "in" and "out" was short, the clutch engaged smoothly and required only light pressure.

Engine flexibility and low-speed torque were very good. In traffic, early upward gear changes were customary; there was little point in revving the engine in the gears unless really hard acceleration was desired. Normal changing-up speeds were no more than 7, 15 and 25 m.p.h., but the ability of the engine to buzz is indicated by a maximum speed in third of over 50 m.p.h.

The hilly area of Surrey failed to produce any gradient capable of troubling the Regal in the slightest with only the driver aboard. Restarts were made on the inside of a hairpin bend having a maximum slope of about 1 in 5; the power margin was so great that a change to second gear could be made almost at once. Second gear was normally used for getting away and, for test purposes, third gear was employed once or twice without the need for much clutch slipping. Although a closer-ratio gear box would give a better performance under ordinary conditions, the present ratios certainly enable really severe going to be tackled with complete confidence, even with a full load.

Comfortable cruising speed on the level lay anywhere between 20 and 55 m.p.h. With two up, the latter speed could be maintained up average main-road hills. Even at the maximum of over 60 m.p.h., the unit remained free from vibration and sang a pleasant song.

A measure of praise must be accorded to the brakes, which were pleasant to use and extremely powerful. Only light pedal pressure was required for normal deceleration, but all three wheels could be locked on a dry road by fierce application; the action, however, was sufficiently progressive for safe operation on slippery surfaces. Under heavy braking, the Reliant held a straight course, nor did it try to stand on its nose—in fact, its braking was fully up to the standard of the best modern cars or solo motor cycles. The hand brake was capable of locking the rear wheels; it held securely on the aforementioned 1 in 5 gradient and was easy to release.

Of prime importance in a vehicle of this type is fuel economy. Owing to the pump-fed carburettor and the cowled engine, it was not possible to fit our test tank for an accurate measurement of the consumption. However, as close a check as possible was made by means of speedometer and fuel-gauge readings; the all-in figure so obtained was about 45 m.p.g. Since the Regal was driven fairly hard and the bulk of its running was in London, amid rush-hour traffic, it is thought that the makers' claim of 50 m.p.g. should be attainable in easier circumstances.

The coachbuilt body was well finished, both inside and out, and was free from squeaks and rattles. Wheels are interchangeable, and a spare wheel is carried conveniently under the bonnet, which also houses the battery, jack and tools. There is sufficient luggage accommodation for two medium-size suitcases in the boot, access to which is obtained by tilting the rear-seat backrest. Weather protection with the hood and side curtains raised was up to normal open-car standards. The hood was reasonably easy to raise and lower, and when not in use fitted snugly out of sight behind the rear seat. The latter, incidentally, provided rather cramped accommodation for two adults but gave adequate room for one adult or two children.

In warm weather, the temperature inside the Regal when closed became rather high, owing to the engine position and the absence of any form of heat insulation on the inside of the cowling. One

With hood and side curtains raised, the Regal has trim lines and provides good protection from the elements

run was made in heavy rain, when it was found that water leaked in at the rear edge of the bonnet and dripped on to the feet of the front-seat occupants.

The headlamps on this particular model were set to point the main beams rather too high for optimum results. Had any long night runs been envisaged, the reflector position could easily have been adjusted on the three-screw mounting. Sufficient light, however, was given by the dipped beams to permit a cruising speed in the region of 50 m.p.h. without offence to oncoming traffic.

At the conclusion of the test, the Regal was handed back with real regret. It had shown itself to be a thoroughly practical and likeable little vehicle. It should appeal strongly to the family man of limited means who requires more protection for himself than is provided by a sidecar outfit. It possesses excellent manœuvrability and steering, thoroughly safe brakes and a lively performance—sufficient virtues to ensure it a welcome place on the roads.

Exceptional manœuvrability made the Reliant three-wheeler an admirable vehicle for town driving   This picture was taken near Buckingham Palace

First published 5 July 1951

32 c.c. Berini Cyclemotor

A Roller-drive Unit with Pleasant Characteristics :
Imported from the Netherlands

LOW-SPEED pulling has been cited as a most desirable feature of the cyclemotor. It is in this direction that the Berini shows up particularly well. Extremely neat and compact in appearance, the 32 c.c. two-stroke unit develops 0.65 brake horse power, and is powerful enough to propel the cycle along pleasantly at about 20 m.p.h. on three-quarter throttle. At speeds in excess of this figure (maximum is about 25 m.p.h.) a tendency to four-stroke was prevalent; however, it is learnt that the carburettors of machines now being marketed are fitted with a different needle and jet to overcome this four-stroking.

In Holland, where the Berini is manufactured, no such trouble has been experienced. The cause has been put down to the different atmospheric conditions in this country, and also to the quality of Pool petrol. Later, a run aboard a machine fitted with the modified carburettor components, revealed that the engine two-stroked satisfactorily throughout the speed range.

Engine construction incorporates a rotary valve, and this contributes largely to the excellent low-speed running under load which could be obtained. To get away from a traffic stop, it was only necessary to give one complete turn of the pedal crank, re-engage the drive by means of the handlebar control and, on the throttle lever being opened, the tiny engine would pull away lustily. On a flat road the engine could be throttled down and the machine would idle along reliably at a fast walking pace.

The characteristics of the Berini make traffic riding easy; if the best acceleration from a slow speed was required, it paid to give a few rapid turns on the pedals, when the revs would mount very quickly indeed. Main-road hill-climbing (for example, on a hill about a quarter-mile long with a gradient of about 1 in 25) was good. When pedal assistance was necessary, only very moderate effort was required to sustain the revs. On another longish hill which was just steep enough to cause ordinary pedal cyclists to dismount, the Berini pulled steadily to the top.

A much steeper hill was tackled—one which only the super-sporting type of cyclist would attempt to ride up. It was found that with a reasonably fast approach a successful climb could be made, provided continuous pedal assistance was given. However, the effort required at the pedals was hardly more than that necessary to propel an ordinary cycle up a very slight gradient.

For cold-starting, the mixture control on the Amal carburettor required to be set in the rich position ("shut"), and the throttle at about one-quarter open; on pedalling away and connecting the drive, the engine would always fire after it had been turning over for five or six seconds; the pedalling effort required was

---

INFORMATION PANEL

SPECIFICATION : Berini 32 c.c. (bore 36 mm, stroke 32 mm), two-stroke engine. Inverted cylinder, with detachable alloy cylinder head. Transverse crankshaft carrying carborundum-faced roller which bears on tyre. Wipac flywheel magneto, driven from mainshaft. Amal carburettor. Weight, 15 lb. Petroil tank capacity, ⅓ gallon ; ratio, oil to petrol, 1 to 25.

PRICE : £24 fitted.

CONCESSIONAIRES : Interpro Engineering Co., 15, Arlington Street, London, S.W.1.

---

surprisingly slight. Almost immediately the mixture control could be set on weak, or "open". Starting with a warm engine was instantaneous on engagement of the drive.

A petroil consumption of 240 m.p.g. is claimed. The machine tested—used mainly in traffic—covered approximately 160 miles to the gallon; the figure may have been influenced by the incorrect carburettor settings. A useful "trap" in the rear of the fuel tank ensured that, on running short of fuel, a forward tilt of the tank would provide enough reserve petroil for a few more miles.

Mounting of the engine unit over the front wheel did not adversely affect the steering of the bicycle, and, if anything, gave improved road-holding at the front end. As will be gathered, there are only two engine controls on the handlebar. On the right side there is a lever for the throttle, and on the left a lever for raising or lowering the engine to disengage or engage the drive.

It was desirable to match approximately engine speed and road speed when engaging the drive, to prevent undue tyre wear. The drive control, which incorporates a spring-loaded cam to lock the lever in the disengaged position, was inclined to be stiff in operation. Adjustment is provided for both the cable and the coil spring to hold the engine down and the roller in contact with the tyre. At no time, even in wet-weather conditions, was any drive-slip experienced. The engine was quiet mechanically, and well silenced.

A description of the Berini was given in the issue of *The Motor Cycle* dated May 24, and a sectional drawing appeared in the June 7 issue.

The neat Berini engine unit weighs 15 lb. A "trap" in the rear of the egg-shape petroil tank ensures a small reserve supply

First published 31 January 1952

48 c.c. Cucciolo Cyclemotor

A Lively Overhead-valve Engine with Two-speed Pre-selector Gear Box Built in Unit

ITALIAN designed and manufactured, the 48 c.c. overhead-valve Cucciolo is a cyclemotor with a difference. Translated, the name means "Little Pup," and certainly the engine is just as lively as any small canine could be. An interesting point was that the machine tested had covered 8,000 miles.

Clipped to the cycle frame bottom bracket and front down tube, the engine has a two-speed pre-selector gear box built in unit, and final drive is through the pedalling chain. Therefore with a free-wheel the cycle will coast if the throttle is closed, regardless of gear position. On the cycle tested, a fixed-wheel was fitted, and in this case advantage could be taken of the engine-braking effect when the twistgrip was closed.

Gears are selected by positioning the bicycle pedals—left pedal forward and crank horizontal for bottom, right pedal forward for top, pedal cranks vertical for neutral.

The engine was readily started from cold by the following method. The carburettor was lightly flooded, and the gears put in neutral by positioning the pedals and then actuating the clutch. Then the machine was pedalled away, and at a speed of 4 to 5 m.p.h. the right pedal was held forward to select top gear and the bicycle allowed to coast. By actuating the clutch (one movement, out and in), and at the same time raising the exhaust valve lifter, the engine was made to revolve. When the valve lifter was released the engine would fire immediately and, with a little pedal assistance, pull away in top gear.

If one wanted to be "lazy" one could, as soon as the engine fired, select bottom gear, engage the gear by actuating the clutch, and pull away quickly in the low gear. Another method of starting was to engage top gear and pedal away with the valve lifter raised, then release it at 4 to 5 m.p.h.

The clutch, though slightly stiff in operation—it was necessary for it to be withdrawn to the full extent of its travel to engage the gears—was smooth and positive in its take-up of the drive.

There are two methods which may be adopted at a traffic halt. Neutral can be selected, the engine kept ticking over and the left pedal put forward for bottom gear preparatory to making a normal clutch start. Or, the engine can be kept ticking over in bottom gear with the clutch held out. The left pedal must, of course, be in the forward position when the clutch is engaged. Holding the clutch out for a few minutes is not detrimental, since it is a metal-to-metal clutch running in oil, though slight clutch-drag is usually experienced. Both methods proved to be entirely satisfactory.

It would hardly be accurate to describe the Cucciolo as a motor-assisted bicycle—rather it is a power bicycle. For at no time during the test was it necessary to use pedal assistance once the engine was running, except when starting by the first method described earlier.

At 5,200 r.p.m. the engine is said to produce 1.58 b.h.p., and this proved sufficient to propel the cycle along a level road at a speed in excess of 40 m.p.h. A cruising speed of 30-35 m.p.h. was maintained quite easily for mile after mile on mildly undulating roads. After running on full throttle for ten miles the engine showed no signs of overheating; indeed, it was possible casually to stroke the cylinder barrel fins without burning one's fingers.

INFORMATION PANEL

ENGINE: 48 c.c. (38 × 42 mm) four-stroke, with pullrod-operated overhead valves. One-piece light-alloy cylinder barrel and head; cast-iron liner. Wet-sump lubrication; oil sump capacity, approximately 1 pint.
CARBURETTOR: Weber, 2-jet, single lever.
TRANSMISSION: Two-speed pre-selector gear box. Gear ratios: Top, 7.5 to 1. Bottom, 13.5 to 1. Nine-plate all-metal clutch running in oil. Final drive through pedalling chain.
IGNITION AND LIGHTING: Flywheel magneto; lighting coils incorporated giving 6 v. 12 w. a.c. output for lights.
FUEL CAPACITY: Half a gallon.
WEIGHT OF UNIT: 17½ lb. (including petrol tank).
ROAD TAX: 17s. 6d. a year; 4s. 10d. a quarter.
PETROL CONSUMPTION: Approximately 140 m.p.g. under fairly hard riding conditions.
PRICE: £40.
CONCESSIONAIRES: Britax (London) Ltd., 115-129 Carlton Vale, London, N.W.6.

Hill-climbing abilities of the diminutive engine were exceptional. Shooter's Hill West, in the south-east London area, is over half a mile long, with an average gradient of 1 in 17 and a maximum gradient of 1 in 6. With a light following breeze and an approach speed of 30 m.p.h., the Cucciolo climbed the full length of the hill in top gear; the speed never dropping below 20 m.p.h. On another run, a stop and re-start was made on the steepest part of the hill. The machine pulled away in bottom gear without use of the pedals, and without the rider resorting to an abnormal amount of clutch-slipping.

On a run up the opposite, or east, side of the hill, bottom gear had to be engaged in the face of the wind, but the speed was maintained at 20 m.p.h.

Petrol consumption during average in-and-out-of-town running worked out at 140 m.p.g. The exhaust was fairly well silenced for normal running, and with the machine pottering along at 25 m.p.h. in top gear was quite unobtrusive. As might be expected with such a potent little engine, the exhaust sounded distinctly "healthy" when full power was used in bottom gear; the exhaust note was then rather like that of a distant lusty single at high revs. During normal acceleration there was a slightly obtrusive harsh-sounding whine from the gear primary drive.

The cycle to which the unit was attached was a Phillips' light-weight roadster, and the hub brakes on the machine were considered to be above average. Stopping distance from 30 m.p.h. was approximately 33ft. Lighting is supplied direct from a generator incorporated in the flywheel magneto. A Britax sprung saddle which was fitted to the bicycle was much appreciated.

At 5,200 r.p.m. the engine, it is claimed, produces 1.58 b.h.p.

First published 27 March 1952

49 c.c. Mini-Motor Cyclemotor

Powerful Two-stroke Unit: Simple to Control: Excellent Hill-climbing Characteristics

ONE of the first cyclemotors to be introduced after the war, the 49.9 c.c. two-stroke Mini-Motor—if one can judge by the number seen on the roads—still retains its initial popularity. The engine at present in production is a slightly detuned version of its earlier counterpart; the compression ratio has been lowered, and the result—as evinced by the unit tested —is an engine which is smooth, flexible, and altogether well suited to the task of propelling any standard pedal-cycle.

On first straddling the machine it was noticed immediately that the layout of the handlebar controls is delightfully simple; they comprise only a combined throttle and decompressor lever, and a transmission engagement lever (in addition, of course, there are the usual brake levers). The transmission engagement lever, when locked in the engaged position by its spring-loaded pawl, performs the function of holding the driving roller in contact with the rear tyre; the lever is intended to be operated only when the bicycle is not in motion.

Disengagement of the drive permits the machine to be used as an ordinary pedal-cycle. In practice, therefore, the power is completely regulated by a single control, the throttle-decompressor lever. This point should make a strong appeal to those with no previous experience of riding or driving a powered vehicle.

Starting the Mini-Motor from cold was easily accomplished provided that the Dellorto carburettor was flooded by operating the priming plunger, and the mixture strength was set to "rich" by rotating the air cleaner on the carburettor in a clockwise direction. Then, with the drive already engaged, it was necessary only to pedal the cycle for five or six yards with the decompressor valve raised, when, with one movement of the control lever, the decompressor was closed and the throttle opened to about the half-way mark, causing the engine to fire and take up the drive.

After the engine had been warmed up and the mixture strength weakened by adjusting the air-cleaner control, perfect two-stroking could be obtained at any sustained speed between 15 m.p.h. and the maximum available (approximately 29 m.p.h.). The engine pulled reliably down to a speed of 5 m.p.h., but if four-stroking was to be avoided in the range between 5 and 15 m.p.h., the throttle opening, and therefore, the speed, had very gradually to be increased. No irregular firing occurred on

---

INFORMATION PANEL

ENGINE: 49.9 c.c. (38 × 44 mm) two-stroke, with cast-iron cylinder barrel and detachable light-alloy head. Petroil lubrication.

CARBURETTOR: Trojan-Dellorto (made under licence) single-jet, single-lever; combined air cleaner and mixture control.

TRANSMISSION: Drive by friction roller on to rear tyre.

IGNITION: Flywheel magneto.

FUEL CAPACITY: Three-quarters of a gallon.

WEIGHT OF UNIT: 24 lb.

ROAD TAX: 17s 6d a year; 4s 10d a quarter.

PETROIL CONSUMPTION: Approximately 144 m.p.g. under fairly hard riding conditions.

PRICE: £21.

MANUFACTURERS: Mini-Motor (Great Britain), Ltd., Trojan Way, Croydon, Surrey.

---

the overrun (with the throttle closed) Best cruising speed was considered to be about 23 m.p.h.

Petroil consumption, which worked out at 144 m.p.g., was checked (a) under city-riding conditions, and (b) at sustained maximum speed on the open road; both results were almost identical. At a more moderate sustained cruising speed the consumption would undoubtedly be much more economical.

Main-road hills could be climbed without pedal assistance. However, to find out the near maximum capabilities of the Mini-Motor as far as hill-climbing was concerned, the machine was set at a climb more than half a mile in length that boasts a gradient of 1 in 6 at its steepest part near the end of the ascent. For the first two-thirds of the climb the pedal assistance required was no more than that which is necessary to propel an ordinary pedal-cycle along a level road. Much greater effort had, of course, to be applied at the pedals for the remaining distance, but at no time did the engine fail to assist the rider.

The drive roller fitted to the machine tested was of the composite type. When main-road hills were climbed during wet weather, no roller slip was apparent. An additional roller is supplied with each unit; of cast iron, it is intended for use in mainly dry climates. Silencing was commendably quiet at medium speeds and reasonably so at maximum speed.

The engine was found to be both smooth and flexible. No roller slip was apparent when main-road hills were climbed in wet weather.

First published 24 July 1952

45 c.c. VeloSolex Motorized Cycle

A Sturdy, Built-as-a-whole Runabout with Adequate Performance and Exceptional Ease of Control

THE VeloSolex motor-assisted cycle is probably the most popular machine of its type in the world, since tens of thousands are in use on the Continent, particularly in France and Holland. The machine is supplied as a complete unit, comprising a sturdy, open-frame bicycle propelled by a 45 c.c. two-stroke engine mounted over the front wheel. Transmission is by means of a composition friction roller bearing on the front tyre. Petrol is carried in a 1¾-pint tank on the right side of the engine. Since the tank is similar in shape and size to the flywheel housing on the other side, the engine has a symmetrical, well-balanced appearance.

The design is simple, for the engine unit does not employ gears, chains or pinions, and there is no petrol tap. The carburation, while novel, is also notable for its simplicity. Briefly, petrol is pumped from tank to carburettor by a membrane pump which is actuated by differences of pressure in the crankcase. In the carburettor, a constant level is secured by an overflow system which ensures that excess petrol is returned to the tank. Thus the normal float chamber, float and needle-valve are obviated.

Controls are few, and simple in operation. There are the normal cycle cable-operated caliper brakes front and rear. The engine control is in the form of a thumb-operated combined throttle and compression release lever on the left handlebar. The control is spring-loaded in the throttle fully open position, and to slow the engine it is necessary to move the lever towards the handlebar grip with the thumb. As the lever is moved over, it first closes the throttle, and then, on the final part of its travel, operates a compression-release valve which stops the engine firing and causes it to act as a brake. A choke lever is fitted to the carburettor close by the rider's right hand, and it can be easily operated when the machine is under way.

Starting was at all times delightfully easy. As there was no petrol tap, the drill was simply to mount the machine and pedal off, with the engine control pulled right over in order to open the compression-release valve; once the machine was on the move, the control was released and the engine could be guaranteed to fire immediately. During the mild weather, in which the machine was tested, it was usually unnecessary to make use of the choke when starting.

On a measured pint of petrol the machine covered 25 miles, giving a consumption figure of 200 miles per gallon.

At its normal maximum speed of about 16 m.p.h. on a level road, the engine ran smoothly and without fuss, and with the feeling that it would run indefinitely at that speed without strain or fatigue. Vibration was felt in the handlebar, but it was slight and mostly absorbed by the rubber grips.

Seat and handlebar heights are adjustable to provide a comfortable riding position, and the three large coil saddle springs insulate the rider from all but the worst road shocks. In fact, the machine, with its 1⅜in tyres, is far more comfortable than the normal clip-on employing ordinary cycle tyres.

The open frame is most convenient for either a man or woman owner. Unlike most open bicycle frames, however, its lateral rigidity is adequate. The bottom bracket is lower than normal,

---

INFORMATION PANEL

ENGINE: 45 c.c. (38 × 40 mm) two-stroke, with cast-iron cylinder barrel and detachable, die-cast, light-alloy cylinder head.
CARBURETTOR: Solex injector, with no float chamber, float or needle; fed by diaphragm pump operated by crankcase-pressure.
IGNITION: Flywheel magneto.
LIGHTING: Lighting coils in flywheel magneto; dry battery for parking lights.
TRANSMISSION: Drive by composition friction roller bearing on the front tyre.
FUEL CAPACITY: 1¾ pints.
FUEL CONSUMPTION: 200 m.p.g.
WEIGHT: 60 lb (complete machine).
BRAKES: Rim-type caliper brakes front and rear.
PRICE: £37 10s; with Purchase Tax (in Great Britain only), £47 18s 4d.

---

thus enabling the rider to employ a comfortable riding position and yet be able to plant a foot flat on the ground when the machine is stationary.

The frame is built in four sections, which facilitates repairs, and brake cables and wires are neatly concealed inside the frame. A sturdy carrier is a feature. Indeed, the whole machine shows abundant evidence of careful design; there is a pleasing "fitness for its purpose" about it.

The VeloSolex is as easy to ride as a bicycle; easier, in fact, since it does not have to be pedalled on the level. Gentle slopes were surmounted by a 13-stone rider without pedalling at about 10 m.p.h., and normal main-road hills called for only light pedal assistance. With the throttle almost closed the machine would run smoothly at little more than a walking pace. Steering was light, and there was no feeling of clumsiness due to the weight of the engine, which is over the front wheel.

The brakes were adequate, though not fierce enough for emergency stops. In fairness, however, it may be stated that the brakes were capable of overriding the engine and would stop the machine even with the throttle wide open.

The engine control was open to criticism in that it was too far from the left handlebar grip for a rider with small hands effectively to operate the brake while holding the throttle in the closed position.

The engine is easily disengaged from the front wheel by pulling with one hand on the carburettor casing protruding above the level of the cylinder head. To re-engage the engine, a support beneath the flywheel casing is released and the unit pushed forward until the drive roller is in contact with the tyre. With the engine disengaged, the machine could be pedalled and steered with no more effort than that required for an ordinary bicycle.

This picture reveals the symmetrical appearance of the 45 c.c. power unit, which is shown locked up in the disengaged position. The petrol pump mounted on the front of the crankcase will be noted.

First published 11 September 1952

32 c.c. Cyclemaster

A Power Wheel of Increased Engine Capacity with Excellent Characteristics for Town and Country Riding

UNIQUE in that it is sold as a powered wheel to replace existing rear wheels of cycles, the Cyclemaster has achieved wide popularity on the roads of Britain and elsewhere. Recently the capacity of the engine has been increased from 25 to 32 c.c. This has been achieved by enlarging the bore from 32 to 36 mm.—with the object of stepping up the power output without increase in piston speed; the stroke, of course, remains as before, namely, 32 mm. Except that the engine casing and cover plate are finished in polychromatic grey instead of black, there is no outward change in the appearance of the new unit as compared with the former 25 c.c. model. An appreciated feature, however, is that the new engine has a flywheel magneto equipped with coils to supply lighting current.

The unit tested was fitted to a Mercury bicycle, a machine which has been specially made for use in conjunction with the Cyclemaster. It is built on much sturdier lines than the average pedal cycle, and is marketed without a rear wheel, so that purchasers are not hampered with a surplus bicycle wheel.

Starting the Cyclemaster was simple and certain in all circumstances. During the test period the weather was, for the most part, hot, and it was necessary only to turn on the fuel, disengage the clutch, and pedal away. When the speed equalled that of a slow walking pace, the clutch was engaged and, provided the throttle was approximately half open, the engine started almost immediately. On one occasion—on a chilly evening—it was necessary to close the strangler control on the carburettor, but the strangler was opened after a hundred yards had been covered and was not needed again.

At speeds under 7 m.p.h. and, of course, on the overrun, there was a tendency for the engine to four-stroke. Above that speed, however, two-stroking was almost perfect provided the engine was pulling, albeit lightly. In spite of the four-stroking tendency, the low-speed pulling characteristics of the Cyclemaster are of a high order. It was possible to throttle down and reduce speed until the transmission was on the point of snatching. When the throttle was opened in such circumstances, the engine picked up with barely a trace of roughness. Speeds of less than a walking pace could be maintained with the clutch fully engaged.

In heavy traffic the clutch was found to be a tremendous advantage. It was possible to come to a halt and remain stationary with the engine ticking over quietly and reliably. On level surfaces it was not really necessary to pedal when moving off, although a few light twirls were sometimes called for on a slight gradient.

Maximum speeds are of academic interest only in the cyclemotor world, but the Cyclemaster several times exceeded 28-30 m.p.h. under favourable conditions. What is more to the point is that the machine could be cruised at 20-25 m.p.h. for miles on

---

INFORMATION PANEL

ENGINE: 32 c.c. (36 x 32 mm) two-stroke, with cast-iron cylinder barrel and detachable, die-cast, light-alloy cylinder head.
CARBURETTOR: Amal. Handlebar lever control for throttle.
IGNITION AND LIGHTING: Wico-Pacy flywheel magneto with lighting coils.
TRANSMISSION: Chain drive through clutch running in oil.
FUEL CAPACITY: 2½ pints (petroil lubrication).
FUEL CONSUMPTION: Steady country riding, 208 m.p.g.; town traffic conditions, 148 m.p.g.
WEIGHT: Cyclemaster power wheel, 34 lb; complete machine 73 lb.
BRAKES: Eadie coaster-hub rear brake; stirrup-type front brake.
PRICE: Cyclemaster power wheel only, £27 10s.; Mercury bicycle £13 19s.

---

end without protest from the engine. In the higher limits of the speed range, the exhaust note was raucous—a fact which limited to some extent the speed used in towns and built-up areas.

Hill-climbing capabilities of the unit are excellent for so small an engine. Provided a run at the hill could be made, a gradient of 1 in 25, more than a quarter of a mile long, could be climbed with only the lightest of pedal assistance. Steeper hills required slightly more energetic help, but at no time was there any need for really hard work. Unless head winds were above average in strength, the machine's performance was not affected to any great extent. When pedal assistance was needed against a wind, the effort required was small.

The coaster-hub rear brake, which is operated by rotating the pedal cranks in reverse, was disappointing. It was found to be difficult to operate the brake with any degree of finesse, and it was necessary to exert considerable effort to slow down the machine quickly. On the other hand, the front, stirrup-type brake was powerful and progressive; in most circumstances it provided commendable deceleration.

The built-in lighting set is exceptionally good. At half-throttle speeds the beam of light was strong enough to maintain daytime averages, and the rear light provided a good warning glow. No provision is made for a parking light.

Owing largely to the 2in tyres and robust frame, the Mercury bicycle is an unusually comfortable machine to ride. The rather large handlebar furnishes a natural wrist angle, and this, in conjunction with the low-mounted saddle, gives an excellent riding position. The model tested had an open-type frame, but a machine with a top rail crossbar is also available at no extra cost.

To sum up, the combination of Mercury cycle and Cyclemaster unit is a first-class example of the cyclemotor type of machine; the new 32 c.c. engine should win even greater favour than its popular predecessor.

The two-stroke engine is neatly enshrouded by the wheel hub. Finish is in polychromatic grey

First published 4 June 1953

49 c.c. Power Pak

A Well-built Unit with Excellent Traffic Manners and Extreme Simplicity of Control

IT has been said that there are four main points to bear in mind when choosing a cyclemotor: the unit should be easy to control; have lusty low-speed pulling; be reasonably economical to run and have good hill-climbing capabilities. To a large extent the 49 c.c. Power Pak possesses all these virtues, and it is unquestionably one of the most appealing cycle engines available in Great Britain.

It would be difficult to imagine a unit more simple to control. Indeed, there is only one control—a twistgrip mounted on the right-hand side of the handlebar. Turning the grip inward opens the throttle; when the grip is rotated the other way, the clutch is automatically withdrawn and the engine allowed to tick over with the machine at rest.

Starting the Power Pak was easy and certain under all conditions. For early morning starts it was necessary to flood the carburettor slightly and close the strangler control on the air intake. Then, with the twistgrip in the "clutch" position, the machine was pedalled off. As soon as a speed of roughly 3 m.p.h. was reached the throttle was opened and, in a matter of a few feet, the engine fired. When the engine had been running for two or three minutes, the strangler could be opened and forgotten for the rest of the day. Even if the machine had been standing for several hours, it was necessary to pedal only for a yard or two before letting in the clutch, when an immediate start was invariable. Thanks to the clutch (known as the Synchromatic Drive), no more effort than that used on an ordinary pedal cycle was involved in starting the engine.

Once the machine was under way, it would buzz along at any speed up to about 23 m.p.h. The bicycle on which the unit was tested was in poor condition; in consequence, speeds of much over 15 m.p.h. were uncomfortable. There is no doubt, however, that on a good bicycle, the engine could maintain a cruising speed of 20 m.p.h. indefinitely.

One of the most endearing characteristics of the Power Pak is its delightful manners in heavy traffic. The engine could be throttled back until the speed had dropped to a crawl. Then, with only a trace of roughness, it could be accelerated fast enough to keep up with leisurely driven cars. Occasionally, a few light twirls of the pedals were needed to help the willing little unit at low speeds, but this was necessary only on an incline.

If a complete stop was called for, the twistgrip was turned clockwise and the engine would settle down to a fast but reliable tickover. When a move was made, it was necessary to start the cycle rolling by pedalling. As soon as the machine was under way (walking speed was quite fast enough) the clutch could be engaged.

INFORMATION PANEL

ENGINE: 49 c.c. (39 x 41 mm) two-stroke, with cast-iron cylinder barrel and detachable, light-alloy cylinder head. Petroil lubrication.
CARBURETTOR: Amal lightweight, with combined air filter and strangler control. Twistgrip throttle control.
IGNITION: Wico-Pacy flywheel magneto.
FUEL CAPACITY: ⅜ gallon.
WEIGHT OF UNIT: 25 lb.
ROAD TAX: 17s 6d a year; 4s 10d a quarter.
PETROIL CONSUMPTION: Approximately 155 m.p.g. under hard-riding conditions.
PRICE: £27 6s.
SOLE CONCESSIONAIRES: Sinclair Goddard and Co. Ltd., 162 Queensway, Bayswater, London, W.2.

Except for periods at the extreme ends of the throttle range, four-stroking was conspicuous by its absence. On the overrun there was inevitably a certain amount of irregular firing of the character associated with most two-stroke engines running under no-load conditions. Another pleasing feature of the Power Pak was that it seemed impossible to over-rev the engine. Even on downhill sections the engine would not scream; indeed, it seemed tireless, in spite of much spirited riding throughout the test.

Main road hills were well within the capabilities of the Power Pak. In order to test the ultimate performance, a hill roughly half a mile long, with an average gradient of 1 in 10, was tackled. This hill forces all but the sportiest of he-man pedal cyclists to walk, but the Power Pak took the first half of the climb in its stride; thereafter, light pedal assistance was necessary for the remainder of the ascent. It should be emphasized that the assistance was really light; in no way could it be compared with the heavy slogging required for an ordinary pedal cycle.

No roller slip was experienced, even in wet weather. No doubt this fact was partly attributable to the Dunlop Motorette cyclemotor tyre, one of which is supplied with each unit. The small weather shield fixed in front of the engine effectively kept road filth from the rider's clothing.

To sum up, the Power Pak is a well-built and delightful little engine from the performance standpoint, and, equally important, it is a unit with which even the most unmechanically minded of riders could feel at home in a commendably short space of time.

The Power Pak tested was fitted with the now well-known Synchromatic Drive

First published 15 October 1953

B.S.A. Winged Wheel

Excellently Engineered 35 c.c. Unit with Gear Drive and Internal-expanding Brake

IN view of the variety of layouts favoured for cyclemotor units, considerable interest attaches to the fact that the B.S.A. concern, for its first venture into the field, favours a powered wheel. The Winged Wheel, as the B.S.A. 35 c.c. engine-wheel unit is called, is neat yet functional in appearance. No attempt has been made to enclose the engine.

A feature reflecting appreciation of the demands made by speeds higher than those normal for bicycles is the provision of a 9½-diameter, internal-expanding brake in the hub casing. Ignition is by Wico-Pacy flywheel magneto incorporating a lighting coil which provides current for headlamp and tail light. A clutch is fitted, and is controlled by a handlebar lever embodying a ratchet to hold it out of engagement as required.

Considering the small capacity of the engine, comfortable

INFORMATION PANEL

ENGINE: 35 c.c. (36 x 34 mm) two-stroke, with cast-iron cylinder barrel and detachable, light-alloy cylinder head. Petroil lubrication.
CARBURETTOR: Amal, with automatic strangler control. Handlebar lever control for throttle.
IGNITION and LIGHTING: Wico-Pacy flywheel magneto with lighting coil.
FUEL CAPACITY: ½ gallon.
PETROIL CONSUMPTION: All in, under hard-riding conditions, approximately 135 m.p.g.
WEIGHT OF UNIT: 26½ lb (including wheel).
BRAKE: 9½in-diameter, internal expanding.
ROAD TAX: 17s 6d a year; 4s 10d a quarter.
PRICE: £25.
MANUFACTURER: B.S.A. Cycles Ltd., Small Heath, Birmingham, 11

---

cruising speeds permitted by the Winged Wheel were commendably high. Speeds of between 20 and 25 m.p.h. were well within the capabilities of the unit; indeed, as is usually the case, the combination of small saddle, rigid front fork and slim tyres was the limiting factor, rather than engine performance.

The gear ratio of 18.7 to 1 is well suited to the engine characteristics; it proved sufficiently high for there to be no indication of fuss at the highest possible cruising speed, yet low enough to provide excellent climb and easy starting.

Provided that there was little unfavourable wind, long, gradual inclines could be surmounted without losing more than 5 m.p.h. A really stiff headwind had to be met before even light pedal assistance was required on such gradients. A hill approximately three-quarters of a mile long, with a gradient in the region of 1 in 14, could be climbed with only moderate pedalling effort on the part of the rider. The first 50 yards of such a hill would normally induce the average cyclist to dismount and walk.

Vibration was virtually non-existent at all speeds. The exhaust note, above 20 m.p.h., was rather sonorous but never objectionable. Fuel consumption, under give and take, town and country riding, averaged 135 m.p.g.

A definite, unvarying routine was found to give the most satisfactory results when starting the Winged Wheel from cold. After the fuel had been turned on and the throttle lever moved to the extreme left to operate the automatic strangler device, a few seconds were allowed for the float chamber to fill (no tickler is provided on the miniature Amal carburettor) before pedalling off. As soon as a speed equivalent to that of fast walking was attained, the clutch was engaged. The engine was then permitted to run for about 100 yards with the choke in use, before the throttle lever was returned to its normal arc of movement.

At speeds above, say, 4 m.p.h., the engine would pull strongly and without fuss. Below that speed power delivery was no more than would be expected from an engine of only 35 c.c., and light pedal assistance was advisable, even if not entirely necessary. Transmission smoothness was of a high order at all but the lowest speeds, when slight harshness was apparent.

The Winged Wheel was fitted in a B.S.A. roadster cycle of sturdy construction and equipped with stirrup-type brakes front and rear. As delivered, the operating lever for the rear hub brake was clipped on the right handlebar, above the front stirrup-brake lever. With this arrangement it was impossible to apply the front brake and the rear hub brake together; however, it was decided to retain the standard layout, since of the two rear brakes the stirrup brake was the more powerful. For normal stopping purposes, the front and rear stirrup brakes were used together. The hub brake on the test model lacked real power, though a slight improvement was apparent after about 100 miles had been covered. Its real merit came to light when the bicycle was ridden in rain. Whereas the stirrup brakes lost power, the internal-expanding brake retained its normal efficiency.

The headlight was found to be adequate for the speeds of which the machine was capable. A good, constant beam of light was obtained at low engine revolutions. A dry battery in the headlamp supplies current for a parking light.

Many times during the course of the test, favourable comment was received from motor cyclists and cyclists alike on the trim appearance and attractive beige enamel finish of the Winged Wheel. After many miles of hard riding, the unit remained commendably clean externally.

The hub of the Winged Wheel incorporates a 9½in-diameter, internal-expanding brake

INDEX BY YEAR

MOTORCYCLE SECTION

1949

Dot Two-stroke (197 c.c.)	2
Norton Dominator Twin (497 c.c.)	6
Vincent Black Shadow (998 c.c.)	4

1950

Ariel Four and Sidecar (997 c.c.)	10
Ariel Red Hunter Twin (498 c.c.)	20
B.S.A. Bantam de Luxe (123 c.c.)	18
B.S.A. Overhead-valve M33 (499 c.c.)	12
Francis-Barnett Falcon 55 (197 c.c.)	24
Indian Brave (248 c.c.)	32
James Captain de Luxe (197 c.c.)	16
Norton Big Four and Sidecar (596 c.c.)	14
Royal Enfield Bullet (346 c.c.)	22
Royal Enfield Twin (496 c.c.)	34
Sunbeam S8 Twin (487 c.c.)	8
Triumph Thunderbird (649 c.c.)	26
Vincent Comet (449 c.c.)	30

1951

Ariel Red Hunter Single (497 c.c.)	50
Bown Two-speed (98 c.c.)	54
B.S.A. A7 Twin (495 c.c.)	38
B.S.A. C11 (249 c.c.)	52
B.S.A. Golden Flash (646 c.c.)	58
Excelsior Talisman (244 c.c.)	42
James Commodore (98 c.c.)	44
Norton Dominator and Sidecar (497 c.c.)	46
Royal Enfield J2 and Sidecar (499 c.c.)	56
Tandon Supaglid Supreme (197 c.c.)	40
Velocette LE (192 c.c.)	48
Vincent Rapide and Sidecar (998 c.c.)	36

1952

Ariel Twin and Sidecar (498 c.c.)	64
Bown Tourist Trophy (122 c.c.)	78
B.S.A. Star Twin (497 c.c.)	68
D.M.W. de Luxe (197 c.c.)	62
Excelsior Talisman Sports (244 c.c.)	74
Francis-Barnett Falcon 58 (197 c.c.)	70
Royal Enfield RE (125 c.c.)	66
Sunbeam S7 with Sidecar (487 c.c.)	72
Triumph Tiger 100 (498 c.c.)	76

1953

Ariel Square Four, Mk. II (997 c.c.)	88
B.S.A. B33 (499 c.c.)	86
B.S.A. C10 Side-valve (249 c.c.)	96
D.M.W. Coronation (122 c.c.)	92
Excelsior Courier (148 c.c.)	102
Greeves de Luxe (197 c.c.)	100
James Cadet (122 c.c.)	90
Norman Two-stroke (197 c.c.)	80
Norton Dominator No. 7 (497 c.c.)	94
Norton ES2 (490 c.c.)	82
Royal Enfield Bullet (499 c.c.)	98
Triumph Speed Twin (498 c.c.)	84

SCOOTER SECTION

1952	Douglas Vespa Scooter (125 c.c.)	104
1953	Lambretta Scooter (123 c.c.)	106

3 WHEELER SECTION

1953	Bond Minicar, Mk. C (197 c.c.)	108
1953	Reliant Regal Three-wheeler (750 c.c.)	110

CYCLEMOTOR SECTION

1951	Berini Cyclemotor (32 c.c.)	112
1952	Cucciolo Cyclemotor (48 c.c.)	113
1952	Mini-Motor Cyclemotor (49 c.c.)	114
1952	Velo-Solex Motorized Cycle (45 c.c.)	115
1952	Cyclemaster Cyclemotor (32 c.c.)	116
1953	Power Pak Cyclemotor (49 c.c.)	117
1953	B.S.A. Winged Wheel Cyclemotor (35 c.c.)	118

VELOCEPRESS MANUALS - MOTORCYCLE

1930'S BRITISH MOTORCYCLE CARBS & ELEC COMPONENTS (BOOK OF)
1930'S BRITISH MOTORCYCLE ENGINES (OVERHAUL & MAINTENANCE)
1930'S BRITISH MOTORCYCLE GEARBOXES & CLUTCHES (BOOK OF)
AJS 1932-1948 SINGLES & TWINS 250cc THRU 1000cc (BOOK OF)
AJS 1945-1960 SINGLES 350cc & 500cc MODELS 16 & 18 (BOOK OF)
AJS 1955-1965 SINGLES 350cc & 500cc (BOOK OF)
ARIEL UP TO 1932 (BOOK OF)
ARIEL 1932-1939 PREWAR MODELS (BOOK OF)
ARIEL 1933-1951 (WORKSHOP MANUAL)
ARIEL 1939-1960 4 STROKE SINGLES (BOOK OF)
ARIEL 1958-1964 LEADER & ARROW (BOOK OF)
BMW R26 R27 (1956-1967) FACTORY WORKSHOP MANUAL
BMW R50 R50S R60 R69S (1955-1969) FACTORY WORKSHOP MANUAL
BRIDGESTONE 90 SERIES FACTORY WSM & PARTS CATALOGUE
BRIDGESTONE 175 SERIES FACTORY WSM & PARTS CATALOGUE
BSA BANTAM ALL MODELS FROM 1948 ONWARDS (BOOK OF)
BSA SINGLES & V-TWINS UP TO 1927 (BOOK OF)
BSA SINGLES & V-TWINS UP TO 1930 (BOOK OF)
BSA SINGLES & V-TWINS UP TO 1935 (BOOK OF)
BSA SINGLES & V-TWINS 1936-1939 (BOOK OF)
BSA OHV & SV SINGLES 250-600cc 1945-1959 (BOOK OF)
BSA OHV & SV SINGLES 250cc (ONLY) 1954-1970 (BOOK OF)
BSA OHV SINGLES 350 & 500cc 1955-1967 (BOOK OF)
BSA TWINS 1948-1962 (BOOK OF)
BSA TWINS 1962-1969 (SECOND BOOK OF)
CYCLEMOTOR (BOOK OF)
DOUGLAS 1929-1939 PREWAR ALL MODELS (BOOK OF)
DOUGLAS 1948-1957 POSTWAR ALL MODELS FACTORY SHOP MANUAL
DUCATI 160cc, 250cc & 350cc OHC MODELS FACTORY SHOP MANUAL
HONDA 50 ALL MODELS UP TO 1970 INC MONKEY & TRAIL (BOOK OF)
HONDA 90 ALL MODELS UP TO 1966 (BOOK OF)
HONDA 125-150cc TWINS C/CS/CB/CA FACTORY WORKSHOP MANUAL
HONDA 250-305 TWINS C/CS/CB FACTORY WORKSHOP MANUAL
HONDA 450 CB/CL 1965-1974 K0 TO K7 WORKSHOP MANUAL
HONDA C100 SUPER CUB FACTORY WORKSHOP MANUAL
HONDA C110 SPORT CUB 1962-1969 FACTORY WORKSHOP MANUAL
HONDA TWINS & SINGLES 50cc THRU 305cc 1960-1966 (BOOK OF)
HONDA TWINS ALL MODELS 125cc THRU 450cc UP TO 1968 (BOOK OF)
INDIAN PONYBIKE, BOY RACER & PAPOOSE ILL PARTS LIST & SALES LIT
J.A.P. ENGINES 1927-1952 & MOTORCYCLES 1934-1952 (BOOK OF)
LAMBRETTA 1947-1957 ALL 125 & 150cc MODELS (BOOK OF)
LAMBRETTA 1957-1970 LI & TV MODELS (SECOND BOOK OF)
MATCHLESS 1931-1939 ALL MODELS 250cc THRU 990cc (BOOK OF)
MATCHLESS 1945-1956 350 & 500cc SINGLES (BOOK OF)
MATCHLESS 1955-1966 350 & 500cc SINGLES (BOOK OF)
NEW IMPERIAL ALL SV & OHV FROM 1935 ONWARDS (BOOK OF)
NORTON 1932-1939 PREWAR MODELS (BOOK OF)
NORTON 1932-1947 (BOOK OF)
NORTON 1938-1956 (BOOK OF)
NORTON 1955-1963 MODELS 19, 50 & ES2 (BOOK OF)
NORTON 1955-1965 DOMINATOR TWINS (BOOK OF)
NORTON 1957-1970 TWINS FACTORY WORKSHOP MANUAL
NSU PRIMA 1956-1964 ALL MODELS (BOOK OF)
NSU QUICKLY 1953-1963 ALL MODELS (BOOK OF)
PANTHER 1932-1958 LIGHTWEIGHT MODELS 250 & 350cc (BOOK OF)
PANTHER 1938-1966 HEAVYWEIGHT MODELS 600 & 650cc (BOOK OF)
RALEIGH MOPEDS 1960-1969 (BOOK OF)
RALEIGH MOTORCYCLES 1919-1933 (BOOK OF)
ROYAL ENFIELD 1934-1946 SINGLES & V TWINS (BOOK OF)
ROYAL ENFIELD 1937-1953 SINGLES & V TWINS (BOOK OF)
ROYAL ENFIELD 1946-1962 SINGLES (BOOK OF)
ROYAL ENFIELD 1958-1966 250cc & 350cc SINGLES (SECOND BOOK OF)
ROYAL ENFIELD 736cc INTERCEPTOR FACTORY WORKSHOP MANUAL
RUDGE 1933-1939 (BOOK OF)
SUNBEAM 1928-1939 (BOOK OF)
SUNBEAM 1946-1957 S7 & S8 (BOOK OF)
SUZUKI 50cc & 80cc UP TO 1966 (BOOK OF)
SUZUKI T10 1963-1967 FACTORY WORKSHOP MANUAL
SUZUKI T20 & T200 1965-1969 FACTORY WORKSHOP MANUAL
SUZUKI TWINS 1962 ONWARDS 125-500cc WORKSHOP MANUAL
TRIUMPH 1935-1939 PREWAR MODELS (BOOK OF)
TRIUMPH 1935-1949 (BOOK OF)
TRIUMPH 1937-1951 (WORKSHOP MANUAL)
TRIUMPH 1945-1955 FACTORY WORKSHOP MANUAL
TRIUMPH 1945-1958 TWINS (BOOK OF)
TRIUMPH 1956-1969 TWINS (BOOK OF)
VELOCETTE 1925-1970 ALL SINGLES & TWINS (BOOK OF)
VESPA 1951-1961 (BOOK OF)
VESPA 1955-1963 125 & 150cc & GS MODELS (SECOND BOOK OF)
VESPA 1955-1968 GS & SS (BOOK OF)
VESPA 1963-1972 90, 125 & 150cc (THIRD BOOK OF)
VILLIERS ENGINE UP TO 1959 INC. 3 WHEELERS (BOOK OF)
VILLIERS ENGINE UP TO 1969 (BOOK OF)
VINCENT 1935-1955 (WORKSHOP MANUAL)
YAMAHA 1961-1967 YA5 & YA6 (WORKSHOP MANUAL & ILL PARTS LIST)
YAMAHA 1971-1972 JT1& JT2 (WORKSHOP MANUAL & ILL PARTS LIST)

VELOCEPRESS TECHNICAL BOOKS – MOTORCYCLE

CATALOG OF BRITISH MOTORCYCLES (1951 MODELS)
MOTORCYCLE ENGINEERING (P.E. Irving)
MOTORCYCLE ROAD TESTS 1949-1953 (Motor Cycle Magazine UK)
SPEED AND HOW TO OBTAIN IT (Motor Cycle Magazine UK)
TUNING FOR SPEED (P.E. Irving)

VELOCEPRESS MANUALS - THREE WHEELER'S

BSA THREE WHEELER (BOOK OF)
VINTAGE MORGAN THREE WHEELER (BOOK OF)

VELOCEPRESS MANUALS - AUTOMOBILE

ALFA ROMEO GIULIA WORKSHOP MANUAL 1300 TO 2000cc 1962-1975
ALFA ROMEO GIULIA TECH MANUAL CARBURETED CARS FROM 1962
ALFA ROMEO GIULIA TECH MANUAL FUEL INJECTED CARS FROM 1969
AUSTIN-HEALEY 6-CYLINDER WORKSHOP MANUAL
AUSTIN-HEALEY SPRITE & MG MIDGET WORKSHOP MANUAL 1958-1971
BMW 600 LIMOUSINE FACTORY WORKSHOP MANUAL
BMW 600 LIMOUSINE OWNERS HAND BOOK & SERVICE MANUAL
BMW 2000 & 2002 1966-1976 WORKSHOP MANUAL
BMW ISETTA FACTORY WORKSHOP MANUAL
CORVAIR 1960-1969 WORKSHOP MANUAL
CORVETTE V8 1955-1962 WORKSHOP MANUAL
FIAT 500 FACTORY WORKSHOP MANUAL 1957-1973
FIAT 600, 600D & MULTIPLA FACTORY WORKSHOP MANUAL 1955-1969
JAGUAR E-TYPE 3.8 & 4.2 SERIES 1 & 2 WORKSHOP MANUAL
JAGUAR MK 7, 8, 9 & XK120, 140, 150 WORKSHOP MANUAL 1948-1961
METROPOLITAN FACTORY WORKSHOP MANUAL
MGA & MGB OWNERS HANDBOOK & WORKSHOP MANUAL
MG MIDGET TC, TD, TF & TF1500 WORKSHOP MANUAL
PORSCHE 356 1948-1965 WORKSHOP MANUAL
PORSCHE 911 2.0, 2.2, 2.4 LITRE 1964-1973 WORKSHOP MANUAL
PORSCHE 911 2.7, 3.0, 3.2 LITRE 1973-1989 WORKSHOP MANUAL
PORSCHE 912 WORKSHOP MANUAL
TRIUMPH TR2, TR3, TR4 1953-1965 WORKSHOP MANUAL
VOLKSWAGEN TRANSPORTER, TRUCKS & WAGONS 1950-1979 WSM
VOLVO 1944-1968 ALL MODELS WORKSHOP MANUAL

VELOCEPRESS TECHNICAL BOOKS - AUTOMOBILE

FERRARI 250/GT SERVICE AND MAINTENANCE
FERRARI GUIDE TO PERFORMANCE
FERRARI OWNER'S HANDBOOK
FERRARI TUNING TIPS & MAINTENANCE TECHNIQUES
HOW TO BUILD A FIBERGLASS CAR
HOW TO BUILD A RACING CAR
HOW TO RESTORE THE MODEL 'A' FORD
MASERATI OWNER'S HANDBOOK
OBERT'S FIAT GUIDE
PERFORMANCE TUNING THE SUNBEAM TIGER
SOUPING THE VOLKSWAGEN
SOLEX CARBURETORS (EMPHASIS ON UK & EU AUTOMOBILES)
SU CARBURETORS (EMPHASIS ON UK AUTOMOBILES)
WEBER CARBURETORS (EMPHASIS ON ALFA & FIAT)

VELOCEPRESS BOOKS & GUIDES - AUTOMOBILE

ABARTH BUYERS GUIDE
COMPLETE CATALOG OF JAPANESE MOTOR VEHICLES
FERRARI 308 SERIES BUYER'S AND OWNER'S GUIDE
FERRARI BERLINETTA LUSSO
FERRARI BROCHURES AND SALES LITERATURE 1946-1967
FERRARI BROCHURES AND SALES LITERATURE 1968-1989
FERRARI OPP, MAINTENANCE & SERVICE H/BOOKS 1948-1963
FERRARI SERIAL NUMBERS PART I - ODD NUMBERS TO 21399
FERRARI SERIAL NUMBERS PART II - EVEN NUMBERS TO 1050
FERRARI SPYDER CALIFORNIA
HENRY'S FABULOUS MODEL "A" FORD
MASERATI BROCHURES AND SALES LITERATURE

VELOCEPRESS BOOKS – RACING

CARRERA PANAMERICANA - MEXICAN ROAD RACE (BOOK OF)
DIALED IN - THE JAN OPPERMAN STORY
IF HEMINGWAY HAD WRITTEN A RACING NOVEL
VEDA ORR'S NEW REVISED HOT ROD PICTORIAL

AUTOBOOKS WORKSHOP MANUALS & BROOKLANDS ROAD TEST PORTFOLIOS

FOR A COMPLETE LISTING OF THE AUTOBOOKS & BROOKLANDS TITLES THAT WE CURRENTLY HAVE AVAILABLE, PLEASE VISIT OUR WEBSITE.

www.VelocePress.com

www.ingramcontent.com/pod-product-compliance
Lightning Source LLC
Chambersburg PA
CBHW080923170426
43201CB00016B/2250